Making a Place for Pleasure in Early Childhood Education

Making a Place for Pleasure in
Early Childhood Education

EDITED BY JOSEPH TOBIN

Yale University Press   New Haven and London

Published with assistance from the foundation established in memory of
Amasa Stone Mather of the Class of 1907, Yale College.

Designed by Sonia Scanlon and set in Berkeley type
by Keystone Typesetting, Inc., Orwigsburg, Pennsylvania.
Printed in the United States of America
by Edwards Brothers, Inc., Ann Arbor, Michigan.

Making a place for pleasure in early childhood education / edited by
Joseph Tobin.
p.   cm.
Includes bibliographical references and index.
ISBN 0-300-06968-5 (cloth : alk. paper)
1. Early childhood education—Social aspects—United States.
2. Teacher-student relationships—United States.   3. Child
development—United States.   4. Sex (Psychology).   5. Pleasure—Moral
and ethical apsects—United States.   6. Child psychology—United
States.   7. Early childhood education—Moral and ethical apsects—
United States.   I. Tobin, Joseph Jay.
LB1139.25.M36   1997   96-41890

A catalogue record for this book is available
from the British Library.

The paper in this book meets the guidelines for permanence and durability of the
Committee on Production Guidelines for Book Longevity of the Council on
Library Resources.

10   9   8   7   6   5   4   3   2   1

Contents

Making a Place for Pleasure in
Early Childhood Education

The Missing Discourse of Pleasure and Desire

Joseph Tobin

On a preschool playground, a four-year-old girl chases boys, kissing them when she catches them.

Enjoying a quiet moment with a student at the end of the day, a teacher's aide in a day care center holds a three-year-old girl on his lap as he reads her a story.

During a class discussion, several third-graders comment that one of their classmates seems more like a girl than a boy because he always likes to "do girl things."

The staff of a child center run by a university discuss how a gay teacher should respond to children's questions about why he's not married.

Told by their teacher to come up with a script for a video, a group of second-graders settle on a story that features alien creatures who, after falling down on their hot planet, get "hot butts" which they soothe by sitting in buckets of ice water.

Those of us who work with young children lament that if we lived in a different, better world, incidents like these would be routine and hardly worth mentioning. But working as we do in the world of early childhood education in the United States in the 1990s, we know that any event suggestive of sexuality is problematic and even potentially dangerous.

It is not just sexuality but more generally pleasure and desire that are under siege in early childhood education. Talk of children "having fun" at school is commonplace; talk of their experiencing pleasure is rare. We speak freely of the needs and wants of children and their teachers, but we only whisper their desires. Bookstores carry whole sections on children's safety but few titles on children's happiness. In discussions of teacher recruitment and retention, we worry about low wages but fail to note the changing codes of practice that are frustrating teachers' attempts to satisfy the desires that drew them into the field in the first place.

In "Sexuality, Schooling, and Adolescent Females: The Missing Discourse of Desire," Michelle Fine (1988) argues that sex education in high schools is characterized by: "(1) the authorized suppression of a discourse of female sexual desire; (2) the promotion of a discourse of female sexual victimization; and (3) the explicit privileging of married heterosexuality over other practices of sexuality." Our thesis in this book is that a parallel phenomenon of suppressed desire, victimization, and heteronormativity characterizes contemporary research, theory, and practice in early childhood education. Ignorance, inattention, fear, and hostility to pleasure and desire are diminishing the quality of life for young children and their teachers. Scholarship in early childhood education has failed to challenge the mean-spirited, misinformed, morally panicked public discourses that are distorting how we care for and teach young children. To turn these dynamics around, we need to shift the terms of the argument. Pleasure and desire, now banished to the dark recesses of early childhood educational theory and practice, need to be brought to the fore. The essays in this book argue for the rehabilitation of pleasure as a goal of early childhood education and for overcoming our fear of thinking and talking about the desires of young children and their teachers.

Following Michel Foucault (1980), we use the word *discourse* throughout this book to refer to a grid of power and knowledge that envelops speech and writing, theory and practice, popular culture, scholarship, professional standards, pedagogy, and the law. To chart contemporary beliefs and practices about children's sexuality we must examine a range of texts, including television specials and newspaper headlines, proceedings of courts and Congress, academic journals and child-rearing manuals, policies of child protective services and the insurance industry, and standards and practices of such professional organizations as the National Association for the Education of Young Children.

Here is an example of how this discourse works. Professor D, a faculty member in the early childhood education department of a prestigious state university, gives presentations and publishes articles on what preschools can do to minimize the risk of child abuse. Eventually, as his reputation grows, he is hired as an expert witness to testify for the prosecution in cases involving the purported sexual abuse of children in child care settings. In one controversial case his testimony that there were preventive measures the preschool could have taken (better sightlines, more careful screening and supervision of staff, tighter rules against teachers touching children) contributes to a resolution in which a substantial settlement is paid to the family by the preschool's insurer. The case receives extensive coverage in the press and in professional publications of child care associations. In addition to his ongoing work as a professor and as a prosecution witness, Professor D begins a consulting business, advising preschools across the country on how to avoid sexual abuse and lawsuits. Insurance rates for child care institutions rise. Professor D is appointed to a national advisory commission, which publishes a report recommending that two adults always be present when children's diapers are being changed, that there be no doors on toilet stalls used by children, and that children sitting on a caretaker's lap must sit "side-saddle." Several states adopt the commission's recommendations as professional standards that must be upheld to receive licensing. Teachers who do not follow these standards (who, for example, continue to hold children on their laps in prohibited ways) risk dismissal or even prosecution.

MISSING

The thesis of this book is that pleasure and desire are "missing" from early childhood education—missing in several related senses of the word.

Missing as in Uncharted, Unexplored, Undiscovered

When educational researchers begin a new study, one way in which they assure themselves that their topic has not been mined out or too thickly settled is to do an ERIC search. My ERIC search using the key words "sex," "children," "preschools," and "early childhood education" turned up more than fifty articles on sexual abuse and sexual protection (including Professor D's publications) but only two on sexual desire or sexual pleasure. I found articles advising directors of day care centers on how to establish clear sightlines so as to keep children constantly visible and how to institute criminal background checks in staff hiring. I found articles on how to spot signs of sexual abuse and on how to teach children to say no to unwanted touching. My literature search suggests that whereas deviant and dangerous sexuality is a popular scholarly topic, the pleasures and desires of young children and their caretakers are missing, waiting to be written.[1]

Missing as in Lost

Some of us are old enough to have been educated in child development at a time when the curriculum included the study of childhood ("infantile") sexuality. In this sense, the study of sex-

---

1. A welcome exception to the panicked discourse on childhood sexuality in early childhood education publications is Susan Miller Corbett's article "Children and Sexuality," published in *Young Children* in 1991.

uality and desire in early childhood education is less an undiscovered new area than a forgotten old one. When the nursery school and the field of early childhood education were being invented in the nineteenth and early twentieth centuries, notions of the body and pleasure were openly discussed. Friedrich Froebel, Maria Montessori, and John Dewey each had a strong sense of the mind-body connection, in contrast to the word-oriented, antisomatic ethos of contemporary early childhood education.[2]

Early childhood education from 1900 until the mid-1970s was heavily influenced by psychoanalytic theorists, who focused on the developmental stages of sexuality in children. Preservice teachers took courses in which they were introduced to psychoanalytic notions of oral, anal, and genital sexuality and to the naturalness and inevitability of sexual curiosity, sexual fantasies, and sexual play in young children. In the 1960s and 1970s a child development course typically included works by or about Sigmund Freud, Anna Freud, Margaret Mahler, Melanie Klein, and Erik Erikson. These writings suggested that more harm was caused by the repression of children's sexuality than by its expression. Students also were introduced to studies by Harry and Margaret Harlow (1962), John Bowlby (1969, 1973), and René Spitz (1965), who argued for the developmental necessity of touching during the infantile and toddler periods.

My point here is not to plead for a return to uncritical acceptance of drive theories, ego psychology, or attachment theories but to note that there was a time when these theories and topics were part of the commonsense knowledge of the field. The age of penis envy and eighth-month anxiety may not have been the good old days, but it was a time when discussion of children's sexuality was unremarkable in a way that it is not today.

2. For a discussion of the logocentric distaste for the body and the expression of emotion in American early childhood education, see my 1995 essay "The Irony of Self-Expression."

Psychoanalytic theories of children's sexuality can be reintroduced to the child-development curriculum without necessarily returning to the writings of Klein and Freud (though I continue to find such a return rewarding). Poststructural and feminist versions of psychoanalysis by Nancy Chodorow (1978), Luce Irigaray (1985), Hélène Cixous (1976), Eve Sedgwick (1990), and Judith Butler (1993) provide alternative readings of children's sexual drives and gender formation. These and other writings that draw on Freudian, Kleinian, and Lacanian psychoanalytic theories can be used to pose critical questions about the care and education of young children.

Psychoanalytic theorizing aside, early childhood education can fight the anticorporeal, antipleasure trend by reemphasizing its Froebelian, multisensorial roots. In the face of the "trickle-down" curricular pressure in American education, early childhood educators can push for a trickle up into the elementary curriculum of such classic, body-rich nursery school activities as sand and water play, finger painting, clay modeling, and body painting.

Missing as in Disappeared

If you talk about sexual desire in early childhood education, you risk joining the ranks of the professionally missing—missing from your job, missing from conference programs, missing from being published in mainstream journals in the field. If it is risky to talk about sexual desire in the high school context, it is far more so in the panic-driven context of contemporary American early childhood education. Many educators have commended Michelle Fine for her bravery in calling for the introduction of discussions of sexual desire and agency in high school sex education. Many of our colleagues, in contrast, have warned us that writing about the pleasures and desires of young children and their teachers is foolhardy and perhaps even perilous to children, teachers, and our careers.

We are aware of these dangers. We know that an interest in children's sexuality may be mistaken for sexual interest in children; that advocacy for children's sexual rights may look like retro-1960s hedonism; that calls for reducing the surveillance and suspicion of teachers may seem to elevate teachers' comfort over children's safety; and that our attempts to expose the hysterical and reactionary dimensions of reports of epidemic institutional child abuse may be seen as undermining the efforts of those fighting against the brutalization of women and children. We are aware of these dangers, and yet we proceed, because we believe that continuing to say nothing is both irresponsible and unwise.

The progressive wing of early childhood education in the United States has said little about these issues, and as a consequence we have seen many of our colleagues chased out of the field. At first it was gay men who were under suspicion. Then, suddenly, it was all men working in the field. Now women are discouraged—even prevented—from holding children on their laps or helping them in the bathroom. The point is not that we should be more upset by the demonization of straight women than of gay men. The point is that the moral panic in early childhood education, which focused first on gay men, is spreading rapidly. It was wrong not to speak up aggressively a decade ago when gay teachers were the focus of suspicion and attack. We have been silent as children's rights have eroded. We have only murmured our concerns as fears of litigation and soaring insurance costs have come to dictate our relationship to young children. It is not too late to begin to speak up and act up to win back children's and teachers' rights to their bodies and desires.

We reject the conventional wisdom that suggests that a loss of pleasure and desire is the price that must be paid to protect children from sexual abuse and their caretakers from accusations. Instead, we ask why as a society we are suddenly perceiving early childhood educational settings to be sexually dangerous, and we call for an exploration of the implications of this sense of danger for the lives of young children and their teachers. The explicit intention of those who lobby for fingerprinting preschool teachers, making toddlers wear swimsuits over their diapers when they run through the sprinkler, prohibiting male care providers from changing diapers, and not permitting children ever to be out of adult sight is to prevent child abuse. The reality, which we know but actively ignore, is that these measures, if carried out, will have virtually no impact on child abuse. We are unwilling or unable as a society to confront sexual abuse within families, where it is epidemic, so instead we try to impose draconian measures in preschool settings, where proven cases of sexual abuse are rare. The result of these new practices being advocated and instituted in preschools is to divert attention from the sexual abuse of children at home and to reduce freedom and spontaneity in the interactions of children and their caretakers.

The core of the problem is that early childhood educational settings lack the clout to resist the imposition of extraneous issues, interests, and concerns. The dynamics of this imposition are complex. To some extent it is calculated, an explicit strategy of forces in the society that are determined to reduce the availability of child care because they believe that mothers should be at home with their young children rather than in the workforce. Stories supporting the notion that preschools are places where terrible things routinely happen to young children serve the political interests of the opponents of child care. For these groups, news events like the McMartin case are windfalls, which they use as the Bush campaign used the Willie Horton case. But for such cynical political strategies to be effective, something in the national collective unconscious must be receptive. Moral panics are built on a foundation of widespread preexisting anxieties, fears, and prejudices. Thus, even those of us who endorse such liberal positions as government-supported institutional child care for working parents are not immune from projecting our anxieties onto early childhood educational issues. Even those members of our society who most desperately need institutional child care may project

onto child care settings their fears of homosexuality, AIDS, predatory male sexuality, cults, psychopathic baby-sitters, and other
real and imagined demons.

I am not suggesting that young children are never sexually
abused in child care settings. I am suggesting, rather, that our
ability to address the reality of child abuse in institutional child
care settings and elsewhere is compromised by the moral panic,
projection, displacement, and wishful thinking that we as a society are bringing to this problem. As we project extraneous anxieties and unrealistic solutions onto preschools, we not only fail to
protect young children from sexual abuse but also reduce the
quality of their lives in the process. While mothers' boyfriends,
fathers and stepfathers, uncles, and other family members prey
on young children in the home and a handful of preschool teachers abuse children in institutional settings, tens of thousands of
early childhood educators are being defined by the society at
large, by parents, and by themselves and each other as potential
pedophiles who cannot be trusted to act in the best interests of
the children for whom they care. In this climate of panic and
accusation, young children are also criminalized: play that in
other eras and other cultures would be considered normal and
unexceptional becomes evidence of their being victims or per-
petrators of sexual crimes. Viewing the actions of early childhood
educators and young children through a lens of potential sexual
abuse leads to the imposition of wrong-headed solutions which
themselves create new problems, impoverishing the lives of children and teachers.

Missing as in Repressed

The study of children's sexuality is also the study of our own
dimly remembered desires as children, and of desires we experience as adults that harken back to our childhoods. It is this combination of simultaneously remembering and forgetting our own
childhood sexual experiences and feelings that makes the whole

terrain of this book uncanny in the sense in which Freud used the term. In his essay "The Uncanny" (1919), he suggested that the *unheimlich,* uncanny, is something that is both familiar and strange, new and yet *déjà vu* (previously experienced). Children's sexuality has the power to produce these uncanny feelings in us because it leads to a collapsing of past and present, childhood and adulthood, us and them. As we witness children playing doctor, we are in two places at once, two people at once, two times at once. We are adults considering how to respond to this form of child's play, and we are also ourselves as children, skin burning as we examine each other in a garage. For most of us, our sexual curiosity and experiences at age three or four are so dimly remembered that they appear as stories heard rather than experienced, something that may have happened to someone else rather than to ourselves.

This doubling, this simultaneity of experiencing the children's present and our own past, is one of the great joys of working with young children. We must guard against the temptation to project our own psychological issues onto children's sexuality, to fail to distinguish our past from their present experience. Yet it is inevitable and not undesirable that we acknowledge and even embrace the continuity between their sexuality and ours. Such remembering of ourselves as young children, conscious or unconscious, informs our responses to children today.

Missing as in Unspeakable/Unthinkable

Repression is not just an intrapsychic, individual process of denying memories of our own private childhood sexuality: it is also a shared, societywide denial of the sexuality going on around us every day in child care settings and other contexts. It is a screening out, a disinformation campaign, a process of actively not speaking, hearing, or thinking about children's sexuality and our own. As Foucault writes of the repression of sexuality in the Victorian age:

[Sex] would be driven out, denied, and reduced to silence. Not only did it not exist, it had no right to exist and would be made to disappear upon its least manifestation— whether in acts or in words. Everyone knew, for example, that children had no sex, which was why they were forbidden to talk about it, why one closed one's eyes and stopped one's ears whenever they came to show evidence to the contrary, and why a general and studied silence was imposed. . . . Repression operated as a sentence to disappear, but also as an injunction to silence, an affirmation of nonexistence, and, by implication, an admission that there was nothing to say about such things, nothing to see, and nothing to know. (1980, p. 4)

Foucault's discussion of the "repressive hypothesis" is complex, with cautionary implications for our project here. For Foucault, the repression of sexuality is neither a historical fact nor a contemporary reality: it is a *story* about history and about reality. Questioning conventional understandings of the history of sexuality, he mocks the heroic, evangelical tone of modern liberal campaigns to overturn the reign of Victorian repression. Foucault suggests that the Victorian repression of sexuality is a modern myth that liberal thinkers encourage in order to create a need for their antirepressive reforms. He argues that the repression of sexuality and the repression of the repression of sexuality are companion discourses that create and sustain each other. For example, if Foucault were reading this introduction he undoubtedly would point out how the earlier section on the dangers of writing about sexuality in early childhood settings serves to construct our project as desperately needed and us as heroic.

How, then, do we talk about the banishment of pleasure and desire from early childhood education without falling into the traps and tropes of the repressive hypothesis? One answer is that it would be quixotic to aspire to escape from something that is so much a part of who we are and how we talk and think. If we agree with Foucault that we are trapped in a web of discourse, the most we can hope to accomplish in our writing is to nudge the terms of the debate in order to complicate taken-for-granted usages, understandings, and practices. A step in this direction would be to talk and write about sex and repression in a way that avoids the sterile, self-satisfied vanguardism that, as Foucault points out, has long characterized our discourse of sexual reform: "We are conscious of defying established power, our tone of voice shows that we know we are being subversive, and we ardently conjure away the present and appeal to the future, whose day will be hastened by the contribution we believe we are making. Something that smacks of revolt, of promised freedom, of the coming age of a different law, slips easily into this discourse on sexual oppression. Some of the ancient functions of prophecy are reactivated therein. Tomorrow sex will be good again" (1980, pp. 6–7).

One strategy we employ to avoid falling into these familiar tropes of heroic antirepression is to view the pleasures and desires of children and their caretakers as ordinary and banal. The essays in this book are not about rare or exceptional events but rather are about prosaic, everyday experiences and feelings of early childhood education. For young children, making butt jokes, talking about a classmate as being "like a girl," playing doctor, and engaging in kissing games are not unusual or strange events needing special explanations or meriting special celebration. It is not unusual for a teacher to enjoy holding a child on his or her lap. It is the teacher's acknowledgment of pleasure in the feel of a child's body and in giving pleasure to a child that is odd and disturbing to us. It is not strange or unusual for teachers to have sexual lives and sexual identities and for children to be aware of and curious about them. We find the topic so awkward not because it is a rare event but because it is rarely discussed.

Perhaps the most useful strategy for avoiding the pitfalls of the repressive hypothesis is to shift our discussions of the presence and absence of sexuality from the Freudian lexicon of repression and denial to the poststructural feminist language of the unsayable, the unthinkable, the inaudible, and the unimaginable. Instead of thinking of the everyday experiences and feelings discussed above as either psychodynamically repressed or haphazardly missing, we should view them as *actively missing,* the result of an active unknowing. As Eve Sedgwick describes it, "Ignorance and opacity collude or compete with knowledge in mobilizing the flows of energy, desire, goods, meanings, persons" (1990, p. 4).

Missing as in Overlooked

The lives of young children and their caretakers are made up of a series of moments that are missing not necessarily because they are disturbing but because they are too quiet for us to hear, too small for us to see, so apparently uneventful that they fall beneath our threshold of attention. We carry with us into early childhood classrooms a priori notions of the events and experiences that count and warrant our attention. Events and experiences hold significance only if our narratives of education and child development name them as stepping stones on the paths toward positive or negative developmental outcomes.

Sharing time (show and tell), for example, counts because our contemporary understanding of child development suggests that speaking about one's experiences to a group is an important step on the way to gaining self-esteem and becoming literate. Telling scatological jokes to classmates on the way to and from the playground, on the other hand, is an event in a child's life at school that is missing from the educational literature because ribaldry and grotesque humor hold no special salience in our conventional narratives of learning and development.[3]

In *Power and Emotion in Infant-Toddler Day Care* (1994) and other publications, Robin Leavitt has argued that an obsession

3. A happy exception to this tendency to fail to take children's humor seriously is Thomas Newkirk's (1992) chapter "Get It?" in *Listening In: Children Talk about Books (and Other Things)*.

with developmental outcomes coupled with the drive to control and regularize children's lives leads to systematic inattention on the part of early childhood educators and researchers to the quality of the moment-to-moment lives of children. For example, Leavitt (1995) critiques the use of the "Strange Situation" as an indicator of healthy child development. In the Strange Situation, a young child is left in a room with an unknown adult for several minutes and then is reunited with her mother. The child's reaction to the mother's return has been used to measure the security of her attachment to the mother (Ainsworth 1979) and to determine whether children in day care settings are at heightened risk of insecure attachment (Belsky 1986). Leavitt challenges these uses of the Strange Situation by arguing that we should be more concerned with the quality of the child's life while apart from the parent than with the aftereffect of separation when the parent returns. "With too few exceptions," she points out, "noticeably absent from the research debate is any discussion of assessing infant child care from the infant's or child's own *immediate* point of view" (1994, p. 9).

Our outcome-driven approach to early childhood education leads us to value activities that we believe will have a long-term payoff at the expense of activities that seem frivolous or pointless because they are not correlated with success later in life. David Elkind (1981) has written persuasively of how this reasoning contributes to the "hurried child" syndrome so prevalent in middle-class America. Preschool and lower-elementary teachers experience pressure to give children an academic fast start at the loss of the chance to be more relaxed with children and to provide time for them to enjoy themselves at school. Throughout the nation, an academic curriculum has been "pushed down" into kindergarten and day care.

Missing as in Depleted (Desire Under Late Capitalism)

The foregoing discussion of desire as being overlooked, silenced, ignored, denied, and repressed would seem to suggest that we are living in a puritanical age. But I do not believe this to be the case. Puritanism is associated with a society opposed to all forms of pleasure and desire. In the world of contemporary American early childhood education, however, some forms of desire are outlawed, but others are actively promoted and encouraged. Our late-capitalist, postmodern, postcolonial society requires not puritans but citizen-consumers with a particular constellation of desires. Preschool is a key site for socializing children into pursuing appropriate, culturally sanctioned pleasures and acquiring appropriate consumer tastes.

Frederic Jameson (1988) has defined the key features of late capitalism as superficiality, the dominance of the signifier over the signified, commodification, and the waning of affect. Each of these characteristics can be found in the patterning of desire in contemporary American early childhood education.

The valorization of signifiers is apparent in early childhood education's logocentrism. In the postmodern preschool world, statements about feeling ("I feel angry") replace expressions of feeling ("Give me the truck, you doo-doo head!"), which replace feelings themselves (anger? envy? desire?). Robin Leavitt and Martha Power (1989) offer a troubling exposition of what they see as the inauthenticity and superficiality of emotional expression in early childhood education. They paint a bleak portrait of day care settings in which child minders aggressively substitute their own interpretations of what children are feeling for children's authentic experiences of their bodies and emotions ("You aren't hungry. You just need a nap"). Leavitt and Power observe caregivers putting great emphasis on simulations—on children's displaying desirable surface emotions at odds with their actual feelings and desires: "Dwain and Gwen [both two years old] were playing in a large gym with the rest of their day care class. . . . Dwain hit Gwen for no readily apparent reason. Gwen started to cry. A caregiver approached . . . them and said, 'Dwain, that's not nice. You shouldn't hit your friends. Now give Gwen a hug and tell her you're sorry'" (p. 38).

Commodity reification, another symptom of late capitalism that can be found in middle-class American preschools, is manifested by a conflation of things with value and by a consumer-oriented approach to the curriculum. Capitalism in its early stages is driven by production; late capitalism, driven by consumption, requires the endless manufacture of consumer need. As Jean Baudrillard (1981, p. 82) argues in an essay on "consummativity," needs are not authentic, innate, spontaneous cravings but functions produced by the demands of the decaying capitalist system. Late capitalism requires consumers who have an insatiable need for new toys, gadgets, trendy clothes, decorative objects, and leisure activities. In late capitalism, the ideal man or woman is not self-made but self-consumed.

Consumer desire is reproduced by the material reality of our preschools. The variety of things and choices offered by middle-class preschools is overwhelming to many children. We create overstimulating environments modeled on the excess of the shopping mall and the amusement park and then complain that children are hyperactive and unable to focus on what they are doing. We have become so used to the hypermateriality of our early childhood care settings that we are oblivious to the clutter; settings that provide more structure and are less distracting seem stark or bleak. Many parents select a preschool the way they settle on an amusement park, shopping mall, or resort: by counting the variety of choices available.

In such a commodified world, a successful, well-adjusted preschooler is one who is an adroit consumer, able to cruise the aisles of the learning centers and to know a good educational toy when she sees one. A key characteristic of consumer society is the notion of scarcity amid abundance. Although an excess of materials is available, consumers must believe that if they don't act quickly and impulsively, the opportunity will pass them by ("Only three left on the lot . . . " "The first two callers . . . "). Learning centers sometimes mirror this sense of consumer frenzy. For example, most preschools put limits on how many children (customers) can occupy a learning center at any one time. To avoid a land-rush approach to deciding who will get access to the most desirable learning centers, many schools use an auction system. At the end of circle time, the teacher presents to the children a set of icons, each representing one of the learning centers that will be available for the next period. In one hand she holds up a fireman's hat, representing the dramatic play area; with her other hand she puts up four fingers, representing the number of children the center can accommodate. The auction begins. Each time a child puts in a bid for the dramatic play area, one of the teacher's fingers goes down. Excited, anxious children frantically attempt to assess the value of this option. The hat looks good, and the dramatic play area is certainly desirable, but is it more desirable than the other learning centers that will come up later in the auction? As higher- and lower-status children make their bids, the value of the dramatic play area rises and falls like that of a commodity in the pit.

The telltale sign that the culture of late capitalism has taken over early childhood educational settings is the waning of affect. A channeling and damping of desire are inevitable features of civilization. To decry the waning of affect in modern society is not necessarily to call for hedonism. It may simply be to appeal for a middle ground between uncontrolled desire and the desireless- ness (the desire to desire) characteristic of alienation in the age of late capitalism. The core of the problem is not that we are civilized but that we have gone too far. In our contemporary educational settings, under the guise of helping children let their feelings out, we interrupt and then attempt to eliminate expressions of plea- sure and desire that we find grotesque, silly, sexual, or sadistic. Mikhail Bakhtin (1984) describes this development as the victory of the marketplace over the carnival, of the mind over the body, and of the individual ego over the communal spirit.

We can take the argument further by adding to Jameson's post- modern perspective a postcolonial analysis. We can then see the rise of consumer desire in contemporary early childhood educa- tional settings not just as a product of late capitalism but more specifically as a symptom of postcoloniality. Kwame Anthony Appiah (1991) reminds us that the *post* in postcolonial, like the *post* in postmodern, is ambiguous—the term should not be read as "no longer colonial." Although the colonial era is over, our economies, our tastes and desires, and our (post)modern consciousness are still inextricably linked to the colonial project.

In *Tango and the Political Economy of Passion,* Marta Savigliano (1995) argues that in the contemporary world economy, passion is a raw material exported from the passion-rich periphery to the passion-poor core. Core colonial powers such as England, the United States, and (recently) Japan import from the periphery not just unprocessed foods (such as sugar, coffee, spices, and narcotics) and fuels (gas, oil, coal, uranium) but passion as well, in the form of prostitution and exotic arts and artists.

Postcolonial citizens, alienated from their bodies and desires, consume rather than produce passion. Our social and economic life is structured on this dynamic of laboring in alienating jobs to produce wealth that is then used to purchase value-added, manufactured, imported, highly processed (refined, acquired) forms of pleasure. The reproduction of the system depends on the production of children alienated from desire, habituated to the cycle of work and consumption. The American kindergarten's daily routine of worksheet activities alternating with learning-center times, snacks, and recess imitates and anticipates the adult cycle of pleasureless office work broken up by packaged pleasures in the form of shopping expeditions, coffee and lunch breaks, and vacations.

Missing as Disembodied

Just as colonialism is based on a dualism—the white colonizers associated with mind and culture and the dark-skinned colonized with the body and passion—women and children in our patriarchal society are thought of as prisoners of their bodies and biology. Elizabeth Grosz (1994) argues that patriarchy and many varieties of feminism share a suspicion and fear of the body born

out of an uncritically accepted Cartesian mind-bind dualism. Patriarchy bases its privileging of male power not on men's brute
strength but on women's inherent inability to transcend their
bodies and their biology. Menstruation, hormone-modulated
emotionality, pregnancy, nursing, and menopause disqualify
women from positions of power and leadership. As Grosz writes:
"The female body has been constructed not only as a lack or
absence but with more complexity, as a leaking, uncontrollable,
seeping liquid; as formless flow; as viscosity, entrapping, secret-
ing" (p. 203).

These notions of leakage and uncontrollability are even more
easily applied to young children in our society than to adult
women. Thus we find young children and women locked in a
daily battle to civilize children's volatile bodies. Children enter
day care as infants and toddlers, all uncivilized bodies and unregulated desire, fluids pouring out of orifices insufficiently closed to
the world. By the time they reach kindergarten, children are to be
moved from sensory-motor engagement with the world to abstract thinking, from unbridled expressions of bodily desire to
socially sanctioned forms of play, from excessive pleasure to good
clean fun.

Day care workers and preschool teachers are charged with the
task of bringing these bodies and desires under control. But this
mandate puts teachers' own bodies and desires at risk of erasure.
The preschool teacher is herself disembodied. As Malcolm Vick
and Erica McWilliam (1995) write, "Our timid educational theories do not equip educators adequately for considering the ways
in which the female and male bodies of teacher and learner in-
trude into the pedagogy itself. Teachers have been rendered 'no/
bodies' in educational settings" (p. 1).

Perspectives

The contributors to this book share many political concerns and
theoretical perspectives. Six of the essays in the book were first

presented, in preliminary versions, at meetings of Reconceptualizing Research, Theory, and Practice in Early Childhood Education (hereafter Reconceptualizing ECE). This organization was founded in 1990 by a group of early childhood education professors who were frustrated by the lack of innovative theory and progressive politics at the American Education Research Association (AERA) and the National Association for the Education of Young Children (NAEYC). We "reconceptualizers" have since become an important voice in early childhood education, especially through the publication of edited books calling for a reconceptualization of "Developmentally Appropriate Practice" (Kessler and Swadener, 1992), "full inclusion" (Mallory and New, 1994), and research ethics and methods (Hatch, 1995; Jipson, forthcoming). This collection follows in that tradition.

The book draws on the work of a core group of poststructural, queer, and performance theories to make sense of key issues in early childhood education. We believe that early childhood educators will benefit from this approach by acquiring vocabulary and concepts that will make it possible to talk about and attend to the "missing" issues of pleasure and desire. Early childhood education (like other educational specializations) imports its theories and research methods. Twenty-five years ago, the key sources were Jean Piaget and Burton White; today, they are Lev Vygotsky, Berry Brazelton, and their colleagues in cognitive psychology and pediatrics. Important though these sources are, overreliance on developmentalist, structuralist, and biologically based theories and an ignoring of poststructural and humanities-based perspectives distort the way we approach questions of pleasure and desire in our work with young children.

For poststructuralists, people in performance studies, and queer theorists, a union with early childhood education offers an opportunity to be less adult-centric and more attuned to questions of practice. For example, Judith Butler, by training a philosopher, and Eve Sedgwick, a literary critic, are concerned with the origins of gender identity, subjectivity, and desire. In recent work, Butler (1990, 1993) and Sedgwick (1990, 1993) trace these processes back into infancy and childhood, but only retrospectively, at a spatial and temporal remove from the lives of young children. We believe that literary and philosophical understanding of gender formation, identity, and desire will be enriched by research like ours, which is based directly on the experiences of young children and their teachers.

In Chapter 1, Robin Leavitt and Martha Power draw on an older critical tradition—existential phenomenology—and a newer one—the sociology of the body—to raise our awareness of the day-to-day, minute-by-minute experience of young children in day care. Citing Jean-Paul Sartre (1956), Maurice Merleau-Ponty (1962, 1964a, 1964b), Anthony Giddens (1991), Norman Denzin (1977, 1989), and Elizabeth Grosz (1994), Leavitt and Power argue for children's rights to their own bodies. They present a disturbing picture of the disciplinary regimes that day care workers force on children and issue an impassioned call to replace body control with body care.

Anne Phelan's chapter on the denial of the body in the lower elementary grades parallels Leavitt's and Power's argument about day care. But where Leavitt and Power emphasize the disembodiment of children, Phelan emphasizes the deeroticization of teaching. Blending the French postmodernist theorizing of eroticism of Georges Bataille (1986), Hélène Cixous (1976), and Michel de Certeau (1984) with the African-American feminist theorizing of the female erotic of Audre Lorde (1984) and bell hooks (1993), Phelan argues for the rights of teachers and children to experience pleasure, erotic and otherwise, in their classroom interactions.

In Chapter 3, on "no touch policies," Richard Johnson draws on the concept of moral panics, which queer theorists apply in critiquing the politics of homophobia and the erasure of desire. Drawing on Michel Foucault's histories of the discipline and control of the body and sexuality, Simon Watney (1994) has suggested that moral panics are not always (are never) what they seem: whether the hysteria is about rock lyrics, pornography, homosexuality, or the decline of the nuclear family, moral panics share the aim of instituting and naturalizing increasingly draconian norms of social and governmental control over the flow of pleasure and desire. Johnson's chapter sees the "no touch" policies that are springing up in child care settings as examples of this cycle of manufactured panic followed by heightened control and erased pleasure for both children and caretakers.

In Chapter 4, "Playing Doctor in Two Cultures: The United States and Ireland," I use Foucault's work on panopticism to analyze the control of bodies and desires in early childhood educational settings. In the late eighteenth century, the philosopher and social engineer Jeremy Bentham, in search of a humane alternative to the dungeon and the stocks, came up with a design for a modern penitentiary. He called his invention the Panopticon because it would allow a single guard, peering out from slotted windows in a central tower, to see all that occurs in a hundred or more small jail cells arranged in a grid before him. Foucault explains: "The panoptic mechanism arranges spatial unities that make it possible to see constantly and to recognize immediately. In short, it reverses the principle of the dungeon. . . . Full lighting and the eye of a supervisor capture better than darkness, which ultimately protected. Visibility is a trap" (1979, p. 200). I analyze panopticism in preschool settings, following Foucault, as both a literal surveillance of visible sexual behavior and a metaphorical surveillance (scrutinizing) of the sexual thoughts and desires of children and the adults who care for them.

In Chapter 5, Donna Grace and I apply Bakhtin's (1984) notion of the carnivalesque and Roland Barthes's (1975) distinction between circumscribed fun (*plaisir*) and orgiastic pleasure (*jouissance*) in a study of children as videomakers. We argue that whereas it is a commonplace of early childhood education to say that learning should be fun, teachers are not so sure what to do when school becomes not just fun but pleasurable. Our chapter describes the tabooed pleasures and unschool-like desires that were released in elementary classrooms when the children were given the chance to make videos. We draw on Bakhtin's theories of carnivals, fairs, marketplaces, and novels as sites of exchange between high and low culture to analyze the negotiations that ensued between the transgressive, exuberant urges of the children and the task-centered, authoritarian press of the school.

Grace and I in our chapter and Phelan in hers use Bakhtin analogically: children are to teachers in school settings as peasants are to rulers under feudalism. Bakhtin identified the carnival-esque as a way of life of the feudal world whose logic and spirit have been largely lost in modern times. For early childhood edu-cators, Bakhtin's ethnography of the carnivalesque ethos of feudal Europe provides a new way of thinking about children's doo-doo jokes, their naughty language, their parodies of Barney ("I hate you, you hate me . . . "), and the pleasure they find in the "shared social body." We suggest that, borrowing from Bakhtin, we can view preschool and elementary classrooms as sites where the low (children) and the high (teachers) meet. Bakhtin helps open up new understandings of children's impulse to make everything irreverent and bawdy and adults' counterimpulse to raise things up. He helps us imagine possibilities for how we adults who work with young children might respond differently, perhaps less like the political leaders of modern society who fear the anger and desires of the masses than like Bakhtin's idealized leaders of the feudal age, who welcomed opportunities to merge with (and be satirized by) the people.

Gail Boldt, in Chapter 6, draws on Sedgwick's (1990, 1993) analysis of the formation and maintenance of heteronormativity and on Judith Butler's (1990, 1993) writings on gender as perfor-mance in her study of gender tensions in an elementary class-room. Following Butler, Boldt sees the boys and girls in her third-grade classrooms as performing—or, as Derrida (1976) would put it, citing—gender. Aware that gender matters, they struggle to master the scripts by which masculinity and femininity are per-formed and to cite the authoritative versions of what it means to be male and female. Sensing that performances of gender sometimes (or always) are doomed to fail, they worry about the adequacy of their gender performances and those of their peers.

The new academic discipline of performance studies is emerging in the interface of gender studies, anthropology, sociology, film studies, theater, dance, and the fine arts. In performance studies, Erving Goffman, Victor Turner, and Jacques Lacan meet Robert Mapplethorpe, Madonna, and Alfred Hitchcock. Early childhood education is well positioned to enter into dialogue with performance studies. Carnivalesque hypermasculinity and hyperfemininity are on full display every day in the dress-up corners and housekeeping centers of our preschools and kindergartens. The polymorphously perverse desires and scatological aesthetics that performance critics celebrate in avant-garde artworks are on permanent display in our children's centers. The gender-bending, power-playing mimesis and hybridity that performance scholars debate in their essays on such films as *The Crying Game* and *Paris Is Burning* are familiar scripts in the block corners and sandbox societies of early childhood education. The exhibitionism and performativity that queer theorists locate in New York vamping and San Francisco camp are always in evidence in our preschools, where children are continually calling out to us, "Watch this!" and "Look at me!"

Peggy Phelan (1993) defines performance as "representation without reproduction." This definition has implications not only for our understanding of children's play but also for our attempts to represent children's experiences in our scholarship. "Representation without reproduction" reminds us that children's words and actions are performances reflecting their ever-changing, necessarily partial understandings of the adult world (see Taussig, 1993). Children use society's words, gestures, and social codes (Bakhtin's "authoritative discourses") to call forth a world that mimics rather than reproduces our own.

How do we adults who study children capture and represent their performances? Except for the occasional piece of children's artwork that makes it home to be exhibited on a refrigerator door, children's expression is mostly ephemeral. Listening in, in the style of Vivian Paley (1984, 1992) and Thomas Newkirk (1992), and tape recording and transcribing, in the style of Courtney Cazden (1988) and William Corsaro (1985), are useful strategies. But in turning performance pieces into transcripts, school ethnographers decontextualize children's words and play. Play in a preschool housekeeping corner is performance without an intended adult audience. The meaning is local, contextual, ephemeral, specific to the particular performance and performers. Our scholarly writings about these performances are in turn performances, mimetic acts that represent but cannot reproduce (fully recontextualize) children's meanings and experiences. As Phelan writes, "Performance's only life is in the present. Performance cannot be saved, recorded, documented, or otherwise made to participate in the circulation of representations *of* representations; once it does so, it becomes something other than performance" (1993, p. 146).

Jonathan Silin, in Chapter 7, argues that the cultural belief in childhood innocence requires the cultural construction of the pedophile. Following Sedgwick's theorizing of ignorance and closeted knowledge, Silin views commonsense understandings of both pedophilia and childhood innocence not just as wrongheaded or misinformed but as symptoms of systematic ignorance. By projecting our fears and desires onto the figure of the pedophile, we preclude the possibility of talking honestly to each other about the pleasures we find in work with children. Are pedophiles and perverts the only adults who desire children, who enjoy touching children and being touched by children? What if I were to acknowledge the emotional and physical pleasure I find in holding a newborn to my chest, in spooning oatmeal into an infant's eager mouth, in the feel of a toddler's hand closing around my finger, in rocking a child in my arms to soothe his tears? Must we cite studies on the disastrous effects of touch deprivation on baby monkeys (Harlow and Harlow, 1962) to justify our touching young children? Must we think of our touching and holding children as acts of altruism? If we can't talk aloud to each other about these pleasures—the erotics of caring for children—all of us who work with and care for young children will be forced to remain in the closet, wondering if we are alone in feeling as we do.

In Chapter 8, "Keeping It Quiet," James King draws on feminist theorists, including Nel Noddings (1984, 1992), Carol Gilligan (1982), and Valerie Walkerdine (1990), to help him understand the constraints and possibilities of being a gay male teacher in the primary grades. Describing himself as "a male apprenticing in feminism," King explores the ironies and paradoxes of how the sex, sexuality, and gender orientation of teachers affect the way they are seen by others and the way they understand themselves.

King, Silin, Boldt, Johnson, and I employ queer theory to recast early childhood educational theory and practice. Queer theory is an emerging reworking of gay and lesbian theory and political action that integrates elements of poststructuralism, feminism, gender studies, and cultural studies. To paraphrase Michael Warner, queer theory is not only a theory about queers but also a queering up of theory (1993, p. 26). Queering up early childhood education means not only paying attention to gay and lesbian perspectives in our research on young children but more generally calling into question "the regime of the normal."

For example, Gail Boldt concludes her essay with a queering up of her own desire as a teacher and a researcher to locate children's gender struggles in traditional narratives with conventional outcomes. She points out that her sympathy and concern for the fate of a boy in her class who prefers playing with girls work to naturalize and legitimate the belief that gender-bending children inevitably grow up to be mistreated, unhappy adults. This belief, in turn, can lead to the conclusion that nonheteronormative children need to be corrected for the sake of their future happiness.

Queer theory, along with postcolonialism, gender studies, and performance studies, challenges us to move beyond the safety of

our conventional notions of identity, ethnicity, gender, and pleasure. And what better place to see identity, culture, gender, and
the formation of pleasure at play than in preschools?

The contributors to this volume have much in common, including a shared interest in poststructuralism, performance studies,
and queer theory. But a close reading of our chapters also reveals
areas of tension and disagreement. These tensions, not coincidentally, are characteristic of tensions we have grappled with in our
Reconceptualizing ECE meetings. Some of these tensions have to
do with the difficulty of balancing the needs of the various stake-
holders in early childhood education. Some have to do with conflicts among theories. And some arise from the attempt to fuse
poststructural theory with progressive/emancipatory practice.

For example, there is a tension between the chapters that are
most concerned with the well-being of children and those most
concerned with the rights and happiness of teachers. Although it
is true that both teachers and children suffer from the erasure of
pleasure and desire in early childhood education, there are situations where the interests of children and teachers differ and even
compete. Robin Leavitt and Martha Power fiercely advocate the
rights of children in day care, in part by providing vivid examples
of the mistreatment of young children by their caretakers. Their
research is disquieting to practitioners who argue, with some
justification, that such exposés function to exacerbate public mistrust of child care workers and to aggravate the already low status
of child care as a profession. Leavitt and Power's chapter, along
with the chapters by Johnson, Boldt, and Grace and me, focus
primarily on the costs to children of early childhood educational
practices that attempt to control or erase sexuality, pleasure, and
desire. Silin's and King's chapters deal primarily with the challenges teachers of young children face as they struggle to stay in
the field during an era when teachers are under suspicion and

attack. Phelan's chapter and mine have sections whose emphasis alternates between the needs of children and those of teachers.

Paralleling this division between the interests of children and teachers is a division between the concerns of parents and teachers. In arguing that fears about the risk of sexual abuse of children in early childhood education are greatly exaggerated and in demanding that teachers be freed from the cloud of suspicion under which they currently work, the contributors may appear insensitive to the concerns of parents who feel that no price is too high to protect their children from abuse. One might argue that the needs of parents, young children, and teachers should not be seen as being in conflict. But in a society as distrustful, stratified, and litigious as ours, differences in concerns among these three constituencies are inevitable in discussions of sexuality and young children. I attempt to demonstrate this point in Chapter 4 by arguing that the relatively high level of trust and the small number of lawyers in rural Ireland makes sex play less of a problem there than in the supposedly more sexually progressive United States, where a game of doctor played in a nursery school has the potential to send children, teachers, administrators, and parents into a frenzy of anxiety and mutual suspicion.

Another dividing line in this book, as in the larger field of early childhood education, lies along the politics of sex and gender. The interests and perspectives of men and women and of homosexuals and heterosexuals at times come into conflict. As I observed earlier, the moral panic sweeping the field first hit gay men, then all men, and finally all teachers. Some of the chapters, like this introduction, are concerned with the demonization of males in early childhood education. The chapters by the four male contributors address the question of what we must do assure that males will not be driven from the field. The chapters by King and Silin focus on the special vulnerability of gay teachers. In the other chapters of the book—those written by women—the teaching of young children is assumed to be a woman's sphere of work. In the chapters by Phelan and Boldt, all of the teachers grappling with difficult situations are women. The interests and concerns of men and women working in early childhood education are not necessarily in opposition. But it is a difference worth noting that men in early childhood education tend to be most alarmed about their greater vulnerability to accusation, suspicion, and dismissal, while women tend to be more concerned with the low status, low pay, and lack of professionalism of women practitioners, who, after all, make up 90 percent or more of the field.

The divergent interests of men and women and gays and straights also come into play at the level of theory. Each of the contributors draws, at least in part, on poststructural theories of sex and gender. But within this larger theoretical world there are important differences and even warring camps. One line of division separates feminist and gay theorists from queer theorists. Feminist and gay theorists tend to endorse notions of identity (as women, as gays) that queer theory calls into question and labels "essentializing." Queer theory, in turn, is seen by some women's studies and gay studies scholars as a political move by academic opportunists to undermine the hard-won space that women and gays have opened up for their work in universities. For example, might not a switch in nomenclature from "women's studies" to "gender studies" mean that a man could win out over a woman in a search for a new faculty member? And might not a switch from "gay studies" to "queer studies" create opportunities for straight faculty (male or female) to secure funds, positions, and publication spaces only recently opened up by and for gay and lesbian academicians? These disputes are complex because the term *queer theory* is used differently in different contexts. Sometimes it is used to call for a union of straight women, lesbians, and gay men to combat patriarchy. In other contexts, queer theory takes the field under the banner of toppling heteronormativity, to deconstruct the categories of male and female, gay and straight, and in the process destabilize and reorient the politics of the women's and gay movements.

We contributors struggle with these issues. Phelan's and,

interestingly (because he's male), King's chapters are grounded most firmly in feminism. Silin and Boldt make the most use of queer theory, especially of its best-known current authors, Eve Sedgwick and Judith Butler. But Silin and Boldt also draw on nonqueer feminist sources. Although Johnson cites queer theory, his argument, like Leavitt and Power's, in calling for the rights of children to their bodies, falls into the more humanist, earnest (and thus not-so-queer) tradition of the women's and gay rights movements. Grace and I, in relying heavily on Bakhtin and Foucault, tend to fall more into the antiessentialist (and thus queer) camp. Although neither Bakhtin nor Foucault is a queer theorist, each can be seen as queering up both traditional and progressive notions of gender identity and sexuality. Basing our arguments on Bakhtin, Grace and I tend to be undisturbed by children's scatological and sexual talk and play, in contrast to the critiques offered by Valerie Walkerdine (1990) and other feminists of sexual play and banter as not-so-innocent expressions of patriarchal sexual violence.

Perhaps the most critical tension facing the contributors to this book is the problem of fusing the generally cynical, antiprescriptive implications of poststructural theory with the need each of us feels to improve the quality of life of young children and their teachers. The Reconceptualizing ECE organization has struggled with this tension from the start. At the end of the first meeting, the organizers for the second year's conference came up with the title: "Reconceptualizing Research, Theory, and Practice in Early Childhood Education: Reclaiming the Progressive Agenda." The colon in this ridiculously wordy title marks the divide between the organization's at times competing and contending camps, a divide that is also represented in this book. The organization has found itself split in planning sessions between those who want to emphasize cutting edge theory and those who want to emphasize political action and implications for practice. These often acrimonious discussions have been fought by individuals who staked out competing positions. But instead of thinking of this as a disagreement between dissimilar individuals or warring camps, I believe it is more useful to think of it as an inherent problem of joining poststructural theory with progressive practice in early childhood education. I will make the case for both sides of this question in a pair of codas to this introduction—arguments for and against being prescriptive.

Coda One: Reclaiming the Progressive Agenda

This book is intended as a call to action. The argument, which builds from chapter to chapter, is that early childhood educators have been too passive, afraid, or unsure of how to stand up to the moral panics that have swept over the field, diminishing the quality of life of children and teachers alike. We have allowed voices and pressures from outside our field to dictate the terms of the debate and, as a result, to distort our practice. Over the past ten years, we have allowed early childhood educational settings to be represented in public debate as sites of child abuse. In so doing we have demonized teachers and children and created space for the establishment of measures that would have seemed unthinkable just a few years before: fingerprinting teachers; outlawing the touching of children; installing surveillance cameras; criminalizing children's sex play.

This book was born out of a determination to recover a sense of balance and sanity. Proponents of harsh measures often argue that "no cost is too high to pay to prevent the sexual abuse of children." It is hard to argue with such logic. But argue we do. Our contributors argue that the costs of the erasure of pleasure and desire from early childhood education are too high for children and teachers to pay. We argue that recently instituted measures to fight child abuse by surveying, prohibiting, and proscribing interactions among children and their teachers are for the most part misguided, wrong-headed, and counterproductive.

Specifically, we call for an end to the crusade that is chasing men in general and gay men in particular from the field of early childhood education; for recognizing the rights of young children to privacy and bodily comfort and pleasure; for reopening a space for children to explore their sexuality; for defending the rights of children and teachers to be mutually affectionate; for ending fears of liability and litigation dominating decisions about best practice; for returning the responsibility for acting in the best interests of children and teachers to early childhood education professionals. We hope that this book will make a contribution toward achieving this agenda.

Coda Two: Q.A.P.

The chapters in this book are more concerned with raising questions than with answering them. We argue that not allowing children to engage in sex play or to be touched by their caretakers is a disturbing trend in early childhood education. But we hesitate to put forward guidelines for what sorts of touch or sex play should be allowed. We expose the relentless heteronormativity of classrooms and point to the pain this causes children and teachers. But we balk at endorsing the introduction of antihomophobic curricula for young children or recommending that teachers intervene aggressively in children's discussions of what it means to be masculine and feminine.

Why this hesitation to offer specific solutions? History teaches us to doubt that well-intentioned interventions necessarily lead to desirable outcomes. Foucault's genealogies of liberal reform movements in psychiatry, penology, and sexology are cautionary tales, destabilizing our certainty that our own emancipatory impulses are to be trusted. We also share a distaste for the social-engineering tendency of early childhood educators who are confident that they know what is good and bad for other people's children.

In 1987 the National Association for the Education of Young Children published the "green book" of Developmentally Appropriate Practice (D.A.P.), a manual of do's and don'ts for child care workers. We have no argument with the green book's assumption that we should pay attention to children's emotional, cognitive, and physical developmental needs and abilities. As early childhood educators, we find many of the recommended guidelines sensible. What we object to in D.A.P. are its prescriptiveness, normalization, ethnocentrism, cocksuredness, and joylessness. Our book, with its doubts, uncertainties, and lack of plans of action, is the antithesis of the Developmentally Appropriate Practice movement.

As a corrective vision to D.A.P. we offer Q.A.P.—Queering Appropriate Practice. Acknowledging the limits of our knowledge and the inadequacy of our answers can be freeing and empowering rather than immobilizing. By destabilizing—queering—the notion that what we do with children will lead inexorably to certain outcomes (traumatization, ego fragility, gender disorders, lawsuits), we can free ourselves to be more spontaneous with children and less anxiety ridden. We are not suggesting letting go of the belief that what we do to and with children matters. Clearly, our choices are critical. But facing up to what we don't know and questioning the hysteria that masquerades as truth these days in early childhood education need not leave us paralyzed.

Finally, we balk at being prescriptive because there is something ironic and even ludicrous about the notion of launching a systematic effort to open up a space for pleasure and desire in early childhood education. To create a curriculum of pleasure and desire would be counterproductive. Soon we would have Pleasure/Desire activity boxes, text sets, and teacher guides. To take too much interest in children's pleasure is to be intrusive. For adults to become too aware of children's sexual play is to change it. Many of us would like to believe that the young children we know have experiences of sex play, but we don't want to see it, to know the details, or to be placed in a situation where we need to comment on it ("That looks like fun!" or "I like the way you're taking turns!" or "Remember, only four children at a time in the sex play area!"). Part of the point of sex games and other "naughty" forms of play is that they are transgressive, performed without permission, outside the gaze of supervising adults. In Chapter 5, Grace and I point out that in bringing children's popular culture into the school curriculum in a video project, we risk colonizing one of the last remaining outposts of children's experience and pleasure.

This book does not attempt to prescribe how to put pleasure and desire back into early childhood education. It does attempt to introduce theory and language for thinking and talking about dimensions of children's and adults' pleasure and desire that are glaringly missing. Whether our effort succeeds in shifting the way teachers of young children think, and act, and whether such a shift would produce salutary effects, remain to be seen.

REFERENCES

Ainsworth, M. (1979). Infant-mother attachment. *American Psychologist* 34: 932–937.

Appiah, K. (1991). Is the post- in postmodernism the post- in postcolonial? *Critical Inquiry* 17 (Winter): 356–357.

Bakhtin, M. (1984). *Rabelais and his world.* (Trans. H. Iswolsky.) Bloomington: Indiana University Press.

Barthes, R. (1975). The pleasure of the text. (Trans. R. Miller.) New York: Hill and Wang.

Bataille, G. (1986). *Eroticism.* San Francisco: City Lights.

Baudrillard, J. (1981). *For a critique of the political economy of the sign.* (Trans. C. Levin.) St. Louis: Telos.

Belsky, J. (1986). Infant day care: A cause for concern? *Zero to Three* 6: 1–7.

Bowlby, J. (1969). *Attachment and loss.* Vol. 1, *Attachment.* New York: Basic.

——. (1973) *Attachment and loss.* Vol. 2, *Separation.* New York: Basic.

Butler, J. (1990). *Gender trouble.* London: Routledge.

——. (1993). *Bodies that matter.* London: Routledge.

Cazden, C. (1988). *Classroom discourse: The language of teaching and learning.* Portsmouth, N.H.: Heinemann.

Chodorow, N. (1978). *The reproduction of mothering*. Berkeley: University of California Press.

Cixous, H. (1976). *The laugh of the Medusa*. (Trans. K. Cohen and P. Cohen). *Signs* 1:875–899.

Corbett, S. (1991). Children and sexuality. *Young Children* 46: 71–77.

Corsaro, W. (1985). *Friendship and peer culture in the early years*. Norwood, N.J.: Ablex.

de Certeau, M. (1984). *The practice of everyday life*. (Trans. Steven Rendall). Berkeley: University of California Press.

Denzin, N. (1977). *Childhood socialization*. San Francisco: Jossey Bass.

——. (1989). *Interpretive biography*. Newbury Park, Calif.: Sage.

Derrida, J. (1976). *Of grammatology*. (Trans. G. Spivak.) Baltimore: Johns Hopkins University Press.

Elkind, D. (1981). *The hurried child*. New York: Addison-Wesley.

Fine, M. (1988). Sexuality, schooling, and adolescent females: The missing discourse of desire. *Harvard Educational Review* 58 (1): 29–53.

Foucault, M. (1979). *Discipline and punish*. New York: Vintage.

——. (1980). *Power/knowledge: Selected interviews and other writings, 1972–1977*. (Ed. C. Gordon.) London: Harvester.

——. (1981). *The history of sexuality*. Vol. 1. London: Penguin.

Freud, S. (1919/1974), *The Uncanny*. In *The standard edition of the complete psychological works of Sigmund Freud*. (Trans. J. Strachey) London: Hogarth.

Giddens, A. (1991). *Modernity and self-identity*. Cambridge: Polity.

Gilligan, C. (1982). *In a different voice*. Cambridge: Harvard University Press.

Grosz, E. (1994). *Volatile bodies*. Bloomington: Indiana University Press.

Harlow, H., and Harlow, M. (1962). Social deprivation in monkeys. *Scientific American* 207: 136–147.

Hatch, A. (1995). *Qualitative research in early childhood settings*. Westport, Conn.: Praeger.

hooks, b. (1993). *Teaching to transgress: Education as the practice of freedom*. New York: Routledge.

Irigaray, L. (1985). *This sex which is not one*. (Trans. C. Porter.) Ithaca: Cornell University Press.

Jameson, F. (1988). *Postmodernism, or the cultural logic of late capitalism*. Durham, N.C.: Duke University Press.

Jipson, J. (Forthcoming). Dangerous research.

Kessler, S., and Swadener, B. (1992). *Reconceptualizing the early childhood curriculum: Beginning the dialogue*. New York: Teachers College Press.

Leavitt, R. (1994a). *Power and emotion in infant-toddler day care*. Albany: State University of New York Press.

———. (1995). Infant day care research: Limitations and possibilities. In S. Reifel (ed.), *Advances in early education and day care,* vol. 7 (pp. 153–177). Greenwich, Conn.: JAI.

Leavitt, R., and Power, M. (1989). Emotional socialization in the postmodern era: Children in day care. *Social Psychological Quarterly* 52 (1): 35–43.

Lorde, A. (1984). *Sister outsider: Essays and speeches*. Trumansburg, N.Y.: Crossing.

Mallory, B., and New, R. (1994). Diversity and developmentally appropriate practices: Challenges for early childhood education editors. New York: Teachers College Press.

Merleau-Ponty, M. (1962). *The phenomenology of perception*. London: Routledge and Kegan Paul.

———. (1964a). *The primacy of perception* (Trans. J. M. Edie.) Evanston: Northwestern University Press.

———. (1964b). *Signs*. (Trans. R. McCleary). Evanston: Northwestern University Press. (Originally pub. 1960.)

Newkirk, T., and McClure, P. (1992). *Listening in*. Portsmouth, N.H.: Heinemann.

Noddings, N. (1984). *Caring: A feminine approach to ethics and moral education*. Berkeley: University of California Press.

———. (1992). *The challenge to care in schools: An alternative approach to education*. New York: Teachers College Press.

Paley, V. (1984). *Boys and girls: Superheroes in the doll corner*. Chicago: University of Chicago Press.

———. (1992). *You can't say you can't play*. Cambridge: Harvard University Press.

Phelan, P. (1993). *The unmarked: The politics of performance*. London: Routledge.

Sartre, J.-P. (1956). *Being and nothingness*. (Trans. H. E. Barnes.) New York: Simon and Schuster. (Originally pub. 1943.)

Savigliano, M. (1995). *Tango and the political economy of passion*. Boulder, Colo.: Westview.

Sedgwick, E. (1990). *Epistemology of the closet*. Berkeley: University of California Press.

———. (1993). How to bring your kids up gay. In M. Warner (ed.), *Fear of a queer planet* (pp. 69–81). Minneapolis: University of Minnesota Press.

Spitz, R. (1965). *The first year of life: A psychoanalytic study of normal and deviant development of object relations*. New York: International Universities Press.

Taussig, M. (1993). *Mimesis and alterity: A particular history of the senses*. New York: Routlege.

Tobin, J. (1995). The irony of self-expression. *American Journal of Education* 103: 233–258.

Vick, M., and McWilliam, E. (1995). Body snatchers: The exclusion of the body from pedagogical space. Manuscript.

Walkerdine, V. (1990). *Schoolgirl fictions*. London: Verso.

Warner, M. (1993). Introduction. In M. Warner (ed.), *Fear of a queer planet* (pp. vii–xxxi). Minneapolis: University of Minnesota Press.

Watney, S. (1994). *Policing desire: Pornography, AIDS, and the media*. Minneapolis: University of Minnesota Press.

ONE

Civilizing Bodies
Children in Day Care

Robin L. Leavitt and Martha Bauman Power

The body:
> source of self;
> lived for self and others;
> Encapsulating and encapsulated
> by social order and chaos   —Virginia Oleson

From birth, children construct themselves subject to the "civilizing" controls of adults (Elias, 1978/1939). Since at least the Protestant Reformation and the age of Puritanism, the process of socialization in the West has involved the strict taming of children's emotional and bodily expressions (Foucault, 1979/1975; Turner, 1984; Weber, 1958). Since Rousseau (1979/1762), however, this obedience training has coexisted with a philosophy of child-centeredness.

The influence of Rousseau notwithstanding, child-centeredness is noticeably absent from the child socialization occurring in group day care programs. Even the Puritans, noted for harsh and restrictive discipline, treated children indulgently for the first year of life, before the radical shift designed to break their inherent willfulness (Demos, 1971). In the United States today, this period of indulgence is considerably shorter, as infants are placed in day care programs as young as six weeks of age and are immediately subject to intense, almost complete control over their bodies (Leavitt, 1994).

Our previous work described the ways in which our youngest children are "disciplined" and the stark emotional culture of centers where alienated caregivers manage children's bodies in time and space (Leavitt, 1991, 1994, 1995a; Leavitt and Power, 1989; Power, 1992; Power and Leavitt, 1993, 1994). In this chapter, we extend this discussion to three- to five-year-old children as well as infants and toddlers and specifically attend to the lived bodily experience of the child. The past quarter century has witnessed the day care center's emergence as a primary institution governing the child-body. Managing the child-body is central to the daily business of that institution, and the importance of this fact should not be underestimated. We believe that how children's bodies are treated and how their bodied lives are lived are indicative of contemporary social, political, and cultural constructions of the child.

The stories we tell here were gathered in fourteen child care programs in three Midwest communities over six years (1989–1995). These programs include community college and university lab schools, Title XX and Head Start programs, privately owned and operated centers, community programs, Montessori schools, NAEYC accredited centers, and for-profit chains. Most of the field notes were collected by twenty-two students, supervised by the authors; some of the field notes were written by us during supervisory visits. We have not attempted to correlate particular programs with particular practices or to speak to all the child care practices within these programs. Our research focus continues to be on problematic experience—specifically, the problems of embodied individuals (Leavitt, 1995b). The field notes focus on widespread and persistent practices in the programs we have observed.[1]

Our interpretations of children's embodied experience draw

1. We thank our student-researchers and the many teachers who allowed them and us into their classrooms. We regret that our critical stance places us in opposition to most of these overworked, underpaid, and undertrained child care workers. We are grateful also to the children, for unknowingly enabling us to tell their stories as we read them. Thanks are also due Jenny Hand, whose assistance has been invaluable.

on recent literature on the sociology of the body (Giddens, 1991; Grosz, 1994; O'Neill, 1989; Shilling, 1993; Synnott, 1993; Turner, 1984, 1992), including poststructural analyses (Foucault, 1979/ 1975, 1980), as well as existential phenomenological philosophy (Merleau-Ponty, 1962, 1964a, 1964b/1960; Sartre, 1956/1943), and symbolic interactionist perspectives (Goffman, 1959, 1961, 1967). Within this framework, we address the child-body's simultaneous status as a social and a corporeal phenomenon (Frank, 1991; Shilling, 1993) in the institution of the day care center. We ask: what is the child's experience when the teacher turns her gaze on the child-body?

THE LIVED BODY

> I live my body. . . . The body is what I immediately am. . . . I am my body.—Jean-Paul Sartre

We are always bodily in the world. Our lived bodily experience is inseparable from lived time, space, and others (Merleau-Ponty, 1962, 1964a; Sartre, 1956/1943). "Experiencing the body," writes Giddens (1991), "is a way of cohering the self as an integrated whole, whereby the individual says, 'this is where I live'" (p. 78). Children in particular have embodied ways of knowing and being in the world, of experiencing and belonging to the world (Crossley, 1995). From perspectives as diverse as those of the philosopher Merleau-Ponty, the psychoanalyst Freud, and the psychologist Piaget, we understand that infants' and young children's perceptual-motor-sensory introduction to the world is an embodied experience. It is sensational. And it has meaning. The child experiences his or her world meaningfully through sight, sound, smell, taste, touch, and action. As Crossley (1995) puts it, "The body's being-in-the-world is at once mediated through physical presence and perceptual meaning" (p. 47). Bodies are both active and acted upon, perceiving and perceived (Merleau-Ponty, 1964a, 1964b/1960). The child's body is more than an object (although it is often treated as such); it is a body-subject, an active body always/already engaged with its environment and in the process of sense-making (Crossley, 1995).

The child's body, then, is both a biological, corporeal phenomenon and a social construction, shaped, constrained, and invented by society. It is the recipient as well as the generator of social meanings, an expression, an instrument of communication, interpreted by the caregivers and for the children. It is with her body that the child "speaks," offering her first gestures to elicit responses from her caregivers (Denzin, 1977). Embodiment is the basis of human intersubjectivity and fundamental to the processes of reciprocity (Crossley, 1995; Featherstone and Turner, 1995; O'Neill, 1989; Sartre, 1956/1943).

Children learn about their bodies and their selves primarily in their day-to-day practical engagements with the object world and with other people (Giddens, 1991; Packer, 1987; Packer and Addison, 1989). This embodied practical engagement is also the source of children's emerging agency. It is with his or her body that the child achieves practical competence and learns to feel at home in the physical and social world. Self-identity and the potential for "bodily well-being" (Freund, 1982, 1988, 1990) is constructed via this emerging, practiced agency.[2] The mastery of bodily functions and coordination and the extent to which children experience predictability and security in daily routines and interpersonal relationships contribute to their sense of self and agency.

In writing about the body, we refer not only to the child's physical body but to his or her self (Berthelot, 1995; Turner, 1984; Sartre, 1956/1943; Synnott, 1993). Moreover, the body-self is a reflexive, social, emotional, and moral self. The self is not given but *becoming*; it is created and sustained in experience

2. Freund was referring specifically to physical health and one's control over the close integration existing between body and mind. We add existential considerations to his notion of "bodily well-being."

and interpersonal relationships (Blumer, 1969; Cooley, 1922; Fontana, 1984; Giddens, 1991; Kotarba, 1984; Lester, 1984; Sullivan, 1953). The body plays an important role in mediating the relationship between self-identity and social identity. The continuous and successful interpretation and monitoring of one's own and others' face and body are central to the smooth flow of social encounters across various settings and to a person's acceptance as a full member of the interaction order (Giddens, 1991; Goffman, 1959, 1967; Shilling, 1993; Turner, 1992). The adjustment to the social demands of particular settings and the acceptance of others are vital to one's self-identity as a competent and worthwhile human being. A child who fails to learn appropriate body management incorporates this stigma into his or her self-identity. The body is not only the source of unending and ever-changing feelings and emotions but is also the criterion by which we evaluate our experiences in the world, experiences that may either threaten the self or open the way to fulfillment (Kotarba, 1984). Thus the child's sense of self is understood in terms of his or her embodied biography (Giddens, 1991; Shilling, 1993; see also Grosz, 1994).

Teachers and caregivers in preschools and day care centers are confronted daily with the bodily presence of eight to twenty or more infants and young children. As "uncivilized bodies," infants and young children are unconstrained by behavioral norms, prone to immediate physical expression of emotions and to satisfying bodily desires without constraint or regard for others (Shilling, 1993). The child-body is "unruly, disruptive, in need of direction" (Grosz, 1994, p. 3). The teachers' task is to "civilize" children as they care for them. Becoming civilized requires learning to monitor, control, and restrain one's body and bodily expressions (Elias, 1978/1939). It also requires the deferment and denial of bodily, sensory, and emotional gratification. The civilizing process involves the inculcation of societal norms, conventions and standards, rules, and codes of conduct with respect to behavior and body management.

Societies everywhere must socialize, or civilize, their members as self-regulating participants in social encounters (Goffman, 1967). We argue that teachers in day care centers *over*civilize the young children in their care—that the expectations, restraint, manipulation, and isolation of children's physical bodies and emotional selves is excessive and objectifying. To these teachers, children's bodily well-being is secondary to their management.

Body Time

Daily practices in the child care center necessarily revolve around custodial routines—that is, care of the physical body: diaper changing, toileting, nose wiping, feeding, washing, dressing. Such "natural" functions as eating, sleeping, and eliminating are socially managed and organized (Shilling, 1993). Routinized control of the children's bodies is crucial to the order and efficiency of the classroom; thus the first step is to get the children on a schedule (Leavitt, 1991, 1994). Teachers implement "regimes": learned practices that entail tight control over physical needs (Giddens, 1991). Foucault described this organization of the child's life in schools as "disciplinary time" (1979/1975); similarly, Goffman (1961) wrote of "collective regimentation" in institutions. Disciplinary time requires both the *correct use of time* and the *correct use of the body* (Foucault, 1979/1975). As the field notes reveal, *when* as well as *how* children walk, sit, sleep, and so on is all important to their caregivers:

It was time for the two- and three-year-olds to leave the playground and go inside for lunch. "Let's go in," the teacher announced. "Go quietly up the stairs. That's right, hold onto the banister. D.J., be nice. You need to be quiet and use your inside voices. Let's walk quietly with our feet. Use your feet. Please be quiet." They arrived at their classroom and the teacher began to set the table for lunch. She paused to yell at the children as they attempted to take toys out of the cabinets. Once the tables were set, she asked the children to sit in a circle on the carpet. During the commotion that followed as the children noisily found spots on the carpet, she said sarcastically, "I like the way you are being real quiet. I like it. You're being quiet." Eventually, the children were permitted to sit down at the table to have lunch. "Raise your hand if you want lunch." Once served, Ned began to eat with his fingers. The teacher stopped him, "Put your hands in your lap, Ned." She repeated this to the other children. "Did I say to eat yet? Shhh." Once all the children were served, she announced, "It's now lunch time, and it would be nice if you would start eating now. Use your spoons. Use your spoons. Use your spoons." As Sally began to converse with her neighbor, the teacher told her, "You need to be eating. You need to keep quiet and eat. Be quiet and eat. You need to eat your fruit and carrots." The children quieted and focused on their eating. . . .

Naptime was ending, and the teachers were moving about the room picking up cots and the children's blankets and pillows. Still sleepy, Lori was stretching on her cot when the teacher approached her and said, "Lori, it's time to get up." When Lori did not respond, the teacher picked her up off her cot and lowered her body onto the tile floor. Lori began to cry. The teacher moved on to four-year-old Kara, who was still sleeping, "Why is she still sleeping? Kara, get up!" she commanded loudly. Gradually awakening, Kara did not respond. The teacher said, "OK, fine, I'll just take your cot." Kara cried out, "No, leave me alone." The teacher tipped the cot over until Kara's body slid off onto the floor. Kara lay there crying, ignored by her teacher, who continued to pick up cots. . . .

Naptime was over. The teacher told the four-year-olds to return their pillows to their cubbyholes and sit in a circle on the floor. The children did this without much fuss. The teacher walked over to the circle of children and said, "OK, who's been a good napper today?" Almost everyone raised a hand. The teacher turned to Michele and asked, "Michele, were you a good napper today? Did you go to sleep?" Michele looked up happily and nodded her head. The teacher disagreed, "No, you were not a good napper, you did not go to sleep when you were supposed to." Michele looked down, ashamed. The teacher said, "Only good nappers get a sticker. Now raise your hand if you were a good napper. If you were not a good napper, don't raise your hand." This time, far fewer children raised their hands. The teacher proceeded to give stickers to the "good nappers."

Children must accommodate their bodies to the temporal order of the day care center. Implementation of this temporal order requires organized transitions from one activity to another. Transition times are considered by many teachers to be particularly problematic periods in the day (Davidson, 1980). Consequently, children's bodies are closely monitored:

It was time for outdoor play. As the children got ready to go outside, the teacher announced, "When you get your coat on, sit on the rug so we can make a count." Some children complied. "Sit on the rug," the teacher repeated. "I like the way some of you are sitting right now. Know what, boys and girls? You need to listen more. It would be nice if you'd be quiet so I can tell you what we're doing next. We're going to go outside. We're going to walk. We're not going to run, we're not going to gallop, we're going to walk." The children lined up in an orderly fashion and proceeded outside with their teacher. . . .

After their alphabet lesson the teacher announced to the fourteen children that it was snack time. "Everybody, hands up and get in line to wash your hands. Line up right here after you wash your hands. When everyone is lined up, we will walk to the table for snack." When the children had finished washing and were lined up, the teacher allowed four children to sit at a table. When they were seated, she permitted two more children to go. Jean Paul, on his own initiative, started to walk with these two children and was stopped by the teacher, "You stay here until it is your turn." She then allowed five other children to proceed. Finally, the last few children were allowed to sit at the snack tables.

When children deviate from the established timetable, both they and their teachers are unhappy:

It was "circle time" for the three- and four-year-olds, and everyone went to a spot on the floor. Sharon was slow in getting to the circle but sat down with the others. As the teacher started the "lesson," Sharon interrupted her, expressing a need to go to the bathroom. I accompanied her to the bathroom, and when we returned, the teacher stopped her lesson, looked at me, and said, "She never goes when she's supposed to. She always has to hold things up because she won't go to the bathroom with all the other girls." She directed a disapproving look at Sharon, then resumed the lesson. Sharon sat in the corner and pouted.

Some children are so well aware of the temporal rules governing their bodies in the day care center and the consequences of not conforming that they discipline themselves very harshly:

The children were transitioning to snack time. Kari sat down and drank the juice in a cup placed before her. Meanwhile, Michael asked the teacher, "Is it *time* to eat? Is it time to drink?" The teacher sternly replied, "No!" Hearing this, Kari's face puckered up and she began to cry. Tears streamed down her face as she sobbed, "I'm sorry." The teacher turned to Kari with concern, "What's wrong?" "I drank my juice," Kari confessed, still sobbing, "I'm sorry." The teacher, surprised, reassured Kari, "It's OK, you're not going to get into trouble." The teacher held Kari on her lap for a few minutes, then released her to finish her snack.

Temporal regimes are established and maintained by teachers in an attempt to manage the children in their care. Children are expected to conform to the schedule and the teachers' notions of timeliness. There are specific times and procedures for eating, sleeping, and using the bathroom, regardless of the physical needs of the child-body. The field notes illustrate how teachers impose an external time clock on the temporal rhythm of the child's embodied world of experience. This is the primacy of institutional time over lived time (Polakow, 1992). The consequences of not conforming to the teachers' temporal regimes include ridicule, punishment, and emotional distress.

BODY RULES

It is not just *when* but also *how* the child-body performs that comes under the scrutiny of the teachers in child care settings. In addition to adapting their bodies to the teachers' timetable, children are expected to learn appropriate "body techniques" (Mauss, 1973, 1979) and "demeanors" (Giddens, 1991). Over time, they are expected to internalize the body management norms and controls taught them by their teachers and caregivers:

> Linnae was sitting in the circle of children gathered on the playground for a game of "duck, duck, goose." The teacher observed Linnae spitting on the sidewalk. "Linnae, I don't like to see that. That's not very ladylike." Linnae put her head down in her hands. After a few minutes, her attention returned to the game. . . .
>
> Three-year-old Brad was the last child up from nap. He had wet his pants while sleeping. The teacher told him, "Take off your wet clothes and put on your dry clothes." She took out a plastic bag and said, "Put your wet clothes in here." The teacher walked Brad to the bathroom, where

he changed by himself. When he came out he gave the bag to his teacher, who said, "Big boy, Brad, that makes me very happy. No more accidents. We're going to stay dry all day tomorrow, right?" Brad nodded.

Like emotion work, defined by Hochschild (1983) as the management of feelings to create the displays expected by others, *body work* is also required of children: the presentation (Goffman, 1959) of body according to the rules governing children's lives in day care centers.[3] *Body rules,* culled from the field notes, include: walk, don't run; walk slowly; walk quietly; keep your hands in your lap/to yourself; keep your feet on the ground; sit cross legged; stay behind the line; move only when I call your name; raise your hand; use the toilet; don't wet/soil your pants; don't spit. Other rules are invented by teachers from moment to moment. Children learn body rules and body work through direct instruction, benign manipulation, social comparison, and the promise of rewards and privileges, as well as the threat of punishment.

In the following situations, children learn body rules through explicit and repeated instruction:

The four-year-olds were eating their snack of pretzels and juice. As each child finished, he or she raised a hand and asked, "May I be excused?" The teacher also reminded them, "You need to *raise your hand* and *wait* to be called on before you *ask to be excused*." Many children, not understanding the two distinct parts to this rule, continued to raise their hands and simultaneously ask to be excused. These children had to remain sitting until they complied with the rule in the correct manner. After some minutes, all the children caught on to the procedure. . . .

3. For elaboration on feeling rules in child care programs, see Leavitt and Power (1989) and Leavitt (1994, 1995a).

During group time the teacher asked the four-year-olds to sit quietly in a circle. The children persisted in their noisy behavior. The teacher, standing before the sitting children, put one hand up in the air, and the other one over her mouth. Jared imitated her, putting one hand up and the other over his mouth. The other children continued to talk. The teacher loudly announced, "My arm is getting tired standing up here. What is the rule when I hold my hand up? It means *be quiet*. Jared is the only one obeying the rules. Good, Jared." The teacher added, *"Everyone's hand should be in their laps."*

In the situations below, the teachers link conformance to body rules with privileges and rewards:

The teacher announced to the class: "I like the way Beth is sitting in her chair quietly while she colors. I think I will give her a sticker." . . .

The children were gathered together waiting to be assigned to play areas. The teacher said to the group, "Whoever is sitting nicely with their legs crossed will get to go first." She then began to call out names and sent each child off to play one by one. Eventually three children were left. (I have noticed on previous occasions that these same three boys are always last.) "Well," the teacher said, "until you boys sit up right I guess you won't be going to 'choice.'" Jason quickly worked his body into the correct position, and the teacher allowed him to go and play. She then turned to her coworker and asked in a loud voice, "Well, who do you think should go next, since neither is sitting right?" David and Jim quickly got their bodies into position. The teacher responded, "Wow, that was quick. Now, who do I choose first?" Just then Jim, in his eagerness, wiggled his body. The teacher then said, "Well, Jim, since you moved, David can go first."

In addition to bestowing dubious rewards, teachers exercise seemingly benign control through games and songs that compel children to follow the teachers' directions. For example, this "fingerplay" was heard often during transitions:

> I raise my fingers way up high until they almost touch the sky;
> I lay them in my lap you see, where they are quiet as they can be.
> Open, shut them, open, shut them, give your hands a clap, clap, clap;
> Open, shut them, open, shut them, lay them in your lap!

Once children's hands are in their laps, they presumably are ready to listen, to eat, or to begin a new activity directed by the teacher. When their bodies are properly positioned, the teacher has the children's attention and compliance.

Teachers also reinforce body rules by comparing noncomplying children to other conforming children:

> The children were instructed to gather about the teacher for an activity. "Everyone needs to hurry up. We do not have all day to wait for you," she admonished the stragglers. As children gathered about her, she commented, "Look at the way Lily is sitting. I like the way she is sitting. Look how nicely Jared is sitting. Sasha, do you think you can sit like Lily and Jared? I will give a worksheet to Yolanda because she is sitting nicely—not to Dane, Allen, and Kevin. I like the way Yolanda is sitting. She is not rocking her chair, she is not disturbing others. She is not talking." The other five-year-olds quickly quieted and sat still.

As these situations suggest, there is often an incongruence between what as yet "uncivilized" children do with their bodies and what adults want them to do. This incongruence highlights the teachers' concern with children's performance, their outward behavior, how they should *act* (Leavitt and Power, 1989). Through direct instruction, benign manipulation, the promise of rewards and privileges, and contrast and comparison with others, children's bodily inclinations are redirected and tamed. They learn body rules and how to do body work. At times body rules are stated explicitly; in a few rooms they are even posted on the wall. At other times and in other rooms, however, the rules are implicit, created and enforced at the whim of the teacher, often to the bewilderment of the child.

BODY TRANSGRESSIONS

For preschoolers, rules are absolute (Piaget, 1965). Body transgressions, or lapses of bodily control, are seldom permitted. Whether or not the children understand the reasons behind the body rules, they internalize and apply them not only to themselves but to other children:

> It was snack time. The toddlers were to wait for permission before eating or drinking. While watching the teacher pass out graham crackers, Martin knocked over his cup of milk. It began to drip onto the floor. All the children looked at Martin. Karen, after a moment's hesitation, called out, "Miss Ann! Martin touched his milk and you didn't tell him he could!" But Karen had broken *another* rule. "Karen, are you tattling?" "But, but, he spilled his milk and we're not allowed to touch our drink until you tell us it's OK," persisted Karen. The teacher replied, "Karen, we don't tattle on each other in this room. Mind your own business. What happens when we tattle?" She waited for Karen to answer, but Karen silently looked down at the table. The teacher repeated, "Karen, what happens when we tattle?" Karen did not answer. All the children looked at Karen, who appeared about to cry. Karen quietly protested, "But the milk was dripping on my skirt." The teacher replied, "I don't care, Karen. *We*

don't tattle. You should have wiped the milk off your skirt with your napkin. Now you won't get any milk either." Turning to Martin, then, the teacher asked, "Martin! Did you touch your milk before I told you you could? You know the rules! *We don't touch our snack until the teacher says so.* You *always* spill your milk. The other children listen when I tell them something. You'd better start listening! Now that you've spilled your milk, you won't get any. It's gone. You're done." The teacher took both children's glasses away.

As this interaction suggests, children not only must maintain bodily control but must be seen by their teachers and peers to do so. They must "stage" their bodies for both adult and peer approval or suffer the consequences. While the children may point out one another's transgressions, it is the teacher who implements the consequences—most often the withdrawal of ordinary classroom privileges and/or "time out." When body performances are not satisfactory and body rules are violated, teachers frequently resort to less benign methods to coerce children's bodies. The consequences of noncompliance are described below.

As the four-year-olds finished their snack they were directed to sit on the floor. They were not allowed to touch anything. They were told to sit still and be quiet. Restless, they were not sitting quietly. The teacher asked them, "Do you guys want to lose movie time today?" They replied, "No!" "Sit down and be quiet, then." After a few moments the children were again talking and moving around. The teacher said, "That's it! You lost movie time." The children protested, "No!" "Well, you better be quiet, then." The children continued talking among themselves. Losing patience, the teacher yelled, "Everyone sit at the table for a time out. You're all in time out for five minutes. But that doesn't start until everyone's head is down." . . .

During story time three children were talking, responding to the pictures in the book. Several times the teacher interrupted herself to tell the children, "Shh!" The children persisted in making comments about the story. The teacher asked her aide to move these children to "time out chairs." The children panicked and began to cry, "I'll be good, I'll be good!" as they were removed to the chairs. The teacher resumed her story, reminding the other children to "be nice." But, the flow of the story now lost, the other children talked and fidgeted. The teacher closed her book and commanded, "Everyone lie down! I will not read this story! Lie down!" . . .

Before the five-year-olds started to eat their lunch, the teacher said, "I do not want to see anyone leaning back on their chair today. The first one who does, I will give them no warning—I will just take your chair away." Midway through lunch Calvin leaned back on his chair. The teacher took his chair away. Calvin started to cry and couldn't eat. The teacher moved him to another room, where he was to stay until he calmed himself. . . .

Five-year-old Kyle was talking while the teacher was reading a story to the group. The teacher paused, looked at the children, and said, "I like the way Judy, Damon, Alex, Darin, Zeb, and Ronaldo are sitting. They are sitting nicely." These children were sitting with their legs crossed and their hands in their laps. Then the teacher asked the children, "Is Kyle sitting nicely?" The children replied, "No." Kyle buried his head between his knees, looking very remorseful. The teacher instructed him to "sit nicely." Kyle crossed his legs, looking contrite. About two minutes later, after the teacher had resumed reading, Kyle cautiously stretched his legs out straight before him. The teacher directed him to stand up in the circle until story time was over, about five minutes later. . . .

Benjamin was running around when he was supposed to be sitting in his chair. The teacher caught him, sat him in a chair, and turned his body to face the wall. "You should be ashamed of yourself." Benjamin put his head down and sat quietly for the duration of his time out. At snack time he was placed at a table with three other boys. The four children were given pretzels, labeled by the teacher as "regular snack." At the other tables, the children were given birthday cake. Benjamin, very upset at being excluded, cried while the children recited their before-meal prayer. He was so upset that he could not say grace. The teacher noticed, walked over to his table and said, "You may not eat snack until you say grace!" Benjamin continued to cry. The teacher looked down at him and commanded, "Say it!" Benjamin whispered in response, but afterward he could barely swallow his snack.

The experiences of Calvin, Benjamin, and Kyle highlight how children's emotional being is connected to their embodied selves in ways that fundamentally shape their abilities to achieve bodily well-being (Freund, 1982, 1988, 1990). Young children do not have what Hochschild (1983) calls "status shields": protection from attacks against their selves. Their embodied experience in these situations, then, is disempowering: there is no sense of body (self) competence. Not only do violations result in shame and punishment, but children who fail repeatedly are labeled "impossible" (Elias, 1978/1939) and, if not stubbornly willful, then increasingly "learning disabled" or afflicted with "attention deficit" and "hyperactivity" disorders. It is imperative that we explore the extent to which these psychophysical disorders are social constructions, created by the civilizing requirements of everyday life in day care programs and schools.[4]

4. For example, Polakow (1992) describes a child in a Montessori program whose boisterousness, playfulness, and friendliness were interpreted by his teacher as indications of "hyperactivity," although she recognized that "clinically, I suppose he's not" (p. 94). She recommended to his parents that he have a psychological evaluation. Polakow noted that this "hyperactive" child "was sent, ironically, to play therapy for treatment!" (p. 94).

When children transgress body rules, when they are unable or unwilling to perform, teachers escalate their control, often taking it upon themselves to manipulate the children physically into correct body position or body action. The children's own body integrity is disrespected as adults assume the right to manipulate their bodies. The malleable child-body is an object for adults to act upon, to mold, to "train":

> The sound of a loud whistle was heard throughout the classroom. The teacher yelled to the group of four-year-olds, "Did you hear the whistle? This is not playtime! Come sit down, NOW!" Most of the children complied and straggled to the circle for story time. "Gerald, you come here right now!" Gerald did not respond. The teacher grabbed Gerald and forced his body into a chair. "You're in time out. You don't know how to listen." Gerald got up off the chair. The teacher, angry now, grabbed him by the arms, "Come on, you're going to the office." Gerald pulled away and fell to his knees, crying, "No, I'll be good. I'll be good." The teacher replied, "Next time you will go to the office." Turning her attention to the group, she said, "If I hear anyone talking, you will go sit down in the office all day. I mean it." . . .
>
> The five-year-olds were sitting at the tables cutting out heart shapes drawn by the teacher. Tony had cut out three hearts, then paused. The teacher approached him and asked, "How many more hearts do you need to cut out?" Tony lifted his reddened finger for the teacher to see and said, "Look what it's doing to my finger." The teacher responded, "Uh-huh. It's not doing anything. Finish your hearts." Later, all the children were done cutting out their paper hearts except for Tony. The teacher said to him, "Tony, everyone else is finished cutting their hearts except you. You have been wasting your time talking." Tony, dismayed, put his head down. The teacher grabbed his hand, put the scissors in it, and manipulated his hand to cut the paper. . . .

Greg, Jake, and Bill were playing with beads on the floor. The teacher approached them and asked them to pick the beads up so that no one would trip over them. Greg protested, "I wasn't playing with the beads." The teacher responded, "You were, too. Go sit in time out." Greg replied, "I wasn't, though." "Greg, I said go sit down!" The teacher took Greg's arm, led him to a chair at a table, and pushed him down into the chair. After about ten minutes Greg started to interact with the other children who were sitting at the table with him. The teacher noticed and pulled Greg away from the table by his arm. "You stand here and be quiet." She left him standing away from the group. Greg, upset, put his thumb in his mouth. The teacher said harshly, "Take your thumb out of your mouth!"

These field notes illustrate how the child's body becomes the focus of the teacher's power. Perpetually discomfited and threatened by the activity, lack of cooperation, and unpredictability of the children, the adults increasingly seek to impose their will physically on the will and bodies of the children. The teacher's body is the "dominating body" (Frank, 1991; Shilling, 1993), and the children's bodies must become "docile bodies" (Foucault, 1979/1975) in the classroom.

RESISTING BODIES

Children are not always passive recipients of classroom body rules; sometimes they actively mediate them. At times, they challenge and resist the teacher's power to define appropriate body work, attempt to escape the teacher's gaze, or seek to redefine body rules in ways that incorporate their own inclinations. With varying degrees of success, they exert their own strategies of control as they struggle over the legitimate uses of their bodies:

Four-year-old Melvin was walking around the room barefoot; all the children had just awakened from nap. The teacher approached him and, bending down to his eye level, asked, "Where are your shoes and socks?" Melvin did not look back at or answer his teacher. She instructed him, "Look at my eyes." Melvin avoided her gaze. The teacher started to count, "One, two, three." Melvin did not respond to this warning. "Melvin, do you want me to go down to the office and call your grandma on the phone?" Melvin shook his head. "OK, then, where are your shoes and socks?" Melvin pointed across the room, "There, over there." "Well, then, go put them on," his teacher said, "or we'll have to go call grandma on the phone." Melvin retorted, "If you call my grandma on the phone you won't be my best friend." Unperturbed, the teacher replied, "Fine, I won't be your best friend, then." Melvin persisted, "You won't call my grandma." "Yes," the teacher insisted, "I will call your grandma," but did nothing. . . .

It was group time in the three-year-old classroom. Wen Fu wandered away from the group, appearing uninterested in the activities. A teacher caught him and pulled him down on her lap. He struggled to get up, but she restrained him physically by wrapping her arms around his body. Wen Fu began to whimper. The teacher said, "What's wrong, Wen Fu? Don't you want to listen to the story? Here, look, they're counting with numbers." Wen Fu continued to struggle and noisily tried to get up. The teacher released him from her hold. He walked away from the group and toward the book area, where he began to look at a book. The teacher let him be. Occasionally Wen Fu would walk over to the group and watch the others, and then would walk away again.

Children are not always as successful as Wen Fu in their attempt to assert their own body power:

Alan turned to Helen and said, "Hit my bootie!" Helen called out to the teacher, "Alan said, 'Hit my bootie.'" The teacher responded, "Alan, stop saying those words." Alan persisted: "Bootie, stinky, pooh-y," giggling after each word. Most of the other children ignored him, but a few giggled with him. The teacher warned Alan, "You better stop saying those words. You know you shouldn't say them." Alan defiantly shouted "stinky" again, to which the teacher responded, "Alan, I told you to stop saying those words. Now go to time out." Alan obediently went over to the time out chair and sat down. After a few minutes he approached the teacher and repentantly said, "I won't say 'stinky' any more." The teacher said, "OK, let's not say those words any more," and allowed Alan to join the group of children at play.

Children's bodies are sites of contestation in the day care center. Often, like Alan, children lose the battle to control their own bodies. At other times, neither adult nor child seems to win or lose; instead, they engage in a dance of ambivalence and a mutual test of each other's persistence:

The four-year-olds were seated at their tables about to begin an activity of puppet making. The teacher distributed dittoed sheets of paper with pictures of police officers. Aaron was seated at a table by himself, squirming in his chair. He squirmed all the way down to the floor. The teacher pulled his body back up and into the chair, "Sit in your chair." Aaron pulled his body away from the teacher, shaking his head no. The teacher grabbed him by his arm and forced him into the chair. In a high-pitched voice she threatened, "Do you want me to take you to the office?" Aaron shook his head. When the teacher walked away, Aaron stood in his chair. Seeing her returning, he quickly sat down. The teacher said nothing. . . .

The teacher asked the three-year-olds to sit in a circle while she read them a story. Some children were slow to comply, but eventually everyone sat down. During the story, Matt rose and went over to the climbing gym. The teacher interrupted her story and called him back to the group. A few minutes later Matt left the group again. This time he did not return to the group when called by his teacher. The teacher asked Matt if he would like to go to the "sick room." Matt shook his head no and stayed where he was. The teacher threatened, "I am going to take you to the sick room and close the door." The child replied in an even tone, "I am going to kill you." The teacher shook her head and rolled her eyes, saying, "Well, that's not a very nice thing to say," but did nothing.

While Wen Fu and Matt seemed to escape the threatened punishment in the situations reported above, they may not be so lucky the next time. The negotiation of body rules seems to vary with each incident and each child. The teacher's stance is often unclear, and enforcement of body rules is always arbitrary as teachers respond to children's attempts to push at the borders of classroom propriety. With every intended and unintended violation, resisting children risk experiencing "transgressive excitement" (see Grace and Tobin, this volume) or transgressive repercussions.

BODY PLAY

Molly was standing in front of the mirror. She was singing to herself and caressing her body. She was smiling and looked happy. (The teacher was absent today.)

Adults' inconsistent attitudes and behavior are also apparent as they structure and respond to children's play. Body pleasure is regulated in the classroom, but not always consistently:

The teacher announced to the preschoolers, "You children are really wound up today. Let's do shaving cream! Put on your smocks and come to the table." The teacher sprayed the fluffy white cream onto the tabletop, saying, "Do you remember the rules about shaving cream? It'll burn your eyes just like soap, so no splattering it on the table. You may not touch anyone else's cream or touch their arms or faces with it. And, most importantly, you cannot get up out of your chair." Barely attending to these restrictions, the children squealed with delight as they squished the fluffy cream between their fingers and raked trails through it. Jeff wrote his name in the cream and read aloud, "J-E-F-F." The children continued to swirl, flip, and feel the cream. The cream began to dissipate. Mimi called out, "We ran out, we ran out!" The teacher said, "No you didn't," as she sprayed more cream on the table. "Feels neat, doesn't it?" she added. "What do you think about how that feels? Kinda soft, huh?" Ned explained to the teacher, "This is my grandma. Her hair sticks all the way up like this," he said as he raised his hands above his head. Tyler began to pat cream on his cheeks. The teacher told him not to put any more on his face and to be careful. Gleefully, Tyler slapped the cream on the table with his open hand, splattering cream over his face and arms. The teacher told him that the rules were no splattering and that he needed to go wash up—he was finished.

The shaving-cream activity illustrates the sensory pleasure children experience as embodied persons. The teacher demonstrated a perplexing balance of indulgence and restriction. Sometimes the adult's need for order and safety seems to dictate her behavior. At other times, her actions seem to reflect uncertainty as to how to interpret and respond to the pleasure children were deriving from physical and sensory play:

Two toddlers, Patrick and Selena, were dancing with each other. They fell and rolled over playfully, laughing at themselves. The teacher noticed that Patrick was lying on his back holding Selena on top of him. The teacher said, "That's not nice. You need to be nice to her." The toddlers continued to play with each other. Patrick asked Selena, "Wanna ride on my back?" Selena climbed on his back and the two crawled around the room. The teacher, watching from across the room, called out, "Selena, don't sit on him!" but did not follow through. Patrick said, "I'm a tiger, grrrrr!" Selena then asked Patrick if he wanted to ride on *her* back. She told him, "Hold on," and they began to crawl around, this time with Patrick on top. The teacher saw this and said, "Patrick, are you doing elephant play?"

In another, more ironic situation, the teacher was leading an activity designed to teach children about their bodies, but when one child began to enjoy it too much, engaging in excessive bodily expression, the teacher disapproved and attempted to subdue him:

The teacher was leading the four-year-olds in a game of identifying body parts. First they were told to wiggle their feet, then their toes. Then they were to wiggle their knees, and lastly their "tushes." They were to do this wiggling while sitting down. Henry energetically jumped up and started wiggling his whole body. He was immediately reprimanded and sent across the room, "We told you the next time you couldn't follow directions you'd be sent to the table for a time out." The teacher continued the game with the other children. Watching, Henry started singing and wiggling in his chair, standing up at some points. The teacher told him, "Henry, you're supposed to be quiet during time out." Henry persisted in his singing. The teacher told him, "I suggest you be quiet." A second teacher added, "You better be sitting there quietly if you want to get up before your mom gets here." One minute before Henry's grandmother arrived to take him home, he was released from time out, after a total of twenty minutes.

Teachers often suppress the effusive, enthusiastic games children play with their bodies:

> Four children had been sitting at a snack table for about five minutes, waiting to be served. At first they amused themselves by talking, but then they began to blow their napkins off the table and giggle loudly at their actions. They all jumped up to pick up their napkins, creating a loud noise as Lena's chair fell over. The teacher went over to them immediately and said, "I think this table needs some quiet time. Go back to the line and have quiet time." All four of the children walked slowly to the line. . . .

> The children were outside playing "duck, duck, goose!" Steve could not sit still while Ruby, circling the group and patting heads, passed him by. Steve rolled on the ground and occasionally stood up. After several verbal reprimands, the teacher removed Steve from the group and put him in time out. Chagrined, Steve put his face in his hands. When, after a few minutes, the teacher asked Steve if he was ready to rejoin the group, Steve quietly replied, "No." . . .

> Lester lifted his shirt and showed his belly to his friends in the classroom. The teacher reprimanded, "You are supposed to keep your shirt down. Go sit in time out." . . .

> The children were returning to their classroom after a play period in the gym. As he walked, Charles cheerfully called, "woo, woo, woo, woo . . . I'm a choo-choo train." He walked fast and bent his elbows at his sides to imitate the motion of a train. "Cha cha cha cha, cha cha cha cha." Charles lowered his voice just as his teacher reprimanded, "Charles! Turn around and walk back to the room. You need to walk slowly and quietly. You need to relax."

In these situations, the children's spontaneous, enthusiastic bodily expression and pleasure are contained and traded for the adult's sense of order, propriety, and control. The oft-stated belief of early childhood educators that play is fundamental to children's lives (Romero, 1989) is practiced with ambiguity as the parameters of children's play are tightly circumscribed.

ISOLATED BODIES

Teachers' uneasiness with the physical play and sensory pleasure of young children extends to bodily contact. Children repeatedly are discouraged from touching each other as well as their adult caregivers. The regimented, disciplined child-body is disassociated from desire and from other bodies and affective relationships (Frank, 1991; Shilling, 1993):

> The three-year-olds were sitting on the floor listening to their teacher read a story. While listening, Lucy absently combed Sherry's hair with her fingers. The teacher noticed and said, "Lucy, *do not touch* Sherry. We need to *keep our hands and feet to ourselves*." . . .
>
> Three-year-old Amy was crawling around the teacher while a story circle was forming. She crawled in the teacher's lap. "I asked you, please, *do not sit in my lap*," the teacher said as she pushed the child away, "I like you, but I want to sit by MYSELF." Persistent, Amy crawled back to the teacher's lap. The teacher exclaimed, "Ahhh!" in frustration, got up, and walked away from the circle of children. . . .
>
> The teacher asked the children, "If you want to have music time, what are you supposed to be doing?" Almost in unison, the children responded, "Sitting quietly." The teacher continued, "Where do your hands belong?" The children replied, "In our laps." The teacher started a record and admonished the children, "You'd better *keep your hands to yourself*." . . .
>
> It was group time and I sat with the children who were gathered on the floor before the teacher. Paulo rested his head on my arm while he listened to his teacher. Noticing this, the teacher said, "Paulo, you need to join us. Sit up

now." Paulo said, "I wanna sit by her!" But he did scoot a little bit away from me. The teacher came over to him, put her arms under his armpits, and moved him about six inches further away from me. Paulo put his arms in his lap and put his head down.

The literal and symbolic lines these teachers drew speak to the "progressive individualization" (Elias, 1978/1939) of the body and the self—the walls constructed between our bodies and those of others. The teachers emphasize the physical isolation of the children. Physical contact, except to manipulate children's bodies into correct position, is improper, too intimate and too disruptive. Teachers touch children primarily to control and manipulate their bodies, to exercise their power, and much less often to express affection, tenderness, comfort, or intimacy.[5] As one teacher instructed the children, *"We don't hold hands and we do not hug. Nothing like that."*

The bodily, social, and emotional isolation of children in day care begins in infancy:

Six-month-old Nathan was sitting unattended in his infant seat. After a while he began to fuss, so I went over to him to pick him up. I was stopped by the caregiver, who said, "You can give him a toy or something to play with, but don't pick him up." I asked her why. She replied that she was trying to "teach him that he can't be held all the time, that he can play by himself, and that he will be safe if he's not being held." I did as she suggested and gave Nathan a toy. He quieted for a few minutes and then began to fuss again. No one comforted him or spoke to him. Somewhat later, another caregiver went over to Nathan and talked to him for a few minutes, gave him another toy, and then walked

5. See Synnott (1993) on touch as an expression of power. See also Henley (1977).

away. Nathan was out of his seat for only fifteen minutes of the two hours I observed this day.

It is not clear whether these teachers implement "no touch" rules because of the "moral panic" (see Johnson, this volume) engendered by the threat of child abuse accusations and concerns about children's sexual play or because of their own discomfort, disinclination, or lack of understanding of the developmental importance of touch (Montagu, 1978, 1979; Barnard and Brazelton, 1990). What is clear, however, is that children experience physical, emotional, and social rejection and separation on a daily basis. From within this isolation, children construct meanings of self and others.

Constructed Bodies, Constructed Selves

"Pay attention, look here, go see where it is, sit straight, speak articulately, don't do that." From early on this is the way people are drawn away from the basic rhythm of their own life. This is called "civilization." There is nothing wrong with being civilized, but there is something terribly wrong with being overcivilized.—Stanley Kelleman

The child's embodied self is constituted within the constraints of the body rules and body work prescribed by the teacher in the micro society of the day care center. The teacher is the child's ever present "looking glass" (Cooley, 1922/1902). Children's identities are connected to their failure or success in managing their bodies in accord with their teacher's demands. Children's anxious protests ("I'll be good!") speak to how their self-assessment is tied to the teachers' appraisals of their body performance. Children are told by their teachers to "be ashamed" of themselves; they learn that not "sitting nicely" is equivalent to not being nice, that "good nappers" are good children, and that "big boys" don't wet their pants. Children's self-pride is linked with the accumulation of stickers and "happy faces." When they conform to body rules, children are rewarded with the "privilege" of eating, drinking, and playing. In these ways, the values and requirements of the day care center are etched on the child-body.

As Silberman (1970) noted about schools, there may be less malice than mindlessness on the part of teachers. They may or may not be fully aware of the implications of their power over the materiality of children's bodies, but most teachers claim explicit and sole authority over the activities of the classroom. As one teacher announced to the children in her care: "You guys need to quit making noise and be quiet. *I'm the one that lets you guys do everything.* You guys need to learn some respect or you'll go to time out."

It has long been considered the responsibility of teachers to continually watch the children in their care (Bredekamp, 1987; Hendrick, 1992; Tobin, 1995). Not to do so would be considered irresponsible, if not negligent. Teachers unceasingly use the power of the gaze to ensure that children are doing *what* they should be doing *when* they should be doing it. Children's sense of spontaneous pleasure is traded not only for safety but for the adult's sense of control, as children are expected to comply docilely with the most minute commands. The extent of the surveillance of children's bodies sometimes seems unlimited:

"Someone smells!" the teacher observed. She approached four-year-old Matt and asked, "Did you go potty in your pants?" She wrinkled up her nose as she asked the question. Matt frowned and nodded his head. The teacher exclaimed, "Gross, Matt!" She continued in a voice loud enough for everyone to hear, "I don't know why you do this. You need to go to the bathroom." Matt looked down at his feet. The teacher grabbed Matt's arm and said, "Stand up." Matt complied and, while the other children watched, the teacher pulled the back of Matt's pants away from his bottom and *looked down his pants.*

The child in day care quickly comes to understand, in no uncertain terms, that his or her body is visible to others and that this visibility makes it subject to others' control. And so the child is drawn into the "drama of social life, the struggle with the other." The child's lived body is "the visible body, the object of social attention, projection, and mimesis. The body is now a form of conduct, of an identification with others that is never quite stabilized but is the basis of the child's joy and sorrows . . . that are the experiences of growing up among others" (O'Neill, 1989, p. 57).

The experiences of the children described here remind us that "the learning of self-controls . . . the civilizing of the human young, is never a process entirely without pain; it always leaves scars" (Elias, 1982/1939, p. 244). The stories we share illuminate the close, complete, and unending control children are expected to sustain over their bodies. We cannot assess the long-term influence on children's self-identities. For the present, our concern suggests that this unceasing surveillance and discipline may become so ingrained in children that they experience it not as a series of temporary confinements but as the very structure of being human (see Bernauer, 1988).

Referring to adult lives and health, Freund (1982) observed that the social requirements for "body discipline," the control and stifling of expression and spontaneous impulses, have escalated to the point of becoming "dysfunctional for the *self*-regulation of the individual's body," with implications for physical, psychological, and emotional health (p. 135). We believe that these conclusions apply to the process of child socialization occurring in child care programs as well. In the interests of "socially expedient appearances" and by means of the adults' "arbitrary exercise of authority," the children's authenticity, reciprocity, and mutuality are repressed (p. 136). Inattention to and disrespect for children's lived, embodied experience amount to the absence of body care and neglect of the children's embodied selves. This is the cost of civilizing child-bodies.

Body Care

All cultures construct codes of conduct to facilitate smooth social interaction and minimize social disruption (Berger and Luckmann, 1967; Denzin, 1977; Goffman, 1967; Power, 1985). Transmitting the rules of appropriate body conduct necessarily involves redirecting and controlling children's behavior and is a fundamental part of their socialization. Struggles between adults and children are inevitable as they negotiate the societal and cultural norms and expectations in day care centers, schools, and homes. But "the destructive effects of civilized or other forms of control are aggravated by the *degree* and intensity of domination and repression that they must sustain" (Freund, 1982, p. 133). This degree and intensity must be addressed as we urge children's caregivers to think about *body care*.

The teacher sets the tone for children's embodied experiences in the day care center.[6] Bodily well-being is "partly a function of a 'fit' between environment and particular individual bodily and psychological rhythm and needs" (Freund, 1982, p. 133). Responsive caregivers engage in a balancing act between supplying the necessary supervision and control that make life less dangerous for young children and encouraging children's delight in their bodies and emerging body agency. *Body care* entails developmental, existential appreciation for children's embodied experience. The meanings of these words come to life in the situations described below, as teachers enter into existential moments of the children's lives.

> The children had just listened to a story about butterflies. Inspired, Daniel stood on his chair pretending to be a

6. We acknowledge the institutional constraints to which caregivers currently must accommodate. Leavitt (1994) discusses how the spatial and temporal dimensions of child care centers might be reconceptualized. Clearly, the attempt to humanize the child care setting also depends on fundamental changes in adults' beliefs about and commitment to children and child care.

butterfly. The teacher picked him up and twirled him around in her arms, saying, "Daniel is a butterfly!" She then gently returned him to the floor. . . .

Michael fluttered around the classroom repeatedly calling out, "I'm Batman!" Each time, the teacher quietly acknowledged him, "I see that you're Batman." After one exchange, the teacher retrieved a large cardboard box that was open on each end. She told Michael it was the "Batcave" and asked if he wanted to crawl through it. Michael and his classmates delighted in repeatedly crawling through the cardboard box. . . .

Jason was running around the room excitedly. The teacher suggested he "slow down and relax" before he hurt himself. Jason slowed down momentarily but soon was again running around the block area. The teacher approached him, knelt down to his eye level and reminded him, "Now, calm down, I'm afraid you're going to hurt yourself." Jason slowed down for a minute and then began to run around again. This time he tripped over a block and fell into a cabinet, hitting his head. Five-year-old Sarah admonished him, "See, the teacher told you you were going to hurt yourself." The teacher, coming over to the two children, picked Jason up and explained to Sarah, "Jason hurt himself and needs comfort right now." The teacher held Jason until he was soothed. . . .

Jody, sucking her thumb, came up to the teacher and said plaintively, "I want my mommy." The teacher responded, "Jody, why do you want your mommy today?" "I want to go home," Jody pleaded. "What time is your mommy coming to get you?" the teacher asked. "Four o'clock." The teacher knelt down and put her hand on Jody's shoulder, "Well, let's see, four o'clock is after lunch and nap. Can you wait until then? Can you play with your friends until then?" Jody nodded, and the teacher gave her a hug. . . .

The children were waking up from their naps. Noticing

Michael's distressed expression, the teacher approached him and quietly asked if he had wet his pants. It was obvious that he had, and Michael began to cry in response to the teacher's query. She said, "It's OK. Accidents happen. You don't have to cry. We'll get you all fixed up." She went to get Michael some clean clothes and had him follow her to the bathroom. "You must have been sleeping hard," she observed as she helped him out of his wet clothes. "Let's get you clean and dry." Michael nodded, allowing the teacher to help him change. "When we're done, you can wash up and sit down for snack, OK?" Michael nodded again.

We stated in the introduction to this chapter our belief that how children's bodies are treated and how their bodied lives are lived are indicative of contemporary social, political, and cultural constructions of the child. Most of the scenes described in this chapter present a stark, disturbing view of the status of the child-body in day care. But alternative constructions of the child with respect to his or her embodied experience are possible. These can rescue the child-body and recognize it as a corporeal, intentional, active, feeling, reflective subject. The field notes just presented suggest that the process of civilization in day care centers need not completely rule out children's spontaneous and individualistic inclinations. Caregivers can become more comfortable with their own and the children's embodiedness and can learn to restrain their panoptic urge to control everything that goes on in the classroom. In so doing, they free themselves and win back children's—as well as their own—rights to their bodies and desires. When caregivers attend to and respect children's embodied experience, they—we—embrace, validate, and empower the body and the child.

REFERENCES

Barnard, K. A., and Brazelton, T. B. (1990). *Touch: The foundation of experience*. Madison, Conn.: International Universities Press.

Berger, P., and Luckmann, T. (1967). *The social construction of reality*. New York: Doubleday/Anchor.

Bernauer, J. (1988). Michel Foucault's ecstatic thinking. In J. Bernauer and D. Rasmussen (eds.), *The final Foucault* (pp. 45–82). Cambridge: MIT Press.

Berthelot, J.-M. (1995). The body as a discursive operator: Or the aporias of a sociology of the body. *Body and Society* 1 (1): 13–23.

Blumer, H. (1969). *Symbolic interactionism: Perspective and method*. Berkeley: University of California Press.

Bredekamp, S. (1987). *Developmentally appropriate practice in early childhood programs serving children from birth through age eight*. Washington, D.C.: National Association for the Education of Young Children.

Cooley, C. H. (1922). *Human nature and the social order*. New York: Scribner's. (Originally pub. 1902.)

Crossley, N. (1995). Merleau-Ponty, the elusive body and carnal sociology. *Body and Society* 1 (1): 43–63.

Davidson, J. (1980). Wasted time: The ignored dilemma. *Young Children* (May): 13–21.

Demos, J. (1971). Developmental perspectives on the history of childhood. In T. K. Rabb and R. I. Rotberg (eds.), *The family in history: Interdisciplinary essays* (pp. 127–139). New York: Harper and Row.

Denzin, N. (1977). *Childhood socialization*. San Francisco: Jossey Bass.

——. (1989). *Interpretive biography*. Newbury Park, Calif.: Sage.

Elias, N. (1978). *The civilizing process*. Vol. 1, *The history of manners*. Oxford: Basil Blackwell. (Originally pub. 1939.)

——. (1982). *The civilizing process*. Vol. 2, *State formation and civilization*. Oxford: Basil Blackwell. (Originally pub. 1939.)

Featherstone, M., and Turner, B. (1995). Body and society: An introduction. *Body and Society* 1 (1): 1–12.

Fontana, A. (1984). Introduction: Existential sociology and the self. In J. Kotarba and A. Fontana (eds.), *The existential self in society* (pp. 1–17). Chicago: University of Chicago Press.

Foucault, M. (1979). *Discipline and punish: The birth of the prison*. (Trans. A. Sheridan.) New York: Vintage. (Originally pub. 1975.)

——. (1980). *Power/knowledge: Selected interviews and other writings, 1972–1977*. (Ed. C. Gordon.) New York: Pantheon/Random House.

Frank, A. (1991). For a sociology of the body: An analytical review. In M.

Featherstone, M. Hepworth, and B. Turner (eds.), *The body: Social processes and cultural theory*. London: Sage.

Freund, P. (1982). *The civilized body: Social domination, control, and health*. Philadelphia: Temple University Press.

——. (1988). Understanding socialized human nature. *Theory and Society* 17: 839–864.

——. (1990). The expressive body: A common ground for the sociology of emotions and health and illness. *Sociology of Health and Illness* 12: 454–477.

Giddens, A. (1991). *Modernity and self-identity*. Cambridge: Polity.

Goffman, E. (1959). *The presentation of self in everyday life*. New York: Doubleday.

——. (1961). *Asylums: Essays in the social situation of mental patients and other inmates*. Garden City, N.Y.: Anchor/Doubleday.

——. (1967). *Interaction ritual: Essays on face-to-face behavior*. New York: Pantheon/Random House.

Grosz, E. (1994). *Volatile bodies: Toward a corporeal feminism*. Bloomington: Indiana University Press.

Hendrick, J. (1992). *The whole child: Developmental education for the early years*. 5th ed. New York: Macmillan.

Henley, N. (1977). *Body politics*. Englewood Cliffs, N.J.: Prentice Hall.

Hochschild, A. (1983). *The managed heart: commercialization of human feeling*. Berkeley: University of California Press.

Kelleman, S. (1981). A somatic image of wholeness. *The Journal of Biological Experience: Studies in the Life of the Body* 3 (Mar.): 3–14.

Kotarba, J. (1984). A synthesis: The existential self in society. In J. Kotarba and A. Fontana (eds.), *The existential self in society* (pp. 222–231). Chicago: University of Chicago Press.

Leavitt, R. L. (1991). Power and resistance in infant-toddler day care centers. In S. Cahill (ed.), *Sociological studies in child development*, vol. 4 (pp. 91–112). Greenwich, Conn.: JAI.

——. (1994). *Power and emotion in infant-toddler day care*. Albany: SUNY Press.

——. (1995a). The emotional culture of infant-toddler day care. In A. J. Hatch (ed.), *Qualitative research in early childhood settings* (pp. 3–12). Westport, Conn.: Greenwood Press.

——. (1995b). Infant day care research: Limitations and possibilities. In

S. Reifel (ed.), *Advances in early education and day care,* vol. 7 (pp. 153–177). Greenwich, Conn.: JAI.

Leavitt, R. L., and Eheart, B. K. (1985). *Toddler day care: A guide to responsive caregiving.* Lexington, Mass.: D. C. Heath.

Leavitt, R. L., and Power, M. B. (1989). Emotional socialization in the postmodern era: Children in day care. *Social Psychology Quarterly* 52 (1): 35–43.

Lester, M. (1984). Self: Sociological portraits. In J. Kotarba and A. Fontana (eds.), *The existential self in society* (pp. 18–68). Chicago: University of Chicago Press.

Mauss, M. (1973). Techniques of the body. *Economy and Society* 2 (1): 70–88.

——. (1979). *Sociology and psychology: Essays.* London: Routledge and Kegan Paul.

Merleau-Ponty, M. (1962). *The phenomenology of perception.* London: Routledge and Kegan Paul.

——. (1964a). *The primacy of perception.* (Trans. J. M. Edie.) Evanston: Northwestern University Press.

——. (1964b). *Signs.* (Trans. R. McCleary.) Evanston: Northwestern University Press. (Originally pub. 1960.)

Montagu, A. (1978). *Touching: The human significance of the skin.* New York: Harper Colophon.

——. (1979). The skin, touch, and human development. In S. Weitz (ed.), *Nonverbal communication.* New York: Oxford University Press.

Oleson, V. (1994). Problematic bodies: Past, present, and future. *Symbolic Interaction* 17 (2): 231–237.

O'Neill, J. (1989). *The communicative body: Studies in communicative philosophy, politics, and sociology.* Evanston: Northwestern University Press.

Packer, M. (1987). Social interaction as a practical activity: Implications for the study of moral development. In W. Kurtines and J. Gewirtz (eds.), *Moral development through social interaction* (pp. 245–277). New York: John Wiley and Sons.

Packer, M., and Addison, R. (1989). Introduction. In M. Packer and R. Addison (eds.), *Entering the circle: Hermeneutic investigation in psychology* (pp. 13–36). Albany: SUNY Press.

Piaget, J. (1965). *The moral judgement of the child.* New York: Free Press.

Polakow, V. (1992). *The erosion of childhood.* Chicago: University of Chicago Press.

Power, M. B. (1985). The ritualization of emotional conduct in early childhood. In Patricia Adler and Peter Adler (eds.), *Studies in symbolic interaction,* vol. 6 (pp. 213–227). Greenwich, Conn.: JAI.

——. (1992). Emotionality in morally salient interactions: The experience of preschoolers. Paper presented at the Midwest Sociological Society Meetings, Kansas City, Mo.

Power, M. B., and Leavitt, R. L. (1993). Moral emotions in early childhood settings. Paper presented at the Midwest Sociological Society Meetings, Chicago.

——. (1994). Moral dilemmas in a preschool setting. Paper presented at the Illinois Sociological Society Annual Meetings, Peoria.

Romero, M. (1989). Work and play in the nursery school. *Educational Policy* 3 (4): 410–419.

Rousseau, J.-J. (1979). *Emile.* (Trans. A. Bloom.) New York: Basic. (Originally pub. 1762.)

Sartre, J.-P. (1956). *Being and nothingness.* (Trans. H. E. Barnes.) New York: Simon and Schuster. (Originally pub. 1943.)

Shilling, C. (1993). *The body and social theory.* London: Sage.

Silberman, C. (1970). *Crisis in the classroom.* New York: Vintage.

Sullivan, H. S. (1953). *The interpersonal theory of psychiatry.* New York: Norton.

Synnott, A. (1993). *The body social: Symbolism, self, and society.* London: Routledge.

Tobin, J. (1995). Post-structural research in early childhood education. In J. A. Hatch (ed.), *Qualitative research in early childhood settings* (pp. 223–243). Westport, Conn.: Praeger.

Turner, B. (1984). *The body and society.* London: Basil Blackwell.

——. (1992). *Regulating bodies: Essays in medical sociology.* London: Routledge.

Weber, M. (1958). *The Protestant ethic and the spirit of capitalism.* New York: Scribner.

Classroom Management and the Erasure of Teacher Desire

Anne M. Phelan

Whenever I am in the classroom with the children, teaching a lesson, or just walking with them to lunch, I feel that I have no control over how the kids behave or conduct themselves. The other teachers in the second grade seem to have very orderly classes, and whenever I pass by one of their rooms the children seem to be working quietly, either individually or in small groups, and on task. In our class, they are almost always loud, and I feel that the other teachers look down on this as "obviously she doesn't have any control over these kids." Because I think the other teachers tend to measure your ability as a teacher on the way you allow your children to conduct themselves, it reflects badly on me if I can't have them all line up the way the other classes do or work quietly like the other classes.—Student teacher logbook, Grade 2

One of the abiding questions in early childhood education concerns classroom management. How do I help the children learn self-control? How do I control a large group of young and active children who are still learning how to control themselves? What will my colleagues think of me if I fail to maintain control in my classroom? What will my principal think? If there is no classroom order, will my children learn? Order and control are pervasive concerns for early childhood teachers in their planning and decision making. Teachers spend a great deal of time teaching students to be responsible, to have self-control, and to behave appropriately in the classroom. As C. A. Bowers and David Flinders (1990) suggest, a teacher's sense of success hinges on the ability to maintain order; firm control of children is one of the most important criteria by which colleagues judge one another's effectiveness.

The preoccupation of early childhood educators with classroom management can be explained in a number of ways. Perhaps it is a function of the socialization focus of early childhood education: young children must learn how to act toward one another and to solve problems, Pam Oken-Wright (1992) suggests, by "learning to use language rather than their bodies to get what they want" (p. 15). Perhaps the preoccupation with control is due to the implicit assumption that order precedes learning. The pressure on kindergarten and first-grade teachers to ensure their pupils' academic excellence and readiness for the upper elementary grades may be a factor. Or perhaps the concern with a well-managed classroom is part of the desire for a pristine world free of violence and full of self-disciplined individuals.

The self-evident nature of the need for order in schools and classrooms is dangerously seductive. It is my view that our preoccupation with orderly conduct in schools is related to a disciplining of student and teacher desires, bodies, and pleasures. The discourse-practices of classroom management have engendered a fear of disorderly classrooms where the playful exists alongside the serious, of disorderly children whose bodies touch, and of disorderly women (and a few men) who experience pleasure from their attachment to and continuity with their students. Simply put, a concern with order belies a fear of the erotic.

Eros is the drive that impels human beings toward union. The desire for union and communion manifests itself in classroom moments of joy, laughter, and pleasure. A shift from the normal state of classroom order to that of erotic desire presupposes a partial dissolution of the binary opposition of teacher and student. During erotic moments, boundaries are blurred and established patterns of relations are disturbed; these are moments of exuberance and excess for teachers and students, moments that are unreserved, lavish, and joyful. Georges Bataille (1986) suggests that eroticism smashes apart the self-contained character of individuals as they are in their normal lives. In education, eroticism takes the form of a desire to break with the established patterns of classroom order which are basic to our discontinuous mode of existence as separate and defined individuals.

To speak of erotic desire in relation to children and teachers is to evoke anxiety, anxiety that diminishes the possibilities of the erotic. For example, on my first day in a Montessori preschool, I made the mistake of sitting on the carpet with a child in my lap and two others pressing closely at my sides. The director chastised the children and then tactfully reminded me of the importance of promoting individuation. Suddenly it was obscene to touch or be touched, to feel the warmth of bodies pressing against one another, a blending not of student with teacher but simply of bodies. Bataille reminds us that "obscenity is our name for the uneasiness which upsets the physical state associated with self-possession, with the possession of a recognized and stable individuality." For a moment, I had forgotten my work as an educator and succumbed to a desire of my own.

Teaching requires women to leave their desires at home. We must, in Trinh Minh-ha's (1992) terms, practice forgetting ourselves, take on the face of alienation, and empty ourselves of our erotic desires. Sarah Freedman (1987) reminds us that this is the cost of the increasing professionalization of teaching as society encourages women to leave their homes to pursue *real* work, "work based on the male model that emphasizes rationality, order, detachment" (p. 458). Classroom management practices erase eroticism and promote order. In doing so, they foster certain self-containing body gestures, sensations, and feelings that combine to construct a political regime of the body. And it is not simply the student body that is in question; teachers' desires are at issue as well.

Why have we come to this? How are teachers' and students'

erotic desires disciplined? What happens when "the world of work and reason . . . do[es] not absorb us completely"? (Bataille, 1986) What of excessive moments when the injunction to be orderly fails? As we embark on these explorations, it is important to remember that in classrooms there are no helpless victims or heroic resisters. As Valerie Walkerdine (1993) reminds us, teachers and students are positioned "in relations of power which are constantly shifting, rendering [each] at one moment powerful and at another powerless" (p. 208). Walkerdine's message is critical if we are to avoid a simplistic analysis that posits the teacher as a powerful agent of an oppressive bourgeois educational system and the children as oppressed innocents.

MANAGING DESIRE IN EARLY CHILDHOOD

Because adults take the schools so much for granted, they fail to appreciate what grim, joyless places most American schools are.—Charles E. Silberman

Students must try to behave as if they were in solitude, when in point of fact they are not. . . . In the early grades it is not uncommon to find students facing each other around a table while at the same time being required not to communicate with each other. These young people, if they are to become successful students, must learn how to be alone in a crowd.—Phillip Jackson

In recent years, there has been a resurgence of the progressive education movement and the concept of child-centeredness. Walkerdine (1987) asserts that there seems to be "an overt message concerning activity, exploration, openness and so forth derived from the child-centered pedagogy." However, she also points out that in primary classrooms "the discourse of good behavior, neatness, and rule-following exists *covertly* alongside overt messages. It would have to be covert because it is the exact opposite of what is supposed to take place." In Walkerdine's study, helpful children were those who played an important part in maintaining "calm, order and the smooth regulation of the classroom" (p. 63). Ten years earlier, Michael Apple and Nancy King (1977) noted a similar phenomenon in kindergarten classrooms—namely, that obedience was valued over ingenuity, and cooperation (in the form of "adequate participation") over excellence.

For Apple and King, as for Walkerdine, the binaries of work/play and order/disorder organize classroom life. For example, when kindergartners were asked in September what children in kindergarten do, they never used the word "work"; by October, half of them responded to the same question with "work." Work, for these children, meant doing something one is told to do. Work is always compulsory, and it begins and ends at designated times (Apple and King, 1977). It is the children's diligence and perseverance that are rewarded, not the work itself.

We tend to define work *in opposition to* rather than *in tension with* the erotic. Work demands rational behavior and the control of impulse and desire; work promises long-term rewards rather than immediate, momentary pleasures. Apple and King (1977) describe one kindergarten teacher's concerns: "The teacher often justified her presentation of work activities in the classroom in terms of the preparation of the children for elementary school and for adulthood. For example, she believed that work activities should be compulsory because the children needed practice following directions . . . as preparation for the reality of adult work. The children were expected to view kindergarten as a year of preparation for the first grade. . . . The teacher spoke of . . . the difficulty that children who were inattentive in kindergarten would have the following year" (p. 353).

Impulse and desire are rewritten as inattention. Momentary pleasures are replaced by the pressure to be ready for the first grade. Kindergarten is no place for the exuberance of life in the here and now; the projected difficulty in first grade is deterrent enough. Children's "work" is robbed "of its erotic value, its erotic power and life appeal and fulfillment. Such a system reduces work to a travesty of necessities, a duty" (Lorde, 1984, p. 55). It is not only work that is robbed of its erotic quality. Play is also recast as an instrument of rationality. The emphasis on children's choice of play activities is undergirded by the notion that "by leaving children alone to grow out of their base animal sexuality and their aggression," one can produce rational individuals (Walkerdine, 1993, p. 213).

The preoccupation with work and order is a reaction to the underlying fear that disorder lurks in the corners and crevices of classrooms. "However reasonable we may grow we may be mastered anew by a violence . . . [committed by] a rational being who tries to obey but who succumbs to stirrings within him[her]self which [s]he cannot bring to heel" (Bataille, 1986, p. 40). The teacher's task is to manage those stirrings in herself and in her students. Classroom-management practices contribute to the production of the regulatory ideal—the self-possessed, rational subject.

The opposition of work and pleasure reflects Jean-François Lyotard's principle of performativity (1984). In the classroom, this principle translates into maintaining the flow of activity. Management refers to the procedures necessary to establish and maintain the flow in a lesson; in this manner work, euphemistically termed *learning,* can occur. The prevention of disorder and restoration of order become central concerns in the maintenance of this work system. The key to the teacher's success in management lies in her understanding of the likely configuration of events in the classroom and her skill in monitoring and guiding activities in light of this understanding (Doyle, 1986). In contemporary educational jargon, teachers establish and maintain learning environments, develop and teach rules and routines, and use desists and other cues and sanctions to restore order when prevention is not enough.

In the following paragraphs, I juxtapose theoretical discourse on classroom management with practices in schools. In each example, we witness the enactment of the dichotomies of pleasure/

work and eroticism/rationality. The values of work, order, and rationality constitute a powerful institutional ideology because they remain implicit, unstated, mundane, and ubiquitous in day-to-day classroom life.

Establishing a Learning Environment

The discourse:

> We are concerned not only with reducing distraction or minimizing congestion . . . but also with ways the environment can foster children's security, increase their comfort, and stimulate their interest in learning tasks.
> —Carol Weinstein and Andrew Mignano

The practice:

> When the students couldn't sit still on the floor in the space that the team used for direct instruction, Cora marked off their areas with tape in a sort of grid pattern, to keep the children in their proper place.
> —Student-teacher's journal, kindergarten

It is hard to argue with Weinstein and Mignano's (1993) concern with the child's security, comfort, and interest or to question a practice by which children are freed from distraction by their neighbors' body movements and are safe and secure in squares of their own. But what are the children learning about themselves and their bodies when they live under these classroom regimes?

Children's bodies, especially in their proximity to other bodies, pose a menace to order. Proximity is taboo in many early childhood classrooms. We teach self-possession and self-control by deriving a list of prohibited behaviors—thou shalt not go near; thou shalt not touch; thou shalt not experience pleasure; thou shalt not speak; thou shalt not show thyself, except, as Foucault reminds us, in darkness and secrecy. We read children's behaviors in terms of dominant child-development discourses of self-possession; we misread individual autonomy as separation and independence from others. Moreover, we read into their behaviors our own fear of merging and loss of boundaries between persons. We develop rules and routines to offset the possibility of disorderly conduct, which we tell ourselves might disrupt the work of teaching and learning.

Developing Rules and Routines

The discourse:

> Clearly defined classroom rules and routines help to dispel
> the "what ifs" and to create an environment that is safe,
> comprehensible, and predictable.
> —Weinstein and Mignano

The practice:

> Two Grade 1 students engage in a ritual of eating lunch in
> the cafeteria with their pants and underpants around their
> ankles, until they are caught.—Student teacher logbook

In recent times, the importance of supervising students in classrooms, on playgrounds, and in lunchrooms has received much attention. The safety and security of children are central concerns. However, this concern means that children are subjected to "compulsory visibility" (Foucault, 1977, p. 191). Weinstein and Mignano (1993) explain that teachers with the most effective management skills "were aware of what was happening in all parts of the room, and they communicated this awareness to students" (p. 50). The rhetoric of concern for children's safety conceals the workings of supervision as "a ritual of power and ceremony of visibility, a technology of objectification" through which children can be normalized to some arbitrary set of criteria (Foucault, 1977, p. 191).

In the lunchroom, supervision of children by teachers, aides, and lunchroom attendants constitutes a "machinery of control that function[s] like a microscope of conduct, [and] the fine, analytical divisions that they create form around [the children] an apparatus of observation, recording and training" (Foucault, 1977, p. 173). The apparatus of supervision allows the enforcement of rules (we don't display our genitalia in the lunchroom) and, subsequently, the differentiation between what is deemed licit and illicit, permitted and forbidden. Children learn that the body is something to be hidden; it is forbidden to derive any pleasure from the feeling of nakedness against a cold bench or from the warmth of another's body. A compulsory visibility that renders the body invisible wins the day. The logic of censorship prevails. Order is restored.

Restoring Order

The discourse:

> The overriding goal should be to keep the instructional
> program going with a minimum of disruption.
> —Weinstein and Mignano

The practice:

> Andrew, a first-grader, regularly danced his way through
> the daily singing of the national anthem. His body became
> eel-like, slithering rhythmically in time with the music.
> Andrew's body moved constantly—in math, during lan-
> guage learning, and on the playground. He cannot focus,
> his teacher said. His body is in constant contact with the
> bodies of his peers, she insisted. His behavior is inap-
> propriate and disruptive, she told his parents. Andrew was
> tested. He was diagnosed as hyperactive with an attention
> deficit—an inability to focus for long periods. Ritalin was
> prescribed.—Field notes

Andrew's inability to focus and his disruptions of the instructional program for himself and his class made him a problem. He had little control over his young, pliable body. Andrew was singled out for observation. The joy he expressed with his body was somehow inappropriate in school. His activity exceeded the definition of normal behavior. His file grew. Through a process of referral, assessment, and examination, Andrew was differentiated from his classmates and judged to be atypical. In Foucault's terms, Andrew's examination combined the techniques of "an observing hierarchy and those of normalizing judgment" (1977, p. 190). The surveillance of teachers and school psychologists qualified, classified, and punished Andrew. The assessment and treatment process served to reestablish normality.

Psychological assessment and examination procedures not only make children highly visible but also entrap them in a grid of documentation. The power of writing becomes an essential part of the mechanism of discipline; children become encased in a mass of documents that capture and fix them. The child becomes a describable, analyzable object. The swelling of knowledge about Andrew made him a *case* in the ignoble archives of the school. The result was the prescription of a drug to muffle his activity and induce passivity. Needless to say, Andrew doesn't dance any more.

Cases like Andrew's allow problems within the school to be interpreted as individual rather than systemic. Individuals can be scrutinized, categorized, and punished while the institutional values of work, order, and the rational subject remain intact.

In each of the foregoing vignettes, the dichotomies of pleasure/work and eroticism/rationality are enacted. Children's bodies emerge as sites of the erotic, as excesses in a world that rewards containment of self and desire. At Andrew's school, "traffic lights" were installed in the lunchroom to ensure order. When the noise rises to a designated level, a red light goes on and subsequently a siren. Strips of tape on a carpet mark sites of direct instruction and preparation for work. This is not to say that total permissiveness should prevail; nor am I saying that children do not have to learn some kind of self-control. My point is rather that when the children in our vignettes exceeded the rational frameworks in which they were expected to perform, their desires became reduced to something dirty and degrading. Teachers, afraid that their classrooms will be overwhelmed by eroticism and disorder, follow strategies of management and containment. They then rationalize management practices in the name of order, security, learning, and the greater good of all the students. Thus, as Eve Sedgwick (1990) has pointed out, ignorance and knowledge collude in regulating the subject: the excesses of the body are either censored or prohibited. If they exceed the school's internal control, they become cases for external referral and treatment.

The principal horror of all this is that children learn to live outside themselves, outside their impulses and desires, on "external directives only rather than from [their] internal knowledge and needs . . . away from those erotic guides . . . to conform to the needs of a structure that is not based on human need" (Lorde, 1984, p. 58). So, too, their teachers.

A Desire of Her Own: The Teacher as De-Eroticized Mother

> I, too, overflow; my desires have invented new desires, my body knows unheard-of songs. . . . And I, too, said nothing, showed nothing. . . . I was ashamed. I was afraid. . . . I said to myself: "You are mad!"—Hélène Cixous

> Teachers cannot simply interact with the children in their classrooms according to their desires. . . . Instead, their behavior often takes on characteristics beyond their immediate aims or intents. They must adapt their style, not only to the children, but to the institution, to the principal's requirements, to the other teachers' attitudes and to the standards according to which they will be evaluated.
> —E. B. Leacock

Teachers are not the villains here. They do not intentionally set out to regulate their students' erotic activity. The logic of order and classroom management regulates teachers as much as children.

Audre Lorde (1984) tells us that Eros, born of Chaos, personi-
fied creative power and harmony. The erotic for Lorde is always an
assertion of "the lifeforce of women." This life force is manifested
in a capacity for joy, intense feeling, and a deep sharing with
others. She reminds us that "the erotic is not a question only of
what we do; it is a question of how acutely and fully we can feel in
the doing" (p. 54). Women have been taught to separate the erotic
demand from the other most vital areas of life, and this situation
largely accounts for the disaffection from teaching that many
teachers feel. The classroom-management discourse has played a
major role in engendering this disaffection; recall the student-
teacher's concerns expressed at the beginning of this chapter.
Without the experience of the erotic, the teacher is divorced from
"the moving force that propel[s] every life-form from a state of
mere potentiality to actuality" (Keen, in hooks, 1993, p. 194).

Teachers become ascetics as they dampen the intensity of their
own feelings and those of the children in their care. What ascetics
feel most intensely is fear. Abstinence of a self-abnegating kind
becomes the ruling obsession. The teacher's denial of herself and
her desires is of concern here. She is asked to shed her subjectivity
and assume an "objective" persona. The teacher's identity and role
become synonymous. But identity and role are not the same:
"Role concerns functions, whereas identity presupposes invest-
ments. While functions can be bestowed, identity cannot. . . .
Identity is contingent in that it is always positioned in relation to
history, desires, and circumstances" (Britzman, 1991, p. 25).

The discourse of classroom management emphasizes "role"
and bestows "functions" on teachers. At best, it ignores and at
worst it erases teachers' desires, enveloping them in a regime of
the body defined in terms of distance/proximity, control/release,
intimacy/autonomy, and seriousness/playfulness. Teachers are
expected to distance themselves from their students, to exercise
self-control, to honor a static notion of autonomy that eliminates
the possibility of intimacy with children, and to maintain a serious
attitude in the classroom. These expectations for early childhood

educators ensure that the classroom becomes, in Patricia Yaeger's words, "a tomb—a space as potentially dangerous for its female owner as for the young it produces" (1992, p. 274).

Dangerous Liaisons: Attachment, Intimacy, and Desire

> I hold you close
> trying to inhale the pink gleam of dawn
> in your sweet flesh.
> You are tender-grasped, yet bruised
> by my intensity.
> I strain to absorb you.
> —Rishma Dunlop

Rishma Dunlop expresses the intense pleasure and joy women have derived from their closeness to the young. The pleasure women receive in this way is significant because they are "no longer objects of the gaze but coagent, if not subject, of the action" (Ty, 1994, p. 100). However, well-learned distinctions between public and private seem to imply that such closeness has no place in the classroom (hooks, 1993, p. 198). At home, women become attached to children; in school, teachers are expected to objectify them. At home, women spend time *with* their children, in school, teachers are expected to *do things to* their students. At home, women like Dunlop are allowed to experience and express intense feelings toward their children; in school, teachers who do not exercise self-control are immediately suspect.

In the classroom-management discourse, the teacher's task is defined in terms of watching, observing, and monitoring development and order (Walkerdine, 1987, p. 61). Teachers observe and characterize such student behaviors as nonattendance, negative physical contact, and talking out of turn. Teachers attempt to use praise and reprimand and, when these fail, assessment and referral so as to produce more appropriate behaviors in their students (Phelan, 1994). Once we require teachers to objectify children in this manner, we remove the possibility of mutuality between them. David Jardine suggests that alienation is far more likely as children like Andrew become "monstrous" in the eyes of the teacher, "an uncontrollable obverse to [her] well-laid plans" (1994, p. 21). Detachment from the object of her gaze eliminates the possibility of the teacher's sharing deeply in common pursuits with the children. The separation between teachers and children reflects the separation of mind and body in Western metaphysics. Women live out this dualism in the classroom. Teachers use their minds to manage children's bodies until children can do so for themselves; in the process teachers are diverted from exploring their own needs and desires.

A teacher's body, like a mother's, is a site of power and reproductive labor. Female power, however, is contained within a discourse of sexuality as individual morality. The assumption is that human beings do not act out of respect for one another. Morality is a test of self-control and self-respect. Hannah Arendt maintained that "exercising self control means follow[ing] certain patterns of behavior, so that those who do not keep the rules are considered to be asocial or abnormal" (in Warner, 1990, p. 41). Early childhood teachers must hide their pleasure and desire from the children lest they be misconstrued. Teachers are in fear that their touch may be framed as molestation, their emotional expression as professionally inappropriate. The downside is that teachers are in danger of forgetting their capacity for feeling. Moreover, "pleasure and desire for women as sexual subjects (rather than objects) remain largely in the shadows," obscured from children's view (Fine, 1993, p. 79). As Jean Baker Miller writes: "When one is an object, not a subject, all of one's own physical and sexual impulses and interests are presumed not to exist independently. They are to be brought into existence only by and for others— controlled, defined, and used. Any stirrings of physicality and sexuality in herself would only confirm for a girl or woman her evil state" (1986, p. 60).

Sitting on the rug with children in my lap in the Montessori classroom, I became a menace to classroom order and to my students' individuation processes. I left school that day feeling hurt and angry, but also ashamed and guilty. Bataille says that desire is always closely linked with terror, intense pleasure, and anguish (1986, p. 39). On that day in the Montessori school contemporary educational notions of autonomy, self-possession, and orderly conduct coalesced to remind me of my function and my "evil state." Just as the children's uninhibited self-expression is denied, so too is the self-expression of teachers.

In contrast to the idea that women's desires exist only by and for others, Jessica Benjamin (1986) describes the intersubjective mode as a context in which desire is constituted for each of the individuals involved. Intersubjectivity is paradoxical in that it is in being with the other that I may experience a profound sense of self: "To me it seems that the clarity of such a moment, the heightened awareness of both self and other, the reciprocal recognition that intensifies the self's freedom of expression, is actually the goal of erotic union. . . . The desire for the heightened sense of self is the central meaning of getting pleasure *with* the other. Here the desire to lose the self in the other and really to be known for oneself can coalesce" (pp. 92–93).

Teachers have learned to defer their desires to preserve the integrity of classroom work. Ensuring the order that work requires relegates teachers to an interventionist mode of existence in the classroom—we do things *to* children rather than *with* them. This state of affairs is painfully evident in the talk of teachers and student-teachers: "Children were running down from the cafeteria, shouting and pushing. We decided that this was to be stopped immediately; therefore, we had a serious talk with the children. . . . The talk was more like a punishment and lecture. . . . Later the children practiced walking back from the cafeteria until they had all done it properly."

Children and adults can get hurt in stampedes; mob behavior is real and dangerous. However, an overwhelming sense of seriousness and a lack of intersubjectivity and shared joy between young children and teachers are evident in the line "the talk was more like a punishment and lecture." It is ironic that primary classrooms are among the most serious and gloomy. Audre Lorde (1984) believes that women's erotic connections function in an "open and fearless underlining of [the] capacity for joy" (p. 56). The absence of joy in the foregoing vignettes demonstrates that the discourse of pleasure and desire remains a whisper inside the official work of public school (Fine, 1993).

In the plethora of teacher narratives in recent educational research, little has been articulated about the erotic life of the teacher. It is as if a veil has been drawn between the speakable and the unspeakable. Desire is associated with nature, human bestiality, and even savagery; teachers as instruments of civilization and culture must be defined as other to nature. Therefore, the teacher is constantly struggling to regain her body, to re/member herself as a desiring subject, and to create a counternarrative that reconstitutes her humanity (Henderson, 1994, p. 337).

In the arena of the erotic the teacher is both manager and managed, at once the Medusa and the abyss (Cixous, 1983). As the Medusa, she is likely to turn her students to stone, erase their desires, and eliminate their pleasure. As the abyss, she is the bottomless pit of care, the mother who must sacrifice her erotic desires to fulfill her role in the classroom. And yet, "You only have to look at the Medusa straight on to see her. And she's not deadly. She's beautiful and she's laughing" (Cixous, 1983, p. 289).

EXCESSIVE MOMENTS: OF PARODY, PLAYFULNESS, AND THE EROTIC

There is in nature and there subsists in [wo]man a movement which always exceeds the bounds and . . . can never be anything but partially reduced to order.
—Georges Bataille

Within the European-American tradition, this need is satisfied by certain proscribed erotic comings-together. These

> occasions are almost always characterized by a simulta-
> neous looking away, a pretense of calling them something
> else, whether religion, a fit, mob violence, or even playing
> doctor. And this misnaming of the need and the deed gives
> rise to that distortion which results in pornography and
> obscenity—the abuse of feeling.—Audre Lorde

Disorderly women and children continually testify to the presence of erotic desires in classrooms. However, as Lorde points
out, these moments are rarely acknowledged for what they are.
Erotic moments are contained, ignored, passed over. What is
needed as an antidote is a language of practice that honors rather
than conceals student and teacher desires. The language of carnival provides us with a way to reconceptualize excessive moments of classroom life.

Mikhail Bakhtin (1984) saw carnival as the "second life" of the
people: "We find here a characteristic logic, the peculiar logic of
the 'inside out,' of the 'turnabout,' of a continual shifting from top
to bottom, from front to rear, of numerous parodies and trav-
esties, humiliation, profanation, comic crownings and uncrown-
ings. A second life, a second world of folk culture, is thus constructed; it is to a certain extent a parody of the extracarnival life,
a 'world inside out'" (p. 11). Carnival allows the people to
"emerge from the routine of life . . . to be free from all that is
official and consecrated" (p. 257). In the Middle Ages, the spirit of
carnival loosened the grip of established norms and relations and
allowed alternatives to emerge. During carnival, the boundaries
between rulers and peasants, teachers and students, churchmen
and heretics were blurred. Carnival "draws attention to [human-
ity's] variety, as well as highlighting the fact that social roles . . . are
made not given, culturally produced rather than naturally mandated" (Holquist, 1990, p. 89).

Herein lies the relevance of carnival to our understanding of
classroom life. Carnival queers things up in classrooms. Carnival
agitates preconceived patterns of behavior and normative social

relations. It promotes a more transgressive mode of being for teachers and learners. To recast the early childhood classroom in terms of carnival is to reinstate the erotic as a vital constituent of classroom life. Instead of containing the excesses of the playful, the communal, and the intersubjective, the logic of carnival celebrates those moments because of their unofficial and antiofficial nature. The classroom no longer appears as a closed and orderly system; rather, it is seen as a complex, ambivalent admixture of order/disorder, pleasure/pain, fear/hope, laughter/misery, and freedom/oppression.

From Seriousness to Playfulness

The boy looked up and screamed, "Suck my dick!"
—Student-teacher, kindergarten

At first glance, the kindergarten day goes on as usual. The teacher maintains order, following her daily teaching routines. Then, suddenly, serious classroom discourse is displaced by what Bakhtin (1984) calls marketplace speech or billingsgate. The subsequent laughter dispels "the atmosphere of gloomy and false seriousness" enveloping teacher and students, lending them "a different look, . . . more material, closer to man and his body, more understandable, and lighter in the bodily sense" (p. 380). The kindergartner's comment positions him as male and the teacher as female. The moment is ambivalent, however. On the one hand, the comment is shocking both in its explicit sexual reference and in the power it asserts over the teacher. Walkerdine recounts a similar incident in which a four-year-old boy told his nursery schoolteacher, "Show your knickers." In both stories, the boys, refusing to be constituted as powerless in their teacher's discourse, recast the teacher as powerless object. Importantly, neither woman stopped being a teacher; rather, "she has ceased to signify as one: she has been made to signify as the powerless object of male sexual discourse" (Walkerdine, 1993, p. 209). An individual can be rendered powerful or powerless depending on the terms in which her subjectivity is constituted.

As another reading of these stories, I suggest that these moments have the quality of parody, a kind of "hyperbolic exposition" (Butler, 1990, p. 147). Parody demonstrates that what we formerly thought of as privileged and natural is in fact artificial and constructed. In the kindergartner's refusal to act like a "normal" four-year-old, he exposes our construction of normality for what it is—a construction. Amid the subversive laughter of the moment, the central protagonists of the classroom-management discourse, teacher and student, are denaturalized; nothing in the classroom seems familiar, and our management strategies appear absurd.

From the Individual to the Communal Body

For a silent moment in a crowded classroom Amy's fingertips touched the teacher's breast.—Field notes, Grade 2

For a moment, the boundary between Amy and her teacher is blurred. In a spontaneous moment both experience an intensity of feeling. The obliteration of the official hierarchy and established order that disallow such physical intimacy between student and teacher opens a space for Amy and her teacher to experience different relations from those they are used to. The erotic involves mutuality and reciprocity (hooks, 1993). The momentary freedom from official discourse and its logic of order allows the previously impossible to be experienced—the student can touch the powerful teacher. The disruption of routine and the freeing of behavior interrupt the teacher's program of action; she becomes the disorderly woman, and she is smiling.

Children and teachers continue to transgress, to cross the boundary of appropriateness, and to remind us that our normative categories are not universal. As Mary Russo (1989) points out: "Play with an unruly [woman/child] is partly a chance for temporary release from the traditional and stable hierarchy; but it is also part of the conflict over efforts to change the basic distribution of power within society" (p. 215). Students and teacher experience the interconnectedness of their lives and contexts and the fragility of the hierarchies in which they are embedded. The classroom becomes "a primary, highly charged intersection and mediation of social and political forces, a sort of intensifier and displacer in the making of identity." The contrast between this state and the young "disobedient" child who speaks the unspeakable "is a scandal to the hegemonic dignity which it can hardly sustain. It is indeed wonderful that so little can make so great a difference" (Stallybrass and White, 1986, p. 25).

The underlying erotic dimension of classroom life is revealed in both the boy's shouting out "Suck my dick" and the girl's touching of her teacher's breast. The utterance and the touch remind us that "an autonomous order is founded upon what it eliminates, it produces a 'residue' condemned to be forgotten. But what was excluded . . . re-infiltrates the place of its origin—it resurfaces, it troubles, it turns the present's feeling of being 'at home' into an illusion, it lurks—this 'wild,' this 'obscene,' this 'filth,' this 'resistance' of 'superstition'—within the walls" (de Certeau, 1984).

The classroom cannot be conceived outside of the world, the web of interrelations, of which it is a part. The kindergartner can amusingly transgress, as well as reaffirm, the boundaries between high and low, polite and vulgar (Stallybrass and White, 1986). The child's transgression interrogates the boundaries of civilized/uncivilized, educated/uneducated. Amy's touch reveals the social repressions that formed it. Transgression constitutes a reversal of the teacher's sublimation, undoing the discursive hierarchies and stratification of bodies and cultures that schooling reinforces.

Despite the classroom transgressions, however, rationality is never completely expelled; during those moments it exists in tension with the erotic. As a result, both teachers and students are re-*mind*ed of their em*bod*iment as human beings.

EARLY CHILDHOOD EDUCATION AS AN EROTIC ENDEAVOR?

> Truth is drawn from pleasure itself. . . . Pleasure is experi-
> enced as pleasure, evaluated in terms of its intensity, its
> specific quality, its duration, its reverberation in the body
> and the soul.—Michel Foucault

Desire. Pleasure. Eros. Whispers in the official work of public
schooling. What would it mean to raise the voice of the erotic?
Must we abandon work and order altogether? Must we construct
a distinct pedagogy of the erotic? I think not. I am suggesting
instead that we recognize the erotic as a part of human experience
as integral as rationality, work, and order. In this sense, the erotic
will always be in tension with rationality in the classroom. As in
Bakhtin's carnival, tension is generative. The acts of disorderly
women and children are disruptions that move us forward (Jardine, 1994). Erotic moments are sites of renewal and regeneration
that ultimately guard us from the homogenization and rational-
ization of culture (Bakhtin, 1984).

Eros and the erotic do not have to be denied for learning to
take place (hooks, 1993). When we eroticize classroom work, we
open up new vistas of learning and creativity. As Rollo May (in
Noddings and Shore, 1984) notes, "Eros . . . incites in man
the yearning for knowledge and drives him passionately to seek
union with the truth. Through eros, we not only become poets
and inventors but also achieve ethical goodness. Love, in the form
of eros, is the power which generates. . . . Such creativity is as
close as men ever get to becoming immortal" (p. 155). For teachers this may mean a renewed affection for teaching and learning.
Schools may be places where women can reconstitute themselves
and recover their bodies. In the subversive, "unofficial" world the
Medusa's laughter is no longer "a product of the masculine prov-
ince of history but of the limitless feminine country of desire"
(Gasbarrone, 1994, p. 16).

Bell hooks (1993) exhorts us to "find again the place of eros within ourselves and . . . allow the mind and body to feel and know desire" (p. 199). The danger of such exhortations, including the many I have issued in this chapter, is that they strike a romantic chord. As such, they can easily be mocked and dismissed. Moreover, they may seem naive about the dangers of classroom eroticism and the ambivalence and multiplicity that characterize classroom experiences. Teachers are in positions of power—not always but certainly at particular times—and we have to be careful about the coercive effects of our desires. Eros without rationality is as dangerous and as limiting as rationality without the erotic. It is important, however, that we learn to live with the generative tension that exists between the two so that we can enter the classroom "whole" and not as "disembodied spirits" (p. 193). We must no longer allow our worries about order to override our desire to teach and to have pleasure in the doing.

REFERENCES

Apple, M., and King, N. (1977). What do schools teach? *Curriculum Inquiry* 6 (4): 341–358.

Baker Miller, J. (1986). *Toward a new psychology of women.* Boston: Beacon.

Bakhtin, M. (1984). *Rabelais and his world.* (Trans. Helene Iswolsky.) Bloomington: Indiana University Press.

Bataille, G. (1986). *Eroticism.* San Francisco: City Lights.

Benjamin, J. (1986). A desire of her own. In T. de Lauretis (ed.), *Feminist studies/critical studies* (pp. 78–101). Bloomington: Indiana University Press.

Bowers, C. A., and Flinders, D. J. (1990). *Responsive teaching: An ecological approach to classroom patterns of language, culture, and thought.* New York: Teachers College Press.

Britzman, D. (1991). The terrible problem of knowing thyself. *Journal of Curriculum Theorizing* 9 (3): 23–46.

——. (1992). *Practice makes practice.* Albany: SUNY Press.

Butler, J. (1990). *Gender trouble.* New York: Routledge.

Cixous, H. (1983). The laugh of the Medusa. In E. Abel and E. K. Abel (eds.), *The* Signs *Reader: Women, gender, and scholarship* (pp. 279–297). Chicago: University of Chicago Press.

de Certeau, M. (1984). *The practice of everyday life.* (Trans. S. Rendall.) Berkeley: University of California Press.

Doyle, W. (1986). Classroom organization and management. In M. Wittrock (ed.), *Handbook of research on teaching,* 3d ed. (pp. 392–431). New York: Macmillan.

Dunlop, R. (1995). Written on the body: Autobiography and the language of teaching. Paper presented at the annual meeting of the Canadian Society for Studies in Education, Montreal.

Feher, M. (1990). Of bodies and technologies. In H. Foster (ed.), *Discussions in contemporary culture,* no. 1 (pp. 159–165). Seattle: Bay.

Fine, M. (1993). Sexuality, schooling, and adolescent females: The missing discourse of desire. In M. Fine and L. Weis (eds.), *Beyond silenced voices: Class, race, and gender in United States schools* (pp. 75–99). Albany: SUNY Press.

Foucault, M. (1977). *Discipline and punish: The birth of the prison.* New York: Pantheon.

———. (1990). *The history of sexuality.* New York: Vintage.

Freedman, S. (1987). Who will care for our children? Removing nurturance from the teaching profession. *Democratic Schools,* Fall 1987, pp. 7–27.

Gasbarrone, L. (1994). "The locus for the other": Cixous, Bakhtin, and women's writing. In Hohne, K., and Wussow, H. (eds.), *A dialogue of voices: Feminist literary theory and Bakhtin.* Minneapolis: University of Minnesota Press. 1–19.

Grice, H. P. (1975). Logic and conversation. In P. Cole and J. L. Morgan (eds.), *Syntax and semantics,* vol. 3: *Speech acts.* New York: Academic Press.

Henderson, M. G. (1994). Toni Morrison's *Beloved:* Re-membering the body as historical text. In D. Stanton (ed.), *Discourses of sexuality: From Aristotle to AIDS* (pp. 312–342). Ann Arbor: University of Michigan Press.

Holquist, M. (1990). *Dialogism: Bakhtin and his world.* New York: Routledge.

hooks, b. (1993). *Teaching to transgress: Education as the practice of freedom.* New York: Routledge.

Jackson, P. (1968). *Life in classrooms*. New York: Holt, Rinehart and Winston.

Jardine, D. (1994). Student-teaching, interpretation, and the monstrous child. *Journal of Philosophy of Education* 28 (1): 17–24.

Keller, E. F. (1985). *Reflections on gender and science*. New Haven: Yale University Press.

Laird, S. (1988). Reforming "woman's true profession": A case for "feminist pedagogy" in teacher education? *Harvard Educational Review* 58 (4): 449–463.

Leacock, E. B. (1969). *Teaching and learning in city schools*. New York: Basic.

Lensmire, T. J. (1994). Writing workshop as carnival: Reflections on an alternative learning environment. *Harvard Educational Review* 64 (4): 371–391.

Lorde, A. (1984). *Sister outsider: Essays and speeches*. Trumansburg, N.Y.: Crossing.

Lyotard, J.-F. (1984). *The postmodern condition: A report on knowledge*. (Trans. G. Bennington and B. Massumi.) Minneapolis: University of Minnesota Press.

Minh-ha, T. T. (1992). *Native woman other*. Bloomington: Indiana University Press.

Noddings, N., and Shore, P. (1984). *Awakening the inner eye: Intuition in education*. New York: Teachers' College Press.

Oken-Wright P., (1992). From tug of war to "Let's make a deal": The teacher's role. *Young Children* (November): 15–20.

Phelan, A. (1994). Unmasking metaphors of management. *Teaching Education* (Spring): 101–111.

Russo, M. (1986). Female grotesques: Carnival and theory. In T. de Lauretis (ed.), *Feminist studies/critical studies* (pp. 212–229). Bloomington: Indiana University Press.

Sedgwick, E. (1990). *Epistemology of the closet*. Berkeley: University of California Press.

Silberman, C. E. (1970). *Crisis in the classroom: The remaking of American education*. New York: Basic.

Stallybrass, P., and White, A. (1986). *The politics and poetics of transgression*. Ithaca: Cornell University Press.

Ty, E. (1994). Desire and temptation: Dialogism and the carnivalesque in category romances. In K. Hohne and H. Wussow (eds.), *A dialogue of voices* (pp. 97–113). Minneapolis: University of Minnesota Press.

Walkerdine, V. (1987). Femininity as performance. *Oxford Review of Education* 15 (3): 267–279.

———. (1993). Sex, power, and pedagogy. In M. Alvarado, E. Buscombe, and R. Collins (eds.), *The screen education reader: Cinema, television, culture* (pp. 207–221). New York: Macmillan.

Warner, M. (1990). *Fear of a queer planet: Queer politics and social theory.* Minneapolis: University of Minnesota Press.

Weinstein, C. S., and Mignano, A. J. (1993). *Elementary classroom management: Lessons from research and practice.* New York: McGraw-Hill.

Yaeger, P. (1992). Poetics of birth. In D. Stanton (ed.), *Discourses of sexuality: From Aristotle to AIDS.* Ann Arbor: University of Michigan Press. 262–296.

THREE

The "No Touch" Policy

Richard Johnson

In a recent discussion of "Male Teachers and Accusations" on the electronic network user group Kidsphere, a number of early childhood educators, most of them male, debated the use of touching in their classrooms. Their exchange can help us understand the anxieties that led to the development of "no touch" policies. A male kindergarten teacher began the discussion:

> A female coworker of mine is married to a teacher. Some time ago, he was accused of sexual molestation of a student. He was charged by the state attorney general, and the charges and his name were published in the newspaper and on the local television newscast. Naturally, he was suspended (with pay) during the investigation. At the grand jury hearing, the case was promptly dismissed as unfounded. However, although his name was cleared, the local school system is unwilling to reinstate him . . . [apparently] because of the publicity.
>
> This scares me because as you all probably know, elementary students like to hug teachers, like affection, and do not want to be treated as though they have some dread disease. As a result of my fear, I don't touch students, except maybe on the shoulder or arm, and I do not show any but verbal affect unless it's initiated by the student. I also am never alone with a student, and any time a student has a problem that may be sensitive, I find a female teacher (regardless of the child's sex) to assist me, so that a witness is there.

Another male kindergarten teacher responded:

This is very scary stuff. I think we have all heard horror stories concerning false accusations made by students
against teachers. As a male teacher (twenty-seven years) I
have thought about this a zillion times. It always seemed
totally unfair that the female teachers could touch their
students, some getting hugged by every student every day
as they boarded the bus. However, as a male teacher, I
always have to keep at arm's length. I think what you said
about not being alone with students is a good rule of
thumb. I don't like it, but that's the way it is.

Another male shared some pointers on the subject of touching
and education:

(1) Never be alone with a student, male or female, without
another teacher or other students around; (2) Never cover
up the window on the classroom door. It prohibits administrators and other teachers from looking in, and unless you
have something to hide, it's not necessary; (3) Keep the
classroom door open as much as possible; (4) If there are
problems in clothing-sensitive areas (such as one day when
I had to help a kindergartner with his belt buckle and pants
zipper in the classroom), elicit the help of a fellow teacher,
preferably one of the opposite sex; (5) Always hug from the
side—avoid frontal hugs whenever possible; (6) For legal
purposes, keep a critical incident file for every student; (7)
Keep in close contact with administration. Take your cues
from them.

Another male primary teacher responded:

In the school where I work I have been told by female
teachers that I often appear to be cold and uncaring toward
students, but with all the court appearances who can blame
me? I do show some verbal emotion toward students, but
only if there is another teacher or student in the room. I

avoid body contact. A teacher in the school a while back was accused of sexual harassment after he touched a female student on the shoulder.

The next teacher added:

One has to be careful these days. It is unfortunate. This advice has worked for me: do not initiate affection. However, if a child, especially a little one, initiates a hug or peck, do not refuse him.

A male preservice teacher wrote:

I am currently in my third year B.Ed. This issue really scares the hell out of me, and I often wonder how far-reaching the implications of withdrawal of affection may be. Often I find myself wanting to give the children a hug but unable to do so because the DANGER/CAUTION sign is always flashing in the back of my mind.

Children need the gift of touch, they need to feel wanted and most of all they need to feel valued. But I'm male, and part of my teaching code prevents me from showing the care that I often want to show.

I often think: do I really want to be the sort of teacher that the judicial system is (almost) forcing me to be? So where do I stand? Well, basically I feel like I'm on some sort of tightrope. Recently, while I was on practicum, a young boy came up to me and gave me a hug. I just froze, my mind racing a million miles an hour. Do I hug him back? If I do, is that taking the student-teacher relationship too far? Why shouldn't I be able to give him a hug? Why should I even have to think about all this stuff?

These comments reveal a teaching profession afflicted with moral panic. Moral panics work to create and support mechanisms of social control (Dodd, 1993; Goode and Ben-Yehuda, 1995). The power of moral panics is such that it matters little whether a real danger exists; once a moral panic is marked and defined, it *does* exist, it does objectify, and it does influence (Phelan, 1993). Moral panics appear in various forms. Some recent types include the panic over AIDS, the withholding of federal dollars from school districts that teach about homosexuality, the blanket statement that watching violent television makes children violent, the push to ban sexually explicit music recordings, and the fingerprinting of all early childhood teachers.

I came to know moral panic firsthand as a preschool teacher in the early 1980s. I was just settling into a comfortable style of day-to-day caregiver-child interactions when television specials and magazine cover stories began to appear on child sexual abuse. Until the panic hit, my primary concern was establishing warm, trusting relationships with the children in my care. Suddenly, self-doubt and self-consciousness infused my physical interactions with children. I started to worry and second-guess myself when I went about my once taken-for-granted routines of changing diapers, wiping runny noses, unbuttoning and buttoning jeans, and supervising toddlers as they frolicked about in sprinkler play clothed only in their underpants. I hesitated before physically calming an out-of-control three-year-old in a "football hold," as I had been instructed to do in my master's practicum.

Suddenly, the sense of touch, which has always been an integral part of my relationship with children (my own and those I care for), was being called into question. Without consciously choosing to do so, I capitulated to the pressure, unsure of what I could do to fight it and afraid to try. I allowed the rising moral panic to change the way I interacted with children. Recent developments in early education have reawakened memories of these early years in my teaching career. I am ashamed that I gave in to the moral panic of the early 1980s. This time, I feel compelled to act before the "no touch" policy, which is becoming more prevalent and familiar in school contexts each day, overwhelms us, intimidating a new generation of teachers.

THE IMPORTANCE OF TOUCH

As is true of most preschool teachers, my practice has been heavily influenced by what I learned in a teacher education program. Then as now, popular early education texts reminded aspiring teachers that "learning to create caring, supportive relationships with children is one of the most essential and rewarding tasks of the teacher. Only when [children] feel safe, cared for, and secure will they have the confidence to learn" (Feeney, Christensen, and Moravcik, 1991, p. 201). During my undergraduate and graduate studies, most of what I learned about the care of children was centered around the importance of building a warm and trusting relationship with each child (Noddings, 1992).

To stress the importance of being a warm and supportive caregiver, our professors guided us through the Harlows' attachment studies, Spitz's work on hospitalism and adult-infant interactions, Bowlby's work on maternal deprivation, and Kennel and Klaus's research on parent-infant bonding. We learned about the damage that can be caused by inadequately formed adult-child relationships (Montagu, 1978). All this research stressed the critical importance of stimulation (especially skin-to-skin touch) for the infant's later healthy development (Kennel and Klaus, 1982).

Incorporating what I had learned about touch and the "caring encounter" (Noddings, 1992) into my daily classroom practice with preschoolers came naturally. I recall guiding two-year-olds to help clean up with a supportive touch on the back as they sought to run elsewhere, tickling infants during play or diaper changing, giving children warm pats on the back, readily accepting children onto my lap during story time, physically removing and then holding aggressive first-graders so they couldn't harm themselves or others, tousling children's hair while joking with them. These memories evoke what I think should be typical interactions of early childhood teachers everywhere.

CHANGING PERCEPTIONS OF SELF

Bronwyn Davies (1993) explains how social discourse shapes subjectivities: "Learning the appropriate patterns of desire enables young women to 'voluntarily' and uncritically take up the subject positions made available to them in the patriarchal gender order, and thus to become other to the men in their world" (p. 145). Davies helps me to see how my subjectivity and practice as a male teacher of young children shifted during this moral panic. The discourses I encountered as a novice teacher in a teacher education program were comfortable and matched my natural style of interacting with children. The discourses I confronted in a society burdened with moral panic about sexual abuse negatively influenced my sense of myself as a teacher. I defined myself and was defined by these discourses. I was learning how to position myself correctly within the discourses created and pronounced by others. I "took up the subject positions made available" by such powerful others as the mass media, the conservative right, and the National Association for the Education of Young Children. My ways of interacting with children were defined and dictated by those others, which are actively involved in the continuing moral panic centered around how teachers of young children touch their students.

"NO TOUCH" AS MORAL PANIC

Cohen's (1972) description of moral panics helps us understand the development of "no touch" in early childhood education. He defines moral panic as

> a condition, episode, person or groups of persons [that] emerges to become defined as a threat to societal values and interests; its nature is presented in a stylized and stereotypical fashion by the mass media; the moral barricades are manned by editors, bishops, politicians and other right-thinking people. . . . Sometimes the panic passes over and is

forgotten, except in folk-lore and collective memory; at other times it has more serious and long-lasting repercussions and might produce such changes as those in legal and social policy or even in the way that society perceives itself. (p. 9)

Such sudden creations of social problems do not occur by accident. The development of a moral panic tends to follow a set sequence. The first thing to occur is the emergence of a problem, often associated with negative influences on the behavior of the young; next is the development of associated community concern, typically dictated by the media and greatly disproportionate to the actual scale of the problem; and, finally, a political reaction, which often involves hasty legislation aimed at stricter control (Shuker, Openshaw, and Soler, 1990; see also Young, 1971).

Goode and Ben-Yehuda (1995) note five central characteristics of the classic moral panic: (1) a greatly heightened level of concern; (2) increased hostility toward those associated with that activity; (3) a high degree of consensus in society that the activity does constitute a real and serious threat; (4) exaggeration of the nature of the threat; and (5) volatility, as moral panics "erupt fairly suddenly . . . and nearly as suddenly, subside."

We see the development of such a moral panic unfolding in an article entitled "The New Untouchables: Risk Management of Child Abuse in Child Care" (Strickland and Reynolds, 1988). The authors suggest steps for the child care administrator to follow to protect the center against unforeseen accusations of child abuse. "Where possible," they advise, "try to have at least two adults with the children at all times. If this is not always possible, try to keep the single caregiver time to a minimum and where possible, rotate those who are left alone with the children."

Suggestions such as these are readily turned into rules and regulations. Advice intended to help administrators avoid problems of liability and litigation becomes policy with little consideration for how it will affect young children and their teachers. In their concern for prevention, the authors, like much of society, are too quick to embrace solutions. A recent *Newsweek* cover story discusses the "fevered pitch" with which America today addresses claims of child abuse. As Nowesnick (1993) points out, "We haven't done very well at preventing it, but we're frantic to root it out and stomp it to death no matter where it lurks—or doesn't." The moral panic I first experienced ten years ago is stronger today, threatening all that we are about as individuals, as caregivers of young children, and as childhood educators.

The power of the moral panic regarding child abuse is reflected in a National Public Radio story entitled "Day Care Center's No Touch Policy" (1994):

SMITH (NPR reporter Tovia Smith): A little boy with dark wide eyes watches an Oreo cookie submerge in a plastic cup of orange juice. There are giggles all around. This is a close bunch. Teachers describe it as a big family, but there are very strict rules here as to how this family interacts.

TANNER (Joan Tanner, director of the center): It's against our policy to pick up the kids. It's against our policy to hold them on your lap.

SMITH: If the policies here seem strict, Ms. Tanner says, it's because the stakes are high.

TANNER: The doors have to be open, and not one teacher is allowed to be alone with one child in the room behind a closed door, because I know just from . . . the sexual abuse cases that are in the newspaper and stuff, that's how it's happened.

SMITH: To keep it from happening here, Tanner requires extensive background checks and references for all employees. She's confident that the teachers she's hired are trustworthy. The "no-touch" policy, she says, is more to protect the center than the children. In the business of day care, Tanner explains, reputation is everything, and reputation is fragile. It would be too easy, she says, for one innocent hug or playful piggyback ride to be misinterpreted.

TANNER: The picking-up thing, I just—I don't allow it, because that's one of those issues where you have, you know, the direct physical contact, body to body, that could be misconstrued, so I—I stop it there.

SMITH: And stop it often. Tanner says she's constantly reminding both staffers and kids to keep their distance.

TANNER: I'll say, "No. No holding." Or, if it's one of the little kids, I might say, "OK, Steven, now you know you need to get down," and then I will privately remind the [caregiver], "Remember, now, we don't do that. I know you're just enjoying this child. However, it could be misconstrued. It could be a problem for you."

DAY CARE WORKER: In college they trained us to have the child beside us, not on our lap, when we're reading books and whatnot, and not to give them that hug or kiss for fear that a parent will walk in and see this, or that some sort of instructor will come in and call us in that we're touching these children in ways that we shouldn't be.

SMITH: While it's understandable that a day care center would be concerned about liability, even attorneys who specialize in child abuse cases consider a no-touch policy an over-reaction.

LYNCH (attorney Thomas Lynch): I think that at some point defensive practice, whether it is in the field of medicine or, in this case, child care, crosses a line where [it] tends to detract from what the ultimate purpose of what you're doing is. And, in this case, if the interaction of appropriate and legitimate touching is taken away, then it seems to me you're taking away from the quality of the day care you're giving.

Can such a blanket policy of "no direct body-to-body physical contact" prevent child abuse? Do hugs automatically imply that providers are sexually attracted to children? What is more important in child care, the business itself ("In the business of day care reputation is everything, and reputation is fragile") or the children we serve? How are misguided educational policies ("In college they trained us to have the child beside us, not on our lap") influencing the current and future generations of child care providers?

From discussions with my graduate students, all practicing early childhood teachers, I have learned that elements of this policy have been filtering through our profession for several years. A recent class discussion revealed that the students work in centers with female-only diaper changing areas, video cameras monitoring daily adult-child interactions, policies requiring that at least two adults must monitor the bathroom during whole-class toileting, and staff in-service instruction on how to hold children in one's lap (children must not straddle the adult's legs or face the adult) and on good and bad ways to hold children.

THE SOCIAL CLIMATE

Like the Kidsphere narratives on "Male Teachers and Accusations," the NPR "No Touch" special was mentioned on an early childhood education electronic network, and interested early childhood professionals and parents quickly joined an electronic debate:

> Just yesterday I read in our local paper about how our elementary school teachers are no longer hugging or touching their students. A male teacher will request a teacher's aide or parent to be with him in the classroom if a female student will be alone with him. They will also take along another adult if they must help a child in the bathroom. . . .
>
> How awful to spend most of your day in a place without touching—not even so much as a reassuring hand on your shoulder. . . . How cold! . . .
>
> The idea of child abuse in that center has never even crossed my mind. Every room has several windows, more

than one teacher, and a video camera which is hooked to two monitors in the director's office so that rooms can be observed at any time.

A male teacher said:

I know that many are still suspicious of men working with young children so I have always been very careful not to put myself in a compromising situation. [But] my lap is still open.

Finally, a father revealed:

It strikes me that trust is the factor most likely to create the ideal circumstances for abuse to occur. I must admit that I am not as trusting of other males as I am of myself with my own children. I remember being scrupulous to avoid any inappropriate stimulation of my infants while making sure they were clean.

The comments from the profession reveal that the moral panic of no touch has already seeped into everyday discourse. The language and logic here are familiar. Just as the director on the NPR story is overly concerned about her center's public image ("reputation is everything, and reputation is fragile"), so the male teacher governs his interactions with children on the basis of public fears and (mis)perceptions ("I have always been very careful not to put myself in a compromising situation"). Just as the director on the NPR story is overly concerned about her staff's physical interactions with children ("no direct body-to-body physical contact"), so a father bases his interactions with his own children on public (mis)perceptions ("I remember being scrupulous to avoid any inappropriate stimulation of my infants while making sure they were clean"). As much as we try to reduce and dismiss the moral panic, reports from the field suggest that we have in fact let it define our moral behavior and distort our understandings of children.

What Do We Know About Child Sexual Abuse and Prevention?

That the number of reported child abuse cases in the United States has increased rapidly has been well documented. In 1989 about 2.4 million American children, most under age five, were reported to have been physically, sexually, or mentally abused (Newman and Buka, 1991). In 1992 this figure was reported to be about 2.9 million.

Child abuse is clearly an issue that warrants great concern (Kelly, Brant, and Waterman, 1993), but there is no reason to single out early education settings as places where it is likely to happen. We have no hard facts about its prevalence in educational settings (Nowesnick, 1993; Stein, 1993). A 1986 study by the American Association for Protecting Children revealed that school personnel were involved in less than 1 percent of reported child sexual abuse cases nationwide (Nowesnick, 1993). Sorenson (1990) found that there were six judicial cases dealing with school-related child abuse in 1987, ten in 1988, sixteen in 1989, and nineteen at the end of 1990—a total of fifty-one in a four-year period.

Historical and current demographic statistics reveal that the overwhelming majority of acts of child abuse occur within the family setting (Elrod and Rubin, 1993; Finkelhor, Williams, and Burns, 1988). For instance, a 1970 nationwide survey found that 87 percent of abusive incidents involved a parent or parent substitute (Trickett and Susman, 1988). A 1990 survey showed that 79 percent of child sexual abusers were related to the victims (Batchelor, Dean, Gridley, and Batchelor, 1990).

Although the growing concern about child sexual abuse has led to an abundance of programs claiming to prevent abuse and the investment of millions of dollars in school-based interventions, we know little about the most effective ways to prevent or ameliorate the problem (Lumsden, 1992). Between four hundred and five hundred child abuse prevention curricula have been designed and implemented into schools and other social service settings, yet statistical data show few outcome effects of these various interventions (Bogat and McGrath, 1993; Daro, 1991; Tharinger, Krivacska, Laye-McDonough, Jamison, Vincent, and Hedlund, 1988). Some of the evaluations of child abuse prevention curricula discuss the inappropriateness of many of the models, especially for young children. Among other concerns specialists note that certain curricula "have the potential for creating a distorted view of sexuality in children's minds" (Lumsden, 1992, p. 44); that curricula which "emphasize 'good' or 'bad' touch may run the risk of confusing young children" (McEvoy, 1990, p. 256); that a four-year-old child who cannot understand Piaget's laws of conservation can hardly be expected to "understand lessons that try to convey the far more subtle change of emotions . . . aroused by a soft touch that at first feels good, then becomes confusing, and finally feels bad" (Gilbert, 1988, p. 6).

Gilbert goes on to point out that we are asking too much when we require children to identify the difference between a "red flag" and a "green flag" touch, teach about private parts with wide-ranging definitions of which body parts are private and which are not, and teach that any physical touch that does not feel good is a "bad touch." Some curriculum models even say that a "parent's affectionate pat on the behind of a four-year-old may appear as an act that violates the dictum against touching private parts, or as one to be consciously appraised by the child to determine its goodness or badness" (p. 14).

It is disturbing to think about the impact child abuse prevention curricula are having on the children they are supposed to protect. As Gilbert writes:

> Preschool children need care and security. At a time in their lives when it is important for them to feel that their parents will nurture and protect them, should children be taught that they must evaluate the boundaries of appropriate adult behavior? The underlying message in the "empowerment"

of four-year-olds is that they must try to control the dangerous outside world. It is an abdication of family and community responsibility—a sorry message for our times.

Real dangers do, of course, exist. A distressing number of children are at risk of physical and emotional injury from adults whose touches are not innocent expressions of affection. To criticize sexual abuse prevention training for preschoolers is not to deny the serious problems these programs hope to alleviate. However, "empowering" four-year-olds, whom we normally forbid to cross the street alone, defies common sense. At best, it is a social placebo that may only bewilder small children while soothing parental anxieties; at worst, it leaves youngsters as vulnerable as ever but psychologically on edge—a little more aware of the dangers around them and a little less able to enjoy the innocence of childhood. (1988, p. 14)

MOVING ON

As I consider the "no touch" stories presented here, I reflect back to my opening comments about knowing this moral panic as a preschool teacher tormented by the hysteria of sexual abuse in child care settings. I don't wish to know this torment, and I don't wish to participate in the seen and unseen hysteria surrounding "no touch." I don't want to allow a "sudden, relatively brief outburst of fear, concern, and anger over a given condition, threat, or behavior to transform the norms and institutions of society in such a way as to make it a different place from what it was before" (Goode and Ben-Yehuda, 1995, p. 226). And yet, if I, as a single early childhood teacher, and we, as a collective mass of caregivers, continue to plead ignorance or helplessness, then together we allow the moral panic to gain momentum, determine the terms of the debate, and continue to change our nurturant and caring subjectivities.

Jonathan Silin warns us of the cost of our ignorance: "Igno-

rance is the process through which we construct dangerous silences, through which we legitimate their power and extend their
dominion" (1994, p. 2). Joseph Tobin (1995) addresses the cost
of pleading helplessness, asking us to rethink our passive acceptance of policies of "no touch," fingerprinting children and staff,
and preventing male teachers from changing diapers, measures
that he argues decrease the quality of life of children and teachers
while having little or no effect on the problem of child abuse. Our
failure to respond aggressively leads to regimes of control by
those outside our field (Foucault, 1979; Stainton Rogers and
Stainton Rogers, 1992; Watney, 1993). As the media and law
draw attention to institutional child abuse, the visibility of the
issue "summons surveillance and the law; it provokes voyeurism,
fetishism, and the colonialist/imperial appetite for possession"
(Phelan, 1993, p. 6).

While we continue allowing trends like these to define who we
are and to govern how we operate, an overwhelming majority of
the research reveals that child sexual abuse is most likely to occur
outside our centers, away from our staffs. The relatively rare incidents of sexual abuse in schools should not define what we can
and cannot do with the young children we serve. Why is it that
licensed child care centers are the educational institutions receiv-
ing the most press about child abuse? Shouldn't home-based family care settings and self-contained classrooms with one teacher
come under more scrutiny? And why are the same schools that
are being defined as sites of potential child abuse problems also
asked to serve as primary agents in preventing and healing child
abuse? Schools are a place where it is safe to talk to children
about sex, as long as it is within the confines of a sex-education,
sex abuse–prevention curriculum (Stainton Rogers and Stainton
Rogers, 1992).

As a field, we must better balance the likelihood of child abuse
in our centers with the costs to our profession of our overzealous
prevention. What is gained by our continued support of a "no
touch" policy in early childhood education? Directors are likely to

spend more money on liability insurance than on salary increases for teachers; talented caregivers are leaving the child care profession en masse, and potential male caregivers are looking elsewhere for employment; children are becoming more distrustful of adults, especially teachers; we continue to betray young children (and what we know about good early childhood practices) as we submit them to a variety of inappropriate sexual abuse curricula; and misinformed legislators funnel millions of dollars into prevention programs that could otherwise be spent on educating our young in more effective ways. The field of early childhood education has much to lose if we support "no touch."

Silin and Tobin challenge us individually and collectively to become more active advocates for ourselves and for the children we serve. We can cast out our fears and ignorance by confronting them. To make a change we must struggle "against our unworthy fears, wrong desires and faulty conceptions" (Aviram, 1990, p. 231). To do anything less is to be complicitous in the continuing devaluation of ourselves as nurturant providers and caring early childhood professionals.

REFERENCES

Aviram, A. (1990). The subjection of children. *Journal of Philosophy of Education* 24: 213–234.

Batchelor, E. S., Dean, R. S., Gridley, B., and Batchelor, B. (1990). Reports of child sexual abuse in schools. *Psychology in the Schools* 27: 131–137.

Bogat, G. A., and McGrath, M. P. (1993). Preschoolers' cognitions of authority, and its relationship to sexual abuse education. *Child Abuse and Neglect* 17: 651–662.

Cohen, S. (1972). *Folk devils and moral panics: The creation of the mods and rockers.* Oxford: Martin Robertson, 1980.

Contratto, S. (1986). Child abuse and the politics of care. *Journal of Education* 168 (3): 70–79.

Daro, D. (1991). Child sexual abuse prevention: Separating fact from fiction. *Child Abuse and Neglect* 15: 1–4.

Davies, B. (1993). Beyond dualism and towards multiple subjectivities. In L. K. Christian-Smith (ed.), *Texts of desire* (pp. 145–173). London: Falmer.

Dodd, P. (1993). Moral panic: The sequel. *Sight and Sound* 3 (4): 3.

Feeney, S., Christensen, D., and Moravcik, E. (1991). *Who am I in the lives of young children?* New York: Merrill.

Finkelhor, D., Williams, L. M., and Burns, N. (1988). *Nursery crimes: Sexual abuse in day care.* Newbury Park, Calif.: Sage.

Foucault, M. (1979). *Discipline and punish: The birth of the prison.* (Trans. A. Sheridan.) New York: Vintage.

Gilbert, N. (1988). Teaching children to prevent sexual abuse. *Public Interest* 93: 3–15.

Goode, E., and Ben-Yehuda, N. (1995). *Moral panics: The social construction of deviance.* Cambridge, Mass.: Basil Blackwell.

Hollander, S. K. (1992). Making young children aware of sexual abuse. *Elementary School Guidance and Counseling* 26: 305–317.

Kelly, S. J., Brant, R., and Waterman, J. (1993). Sexual abuse of children in day care centers. *Child Abuse and Neglect* 17: 71–89.

Kennel, J. H., and Klaus, M. H. (1982). Caring for the parents of premature or sick infants. In M. H. Klaus and J. H. Kennel (eds.), *Parent-infant bonding* (pp. 151–226). St. Louis: C. V. Mosby.

Lumsden, L. S. (1992). Stemming the tide of child sexual abuse: The role schools can play. *Oregon School Study Council* 35 (5): 1–53.

McEvoy, A. W. (1990). Child abuse law and school policy. *Education and Urban Society* 22: 247–257.

Montagu, A. (1978). *Touching: The human significance of the skin.* San Francisco: Harper and Row.

National Public Radio. (1994). Day care center goes to extremes to protect reputation. Morning Edition, Jan. 4. Washington, D.C.

Newman, L. F., and Buka, S. L. (1991). *Every child a learner: Reducing risks of learning impairment during pregnancy and infancy.* (Report No. SI-90-9). Education Commission of the States, Denver.

Noddings, N. (1992). *The challenge to care in schools: An alternative approach to education.* New York: Teachers College Press.

Nowesnick, M. (1993). Shattered lives. *American School Board Journal* 180: 14–19.

Phelan, P. (1993). *Unmarked: The politics of performance*. New York: Routledge.

Shuker, R., Openshaw, R., and Soler, J. (1990). *Youth, media, and moral panic in New Zealand: From hooligans to video nasties*. Palmerstown North, New Zealand: Massey University.

Silin, J. G. (1994). What can we know? Advocating for young children. Paper presented at the American Educational Research Association Meeting, New Orleans.

Sorenson, G. (1990). Sexual abuse in schools: Reported court cases from 1987–1990. *Educational Administration Quarterly* 27: 460–480.

Stainton Rogers, R., and Stainton Rogers, W. (1992). *Stories of childhood: Shifting concerns of child concern*. Toronto: University of Toronto Press.

Strickland, J., and Reynolds, S. (1988). The new untouchables: Risk management of child abuse in child care—before establishing procedures. *Child Care Information Exchange* 63: 19–21.

Tharinger, D., Krivacska, J. J., Laye-McDonough, M., Jamison, L., Vincent, G. G., and Hedlund, A. D. (1988). Prevention of child sexual abuse: An analysis of issues, educational programs, and research findings. *School Psychology Review* 17: 614–634.

Tobin, J. (1995). Post-structural research in early childhood education. In J. A. Hatch (ed.), *Qualitative research in early childhood settings*. (pp. 223–243). Westport, Conn.: Praeger.

Trickett, P. K., and Susman, E. J. (1988). Parental perceptions of child-rearing practices in physically abusive and non-abusive families. *Developmental Psychology* 24: 270–276.

Watney, S. (1993). *Policing desire: Pornography, AIDS, and the media*. Minneapolis: University of Minnesota Press.

Young, J. (1971). The role of the police as amplifiers of deviancy, negotiators of reality and translators of fantasy: Some consequences of our present system of drug control as seen in Notting Hill. In S. Cohen (ed.), *Images of deviance*. Baltimore: Penguin.

FOUR

Playing Doctor in Two Cultures
The United States and Ireland

Joseph Tobin

I can pinpoint the moment when the idea for this project was born. It was a Friday afternoon in January 1990. Ten early childhood education majors and I were sitting around a table for the second meeting of our student-teaching seminar. A student reported on a problem at her child care center: "There's a four-year-old girl in my group who runs up to the boys during free play and kisses them. And I don't mean just a peck on the cheek. She kisses them right on the lips. We were hoping the problem would fade away, but now she's got some of the other girls doing it." When I asked why she found this problematic, she responded, "We've had kids out sick all winter with strep and colds. The director told the kids the other day, 'No more kissing! Kissing spreads germs.'" In the discussion that ensued, several students echoed the remark about kissing and the spread of germs. When I asked if contagion was their only concern, a student responded, "I'm more worried about this little girl being so sexually advanced. I wonder if maybe someone hasn't been kissing her that way at home, if maybe someone hasn't sexually abused her."

The class split down the middle between those who felt that such aggressive kissing should alert us to the possibility of sexual abuse and those (including me) who argued that there is nothing unusual, suspicious, or symptomatic about a four-year-old girl kissing boys on the lips. As the students debated the matter, I asked myself the question that ultimately became the focus of this book: why would something as ordinary and innocent (at least to me) as a preschool kissing game strike so many of my students as dangerous?

In the weeks that followed students described other situations they found problematic: children playing doctor; a field trip to a dairy farm; a male teacher holding a little girl on his lap. The common feature of these situations was sex. Children's sexuality, sexual play, sexual knowledge, adults touching and being by touched by children—these struck my students as dangerous and threatening to children, their caretakers, or both.

Week after week, I found myself disagreeing with my students. I didn't share their sense of danger, and I couldn't identify the root causes behind their concerns. As the term progressed it became clear that this was not, as I first suspected, a matter of inexperienced student-teachers overreacting to situations that more experienced teachers would take in stride. It turned out to be just the opposite: the directors and experienced teachers they worked with were impressing on the students a sense of the danger in children's sexuality. It was I, the students tactfully suggested, who was out of touch with prevailing practice in early childhood education.

Something else happened in that spring of 1990 that drove me to pursue this study. As I listened to my students describe how they and their host teachers responded to children's sex play, I began to feel that the world of early childhood education was being overrun by an epidemic of worry, anxiety, and concern surrounding sex—that the early childhood education community was divided into those who were suffering from a culturally constructed hysteria, a moral panic about children's sexuality, and those who, like me, were not only free of this disease but perhaps even immune to it. And then one afternoon I discovered that I, too, was infected. That year I spent several hours each week with a class of four-year-olds, working on a curriculum for the "Japan Class" of the University of New Hampshire's Child Center. One afternoon I stayed late, reading stories to the last children to be picked up. As I read, tired children leaned against me. One girl settled into my lap, with her thumb in her mouth and her eyes half-closed, barely listening. Parents drifted into the room, calling out their children's names to take them home. Out of the corner of my eye I spotted a woman entering the room who I thought was the mother of the girl in my lap. In a flash I straightened up and relocated the little girl on the rug in front of me. When the child ran over to greet her mother, I followed. Unsure whether this mother knew who I was and why I was there, I awkwardly introduced myself.

I was shaken by this event. A woman entering the classroom to pick up her daughter had inspired a sense of panic in me. Worse, my panicked feeling had led to a panicky reaction—pushing the girl from my lap, as if we were doing something shameful, and then explaining myself as if I were somehow suspect. I felt humiliated by having allowed myself to feel so afraid, guilty about how my initial action may have been experienced by the little girl and whether she experienced my pushing her away as a rejection. I worried about what this incident foretold about my future in early childhood education. To learn more about how a similar moral panic is affecting the lives of young children and their teachers, I decided to expand the discussions I had begun with my students and their host teachers that spring in New Hampshire to a wider representation of early childhood educators.

METHOD

The research method I settled on was to assemble focus groups of preschool teachers to discuss a series of stories, each dealing with a problematic issue involving young children, their teachers, and sex. To the stories my seminar students had told in class I added stories I had gathered from discussions with teachers and the story of my pushing the child off my lap. Since teachers' reactions to these stories rather than the stories themselves would be the primary data for this study, I removed confusing and idiosyncratic features, rewriting the stories so that they would function effectively as projective devices, like inkblots or TAT pictures.[1] Like the videos that we used in our *Preschool in Three Cultures* study (Tobin, Wu, and Davidson, 1989), the stories were constructed to encourage teachers to come up with thoughtful responses that would reveal core beliefs, values, and concerns.[2]

From *Preschool in Three Cultures* I also borrowed the idea of bringing in voices from outside the contemporary United States to question the taken-for-grantedness of our beliefs and concerns. The intent here is to use anthropology as a form of cultural critique (Marcus and Fischer, 1986), to use an ethnographic look at another culture (in this case, Ireland) in order to make our familiar beliefs, practices, and concerns exotic. If my hypothesis is true that Americans at the end of the century are engulfed in a culturally shared panic involving young children, their adult caretakers, and sexuality, then a cross-cultural or historical comparison is needed to show us that things can be otherwise: from within a moral panic, and indeed from within any cultural mind-set, it is hard to gain a sense of perspective.

I selected Ireland for the culture of contrast because Ireland has been represented in the social science literature as the most sexually repressed country in the Western world. If a culture as (supposedly) sexually open as the United States is experiencing a

1. As I pilot-tested written versions of these stories on groups of students and teachers, I learned that I needed to edit and in some cases rewrite them. For the stories to stimulate discussion, they needed to be both succinct and ambiguous. There needed to be enough details to make the stories real and compelling, but not so many that the stories would become idiosyncratic or hard for outsiders to enter into. (For instance, I changed the male teacher with a child in his lap into an afternoon aide rather than a visiting Japanese culture specialist.)

2. This use of stories in research is similar to the use of "critical incidents" as a qualitative research method and to the problem-based learning approaches that are being used increasingly in colleges of education, as they have been used for years in legal and more recently in medical education. In each of these contexts, there is a need for the authors of the incidents to balance verisimilitude and specificity with generalizability. The stories I used in this study for research purposes could also be used for teacher education and staff development.

moral panic over children's sexuality, then what might be the attitude toward children's sexuality in a culture as (supposedly) sexually repressed as Ireland?[3]

Outsiders' writings on Irish sexuality have been controversial. The culture-and-personality theorist Nancy Scheper-Hughes has been criticized in Ireland for her suggestion that the rural Irish are sexually maladjusted. In *Saints, Sinners, and Schizophrenics* (1979), she reports that she found in the rural traditional culture a "strong current of sexual repression and personal asceticism" and "an excessive preoccupation with sexual purity and pollution" (pp. 9–11). In "The Erotics of Irishness" (1990) the feminist postmodern literary critic Cheryl Herr, while not endorsing Scheper-Hughes' methods, concurs that the Irish are disconnected from sexual desire and from their bodies: "We see displayed the neutralization of the body in this island culture," she remarks. "Ireland has literally eroded, in the sphere of representations that constitute social identity, a comfortable sense of the body." Moreover, she observed, "Censorship in Ireland is not really a political or legislative issue at heart; it is a symptom of a specific kind of psychological development on individual and group levels" (pp. 5, 6, 14).

I do not aspire to illuminate the darkest chambers of the Irish psyche or the deepest strata of the Irish transhistorical cultural

3. The study was conceived and carried out as a three-way comparison of attitudes toward children's sex play in the United States, Ireland, and Japan. For the present, at least, I have dropped Japan from the analysis. I had the eight stories and the instructions translated into Japanese and the Japanese recording sheets translated into English. But because I was not sufficiently fluent in Japanese to pick up nuances of the focus group discussions, the Japanese data are not as detailed as the Irish and American material. A more serious methodological problem is one of cultural translation. Japanese focus group members found many of the stories to be bizarre. My sense is that sexuality is patterned so differently in Japan than in the West that the comparison with Japan tells us more about broad cultural differences in beliefs about the body, privacy, and pleasure than about the narrower issue of dealing with children's sexuality in preschool settings, which is my primary concern here.

semiotic as these writers do. My analysis of Ireland is much more modest. And because my central goal is to explicate and critique contemporary American beliefs and practices, the discussion of each issue is more fully elaborated in the American than in the Irish setting. Although I introduce some provocative ethnographic data from Ireland and hint at some interpretations, the story of Irish childhood sexuality needs to be told by someone far more knowledgeable about Irish culture and society than I am.[4]

This study is based on twelve focus groups conducted in the United States and eight in Ireland.[5] The U.S. groups were held in Durham, New Hampshire; Honolulu; and Chicago. Participants included teachers and directors from a variety of early childhood educational settings, including Head Start, Montessori, private,

4. Maureen Gaffney of Trinity College in Dublin helped to facilitate the focus groups and to guide my understanding of Irish society. I am also grateful to the staff of Bernardo's and to members of the IPPA in Dublin and Sligo.

5. In each country I put preschool teachers and administrators together in groups ranging from five to eight members and gave them these instructions:

1. One member of the group will read the first story aloud. This group member will then become the recorder for the group discussion.
2. Have a ten-minute discussion of the story: What do you think about the situation described? Do you agree with how the teacher in the story dealt with the situation? Do you ever encounter similar situations?
3. During the discussion, the recorder should write down the points that are made, noting agreements and disagreements. It is not necessary to write down every word.
4. Move onto the next story and repeat steps 1–3, taking turns at being the recorder.

In sites where there were no more than eight people present, I sat in, facilitating discussion and writing a transcript to complement the recorder's notes. When there were more than eight people, and thus more than one group running at a time, I moved from group to group, answering questions and keeping time.

Some recorders did a better job than others. Most recorders got caught up in the conversation and had occasional lapses in writing things down. My transcripts turned out to be much more complete (closer to verbatim) than the recorders' notes. The sensitive nature of the topic led me to decide against video- or audiotaping the sessions.

church-related, and university-attached preschools. In Ireland, discussions were held with play group leaders and preschool teachers working in middle- and working-class neighborhoods in the city of Dublin, in housing projects on the outskirts of the city, and in County Sligo.

A CONCEPTUAL FRAME FOR ANALYSIS

The focus group discussions generally took about ninety minutes, with approximately ten minutes spent discussing each of the eight stories. The twenty focus groups collectively produced more than fifteen hundred recorded comments, presenting me with a formidable task of analysis. It would be interesting to look at regional, class, and cultural differences within the U.S. sample by doing separate analyses of the responses from each site. However, in this chapter I have collapsed the responses from the various sites in the United States and have looked for patterns across the data because I am concerned here with describing and understanding a broad cultural discourse.

My first readings of the transcripts suggested that while there was considerable variation within and among the focus groups in what people said, there was also a very clearly articulated shared social discourse. For example, while group members disagreed strongly with one another about whether a teacher was right to intervene in a childbirth game or whether they would tell a male aide to stop holding children on his lap, the terms of their disagreements were shared and familiar. That is, American respondents often said such things as "I disagree with what you just said" or "I would handle the situation very differently," but no one said "I don't understand your concern" or "I've never thought about a situation like this as a problem." On the other hand, many (but by no means all) of the Irish respondents were perplexed about why Americans found some of the situations described in the stories threatening. My reading of the Irish transcripts suggests a divide within the responses, with the Dublin informants closer to the panicked American discourse and the Sligo informants farther from these concerns.

I am not interested in psychoanalyzing the unconscious motivations and defense mechanisms of my informants as individuals. I used group discussions rather than individual interviews as a research method because my object of study is a public discourse rather than intrapsychic dynamics. In my analyses of statements made in the focus group discussions I paid little attention to who said what and instead treated the discussions as complex collaborative texts. Even where individuals take up sharply opposing positions, I think it most useful to think of their arguments as expressions of culturally shared conflicts and ambivalences.

My reading of the U.S. focus group responses suggests a thesis: the core concerns Americans have about sexuality in preschool settings reflect the projection of larger social problems onto early childhood education. With a constituency composed chiefly of underpaid women, young children, and their preoccupied, anxious, and sometimes guilty parents, preschools are a vulnerable sector of society, lacking the power and voice to resist the projection of extraneous issues, interests, and concerns.

To support my argument that Americans are, indeed, projecting larger social issues and anxieties onto the preschool setting—and that, on the whole, the Irish are not—I will present the focus group responses not story by story, but projected issue by projected issue. Working back and forth between the data, the theory, and my evolving hypothesis, I derived eight content categories. Five of these categories fall under the larger heading of "dangers": sexually transmitted disease, gynecological maladies, (excessive) female desire, dangerous sexual knowledge, and homophobia/androphobia. The other three categories are solutions or reactions to the perceived danger: panopticism (visibility/surveillance), litigation, and nostalgia for simpler times. I link these eight content categories into a narrative: Preschools are sites of danger. Some of the danger comes from children, who suffer from sexually transmitted diseases and gynecological problems and have dangerous sexual desires and knowledge. Some of the danger comes from teachers, especially if they are homosexual and/or male. A solution some teachers and directors turn to is panopticism. But this solution further disempowers the profession, as teachers find themselves objects of the suspicious gaze of the larger society, manifested as parental distrust and threats of litigation. Some teachers and administrators stand up to the distrust and threats; most give in. All are nostalgic for simpler times, when sex was less dangerous.

The Symptomology of Endangered and Dangerous Children

Story 1: There's a four-year-old girl in my group who runs up to the boys during free play and kisses them. And I don't mean just a peck on the cheek. She kisses them right on the lips. I was hoping the problem would kind of fade away, but now she's got some of the other girls doing the same thing.

In their discussions of several of the scenarios, American informants used the logic and language of medical and psychological symptomology. The little girls in these stories were seen as having clinical conditions, conditions that could or should be referred to medical specialists. Like my seminar students, many of the American respondents associated kissing games with germs, contagion, and sexually transmitted diseases. Germs were cited in nine of the twelve U.S. focus groups. In three groups, the mention of spreading germs through kissing escalated to a discussion of sexually transmitted diseases. The most striking example of such a jump was this sequence of comments made by a group of Honolulu early-childhood-education graduate students in the spring of 1992:

TEACHER A: I worry about germs. I'd tell them, "You can kiss on the cheek, but not on the mouth. You have yucky germs in your mouth."

TEACHER B: I heard somewhere that actually you have lots more germs on your hands than in your mouth. You're more likely to get sick from shaking hands than from kissing.

TEACHER A: We make the children wash their hands several times a day, but it's a constant battle. A lot of them just run in and out of the bathroom and pretend they washed their hands. Or they just stick one hand under the faucet and think their hands are clean.

TEACHER B: That's why so many preschool children and teachers are sick. There are germs being spread all over the place because the kids have such bad hygiene. Someone did a study of germs in a preschool classroom using like an infrared device to show how the children spread germs, and germs were literally all over the place. The whole room was red in the picture.

TEACHER C: It's scary, all the new germs out there they don't have medicines for. There's even resistance to the old germs that used to be handled by antibiotics. I was reading something the other day about how common herpes is, and that once you get it, it's almost impossible to get rid of it. I mean the kind of herpes you get in your mouth, on your lips.

TEACHER D: With this whole Magic Johnson thing, you can't help but think about HIV.

TEACHER B: But it's a myth that you can get AIDS by kissing.

TEACHER D: Right, I know, but the whole safe sex and AIDS thing, and we have to be really careful. I just mean that somehow this story just brings to mind the whole thing with Magic and AIDS.

TEACHER E: And now there's that book that says Wilt Chamberlain had sex with thirty thousand different women!

TEACHER D: You know how doctors and dentists and nurses have to wear rubber gloves with all their patients. I bet we'll be next. I can just see me putting on gloves to wipe the kids' noses and make their snacks.

Taken one by one, these comments are reasonable and unexceptional. But the conversation taken as a whole follows the (il)logic of association, displacement, and substitution characteristic of dreams, hysterical symptoms, and moral panics. The conversation moves from children's kissing, to children's inconsistent hand washing, to children and teachers getting sick, to (oral) herpes, to AIDS, to sexual promiscuity, and finally to teachers' needing to wear rubber gloves. Topical jumps and shifts are characteristic of informal human communication. But the associative jumps in this conversation have a logic and directionality characteristic of an anxiety-driven, culturally shared hysteria in which a larger societal panic about adult sexuality and AIDS is projected onto the benign bodily contacts of young children.

This conversation gives us insight into the projective mechanisms that lead teachers to regard as dangerous a kissing game that in other times and contexts would be seen as benign. The conversation leaps from minor worry to apocalyptic disaster, from the common cold to the AIDS epidemic, from a little girl kissing several boys to a man having sex with thirty thousand women. This is how moral panics work: by synecdoche (the substitution of parts for whole and whole for parts) and the erasure of distinctions between dissimilar actors and actions. In this conversation the child's mouth becomes a synecdoche for the sexually vulnerable and dangerous adult body. Critical distinctions are erased between the sexuality of children and adults, as indiscriminate kissing by a four-year-old girl is linked to Wilt Chamberlain's improbably prodigious sexual promiscuity. There are substitutions of the mouth for the genitals, of the relatively benign germs of the cold and the sore throat for the deadly viruses of sexually transmitted diseases, of the beginning (kissing as foreplay) and the end (sexual intercourse). In the leap from a little girl to Magic Johnson to Wilt Chamberlain to the gloved preschool teacher we have a collapsing and confusion of perpetrator and victim and of guilt and innocence (guilty victims and innocent vectors) characteristic of the moral panic and projection surrounding AIDS.

The moral panic in the American discourse about kissing games becomes clearer when contrasted with the Irish early childhood educators' responses to the same story. Of the fifty-five comments that they made in response to the kissing story, only one even remotely referred to any kind of germ: "I don't kiss children on the lips because they usually have snotty noses or dirty mouths." The conversation of a group of five Dublin teachers is typical of the Irish lack of concern about kissing games:

TEACHER A: Kiss chase is our big game. The girls think it's brilliant.

TEACHER B: Ours is "kiss and strip." They kiss and pretend to take their clothes off and touch each other.

TEACHER A: The one rule we put in is that if you don't want to play kiss chase, you have to announce so at the beginning of the game.

TEACHER C: Our kids call it "television kissing." When a child does it to me, I say, "I don't like that television kissing."

> *Story 2:* Emily touches herself a lot. When she's excited, she keeps touching herself with one hand. During story time, she rubs her legs together with a sort of far-off look in her eyes. Even at lunch she'll have a hand in her pants sometimes. I don't mean she's doing it every minute, but it's not like it's only now or then, either.

Just as the U.S. focus group respondents turned the story of the kissing girl into a discussion of infectious disease, so they turned the story of the masturbating girl into a discussion of gynecological disorders. In all twelve of the U.S. focus groups the most frequent explanation for the girl's activity was that she was scratching a vaginal itch:

- Could be some type of infection or rash.
- Vaginal irritation? Improper hygiene?
- Why is she doing it? Irritation?
- I'd suspect a medical problem.
- Could be a medical problem: rash, yeast infection, bladder infection.
- Talk to parents. Maybe she has an infection.
- Vaginal infection? Medical problem?
- Irritating underwear.
- Have parent check with doctor.
- Tell/suggest that parent take child to doctor to check for pinworms, yeast infection, etc.

Even the director of a preschool who disagreed that the girl's problem was gynecological acknowledged that the turn to gynecological explanations was inevitable in today's climate: "I would just leave the girl alone or at most speak to her about doing her masturbating during more private times of the day. But I can hear my teachers now: 'It must be physical.' 'Send her to the doctor.' Anything to avoid dealing with sexuality."

As the director implies, the psychological mechanism operating here is denial: *anything to avoid dealing with sexuality*. Rather than discuss the story in terms of masturbation, most of the respondents preferred to think of Emily as having an infection. By suspecting an infection, they can avoid the responsibility of dealing with the child's sexuality. Instead of coming to terms with their feelings about children's masturbating in early childhood education settings, these respondents transform ordinary sexuality into a gynecological disorder. This is consistent with Foucault's (1979) discussion of the medicalization of sexuality and the body as mechanisms of social control.

Because Emily is a fictional character rather than a real preschooler, there is no right answer to the question, "Does Emily have an infection or is she masturbating?" I wrote the vignette to elicit attitudes toward masturbation; it never occurred to me that it would be discussed as anything else. But because I wrote, "Emily always has her hands in her pants" rather than "Emily is always masturbating," I created ambiguity, which left room for the gynecological explanation. I maintain, however, that this explanation requires an active denial of the vignette's sexual theme: though the story does not mention the word *masturbation,* it does refer to Emily's "far-off look" and to her being "excited," a look and a mood more plausibly connected with sexual pleasure than with a yeast infection. I read in the absence of a discussion of masturbation a mechanism of denial characteristic of a moral panic about children's sexuality: children's sexuality has become so dangerous that it must be denied, ignored, or, as in Emily's case, converted into a medical problem that can be referred for treatment. Again, the contrast with Ireland is dramatic. Of sixty-two Irish responses to this story, only one mentioned the possibility of a vaginal infection.

Of the minority of American respondents who *did* interpret Emily's behavior as masturbation, several were very concerned:

- I would worry about frequent masturbation.
- Yes, we would all worry.
- I would ask the teachers to keep a log: frequency, duration, times, pattern, intensity.
- Gather information—keep a log—what triggers it.
- Unloved? For attention? It's one of the tell-tale signs of abuse.
- Send her to a counselor for disclosure. You don't want to contaminate disclosure by talking to the girl first.
- Talk to her. Things about home, recent events, siblings, trips, anything out of the ordinary.

Clearly, at the heart of this concern is the sexual abuse of children. Disclosure, logs, tell-tale signs—this is the language of the courts and child protective services, of the legal and social work apparatus that battles child sex abuse.

If the story that provoked these reactions had been about a

sexually abused girl, this language would make sense to me. But where did these respondents find indications of abuse? In the story of the masturbating girl, as in the story of the kissing girl, behaviors that to me seem typical of young children became danger signs to many of my American respondents. In each of these stories, an expression of sexual desire by a young girl was marked as dangerous. The logic seems to be that, first, these girls were desired (abused), and this abuse in turn stimulated the release of unnatural, dangerous desires.

Because Emily is a fictional character who appears in a text barely sixty words long, we cannot say that she was or was not abused. Nor can we know how these teachers would react to the reality of a girl masturbating in their classroom. Presumably their reaction in real life to a girl like Emily would be based on intuition and contextual knowledge that they cannot bring to a vignette. Still, it is striking that eight of the twelve American focus groups brought up sexual abuse as a possible explanation of Emily's masturbation. In six of the twelve groups similar concerns were raised about the kissing girl, who, like Emily, was identified as a possible victim of abuse:

- Anything out of the norm, I would worry.
- My concern is the child's being sexually abused.
- Children who've been abused often become sexually aggressive.

I do not doubt that some girls who have been the victims of sexual abuse become sexually aggressive. But this phenomenon should not suggest the converse: that little girls who are sexually assertive or curious have necessarily been abused. Girls' masturbating and chasing and kissing boys are not strange or bizarre behaviors that should lead us to search for an explanation in trauma. To see the girls in my stories as victims of sexual abuse may look like sympathy and concern. But the logic and politics of victimization can work to undermine rather than support the dignity, agency, and rights of those we are trying to protect. Reading these stories as sagas of abuse and victimization works to interrupt and demonize female sexuality. This is an old story; female sexuality in our culture has long been under attack. Feminists in the 1970s and 1980s, challenging the notion that (good) girls and women are without desire, attempted to overturn the shame girls and women have been made to feel about their bodies and their sexual desires. But in the 1990s, the moral panics surrounding pornography, AIDS, teen pregnancy, and sex abuse have combined to reinvigorate the long-standing suspicion of female desire.

The image of the masturbating girl is profoundly disturbing. The sexuality of little girls confuses us. It's not that we want girls to be sexless. Little girls are expected to have clear gender identities, to rehearse adult sexual roles, and to mimic heteronormative desires. Playing out flirtatious, sexual, romantic, heteronormative scenarios in the housekeeping corner (for instance, dressing up to look sexy in high heels and makeup or "cooking dinner" at a toy stove while waiting for a "husband" to come home) is generally accepted behavior for little girls. But when girls touch their own bodies, we are horrified. Why? Perhaps because they are displaying female desire, which we have a hard enough time accepting in grown women and adolescent girls, much less in preschoolers. Perhaps because by masturbating in our presence, the little girl produces in us an uncomfortable association with the masturbating woman who is a key figure in our culture's pornography. (In her essay "Jane Austen and the Masturbating Girl" [1991], Eve Sedgwick exposes the sadomasochistic pleasures our society derives from stories of naughty girls who need to be taught a lesson.) Or perhaps, to employ another Sedgwick mode of explanation, because in pleasuring herself, the little girl, like the lesbian, threatens patriarchy by functioning outside the circulation of phallic desire.

In discussions of the kissing and masturbating scenarios, Irish and American respondents raised feminist critiques that were trenchant, if less provocative than Eve Sedgwick's:

- If Emily were a boy would we be worried?
- Why are we more concerned with girls doing it? Boys do it all the time and we think nothing of it.
- The boys have their hands in their pants all day long.
- Some boys, you'd think their hands are attached permanently down there.
- That's where boys' hands go when they're anxious or excited.
- I have several boys like that in my class. I only say something when we're cooking: "OK, thumbs out of the mouths and hands out of the pants."

These responses show the awareness of teachers in both cultures of the double standard that governs reactions to children's (and adults') sexuality: If the masturbating and kissing children in the stories were boys, would we be as likely to wonder about abuse? No. The figures of the masturbating and kissing girls touch core cultural taboos, loathings, and fears. Where we as a culture hope, expect, and need to find innocence, we instead find desire. The feminist teachers are caught in a bind: as women and as feminists, they know that girls are more sexually vulnerable than boys. They are aware of the dangers that girls will be sexualized by the male gaze, objectified by male desire, and vulnerable to having their sexual identities constructed negatively (as the abject Other) under patriarchy. On the other hand, these feminist early childhood educators feel it is unjust that the sexual activities of little boys are normalized and accepted while the sexual activities of little girls are constructed as dangerous and unnatural.

The Girls Who Knew Too Much

Story 3: The other day, two girls and a boy were playing "doctor." Actually, they were playing "delivery room." One girl, who was being the patient, lay on her back and said, "It's time for the baby." Then the other girl, who was the nurse, and the boy, who was the doctor, got ready to "deliver" the baby. I was watching from across the room. At first I was thinking this was cute, but then the nurse told the doctor, "Pull down her underpants so we can get the baby out," and that's just what they did. When they pulled her underpants down I could see that she had put a little baby doll in her underpants and was now holding it between her legs. At that point I came over. The "nurse" told me, "Get away, we're birthing a baby," but I told the "patient" she had to put her underpants back on immediately.

It is not just children's sexual desire and pleasure that worry early childhood educators but also their sexual knowledge. If the focus group discussions of the kissing and masturbation stories are classically Freudian in their hysterical conversion of tabooed desires to bodily (somatized) symptoms and in their concern with female immodesty, reactions to the delivery room story are Lacanian in their anxiety about the interplay of knowledge, ignorance, and innocence. In several of the discussions, the conversation turned to the question of how these children knew so much:

- What graphic, vivid language they use!
- Too much maturity for kids of that age.
- Where did they get all this knowledge of where babies come from?
- Kids these days see everything—even films of babies coming out of the birth canal.
- I would question how these children would have such knowledge. I mean actual physical knowledge of the birthing process.
- Maybe one of them was in a delivery room with their parents.
- Maybe they saw a baby book or saw a birth on TV and are acting it out.
- Something about this gives me an uncomfortable feeling. These girls seem to know a bit too much for, how old does it say they are? Four years old?

Similar concerns were expressed in reactions to the kissing story:

- She's too precocious.
- I would want to talk to this child's parents.
- I would want to know what's she seeing at home.
- Is there a baby-sitter who has a boyfriend?
- Is the child seeing adult sexual behavior?
- I would want to know where it's coming from, how she knows so much about kissing.

The core concern here is that excessive sexual knowledge is dangerous. This is knowledge in the Edenic sense, the kind of knowledge that comes from eating forbidden fruit (or watching someone else do so). These girls who know how to play doctor so expertly are suspect. Sexual knowledge is dangerous because it suggests a lack of innocence. These girls suffer from lack of a lack. In *Looking Awry: An Introduction to Jacques Lacan Through Popular Culture* (1992), Slavoj Zizek discusses the characters in Hitchcock films who are in danger because, by chance, they have come to know things they should not know. Children shouldn't know too much about kissing or the anatomical details of birth (much less of sexual intercourse). This knowing becomes dangerous to others but mostly to the child who knows and who for this reason comes under suspicion of needing treatment.[6]

This is consistent with Jonathan Silin's argument in Chapter 7 about the role our passion for ignorance plays in the education of children. We have a need for children to be ignorant. In the face of evidence that they in fact know a lot about sex and birth and even about AIDS and death, we continue to insist that they don't know, can't know, shouldn't know. The child who palpably knows

6. Laura Mulvey (1975) points out that in film noir it is the woman who sees, the woman who turns the table on the male gaze, *the woman with glasses* who is dangerous. Seeing and knowing are connected in complex ways. Seeing too much, for example, is one way little girls come to know too much.

becomes a threat to our belief in children's ignorance. She is a problem that must be dealt with.

If, as Silin suggests, ignorance in children is equated with innocence, then precocious sexual knowledge suggests defilement and culpability. A preschool child's knowledge of sex suggests that something is amiss. The child who knows too much is immediately suspected of being a victim of abuse. But like a rape victim, the little girl who is under suspicion of being abused is also seen as ruined and dangerous because of her loss of innocence. The little girl who lacks innocence becomes monstrous, aberrant.

In every focus group there were some respondents who challenged the sentiment that there was something wrong with the children's playing the delivery room game. Several teachers, defending the game as developmentally appropriate for four-year-olds, said they would be very hesitant to intervene in children's dramatic play "unless it really got out of hand." Among these respondents were feminists who approved of the children's having knowledge of childbirth. These respondents were bothered instead by the gender stereotyping: "The only problem I have with this is why isn't the girl the doctor and the boy the nurse?" An Irish respondent made the same point: "It's interesting that it's still sex-stereotyped. The boy is the doctor, the girl the nurse. That would be more concerning to us than the sex play."

Key differences between American and Irish early childhood educators in their attitudes toward children's sexuality can be seen in the way they assessed the kissing, masturbating, and delivery-room scenarios. In discussions in both countries, there was disagreement about whether teachers should intervene in children's sex play. Many Irish respondents, like their American counterparts, said they would. But few Irish respondents shared the American concerns that the children in these stories were abused, dangerous, or in need of clinical assistance. In the Irish focus group discussions there was strikingly less projection of larger societal panics about AIDS and abuse onto these scenarios.

As writings by Nancy Scheper-Hughes (1979), Cheryl Herr

(1990), and others suggest, we would expect to find more anxiety about sexuality in Ireland than in the United States. Why, then, aren't the Irish more worried about these stories? Some of the Irish respondents were critical of the little girl's having her hand down her pants in public and of the kissing and doctor games while others thought it all acceptable. But to both groups, masturbating and kissing and playing doctor games were just things young children do rather than indications of danger.[7] Where Americans associated children's sexual play with infection, contagion, and abuse, the Irish tended to describe it as simply "dirty" or "bold":[8]

- My sister-in-law slaps her two-year-old's hand when she touches herself. It's dirty.
- When I was young my mother would be down on me like a ton of bricks: "Stop that dirty thing immediately! Don't be 'at yourself.'"
- My sister would masturbate and the lads in the house would give her a clip.
- My mother would say, "That dolly might be dirty. Keep it outside your knickers."
- My own little girl is exploring her bottom with her legs in the air, and suddenly I become my mother and say to my daughter, "Don't be bold. Put your legs down!"

7. This is consistent with queer theorists' suggestions that in other times, in other places, same-sex sexual relations were things people did rather than who they were.

8. "Bold" is used in Ireland in situations where Americans would say "bad" or "naughty." Scheper-Hughes (1979) writes: "The cardinal sin of early childhood is 'boldness,' and a *bold* child is, by definition, one who questions the orders that come down to him, who does not do as he or she is told, or who does not demonstrate proper shy and deferential comportment before the elders" (p. 154). I found Irish parents and teachers to be ambivalent about children's displays of boldness (sexual and otherwise). When telling a child that he or she is being bold, the adult's tone often reveals a characteristically Irish amalgam of condemnation and approbation. As Scheper-Hughes notes, the bold child "is privately admired for his or her 'spunk.'" (156).

It is significant that in these comments the Irish teachers refer to how these situations would be handled by other people—sister-in-law, mother, brother. The key figures here are their mothers, ambivalent figures who are simultaneously praised for their commonsensical, unequivocal approaches and ridiculed for being old-fashioned and ill-informed:

- On an excursion to the park we saw two ducks mating. The children were fascinated. Then a lady came and hit them—the ducks, not the children. "Stop that!" And I thought, that's just what my mother would say.
- At the beach my son took his clothes off to go swimming. My mother was horrified!
- If my mother saw such a scene in a parish preschool, she'd be giving out to the priest.
- My son was doing it once when my mother was there, and she was disgusted, "Why are you letting him do that?" I said, "Mammy, if he doesn't learn to handle it now, he'll be in trouble as an adult."
- When I was growing up my mother wouldn't have hesitated a second in a situation like that. She'd have said, "Stop that! It's bold." But these days you'd be thinking you'd not want to traumatize a child.

Although these Irish early childhood educators ridicule their mothers' harsh, old-fashioned approaches to children's sexuality, in the laughter they shared as they talked about their mothers and the Irish past there is a subtle, begrudging acknowledgment that there was something straightforward and reassuring in their mothers' openly critical approach, something they worry they may be in the process of losing and that Americans already have lost. It's as if these Irish teachers are citing the Foucaultian paradox: children's sexuality was less endangered in earlier eras, when it was seen as lowly and dirty, than under modern, liberal regimes, where it supposedly is accepted but in actuality becomes subject to the clinician's gaze and the interventions of the helping professions. Liberal American society, seeming to accept sexuality and bring it out of the realm of superstition, religion, and the gutter and into the light of scientific discourse and understanding, creates categories of sexual deviance and mechanisms for the control and erasure of sexuality. A danger of this Foucaultian reasoning is that in exposing the quietly repressive mechanisms of the modern, liberal present, we sentimentalize the brutally repressive mechanisms of the past. While most of my Irish informants were glad to be free, at least for a while longer, from the excesses of American social liberalism, none wished to return to what they saw as the ignorant, judgmental, guilt- and shame-inducing sexual attitudes of their mothers and grandmothers.

Dangerous Adults: Pedophiles, Homosexuals, Men, and Other Teachers of Young Children

Story 4: At the center where I'm the director, we don't have any male full-time teachers, but we have one male teacher's aide who comes in three afternoons a week. One day last week, near the end of the day, he was reading a group of kids a story, and one little girl was leaning up against him, with her thumb in her mouth, almost like lying in his lap. On one hand, it gave me a nice feeling to see her so relaxed with him and affectionate, but on the other hand, something about it made me uncomfortable. I wish it didn't but I have to admit it does.

The companion figure to the sexually vulnerable and dangerous child is the sexually dangerous and vulnerable teacher. The story of the teacher's aide with a girl in his lap clearly brought out the contradictory concerns that males in early childhood education are simultaneously dangerous to children and vulnerable to the accusation of being dangerous to children, as we can see in the comments made in response to this story by a female teacher in

Honolulu: "The director of our center isn't letting the two male teachers change diapers or take kids to the bathroom. She transferred the one guy who used to work with the twos to work with the older kids so he wouldn't have to change diapers or deal with kids in the bathroom. He didn't want to switch, but the director said he had to for his own sake, to protect him from accusations. He said he was willing to take the chance, but she said she couldn't let him, because she has an obligation to protect him, and even if he is willing to take the risk, she has to look out for the interests of the program." In several of the U.S. focus groups, this scenario produced heated debate between those who felt the director was failing to back up the male aide and those who felt that the director had reason to be concerned:

- Because of the way society is today, there is a need to pay attention to appearances. I'm not saying you can't show affection, but you have to think about how it might look.
- I think the problem here isn't the male teacher. It's this director's mistrust of men. I think she needs to talk to someone to clarify her views before discussing it with him.
- It's a shame because children need more male role models. But the reality is that hiring males these days to work with young children is a chance a lot of centers just can't afford to take.

While these respondents took sides, others found themselves caught in the middle:

- I feel bad for everyone involved—the little girl, the man, . . . the director. There's no villain here.
- You don't want to overreact, but you can't underestimate how crazy it has gotten. A true story: A male teacher I know mailed himself photos he had taken of the kids in his group in T-shirts and diapers. The package came open in the mail. The Feds showed up. These are pictures of babies in diapers and this guy is being investigated for pornography!

- When my friend John hugs kids, their faces are in his crotch, and he says, "What do I do? You know, they grab one leg." I don't know what to tell him. *I* totally trust him, but if a parent who didn't know him well walked in and saw him with a kid's head in his crotch—if they already are prepared to look for the worst, they'll find it.

As a culture, we find ourselves on a slippery slope. Once we acquiesce to having personnel decisions made on the basis of the potential or imagined dangers that employees present to the children they care for, where will we draw the line? Who is completely safe? Who is beyond suspicion? The hysterical nature of this discourse is revealed in the chain of signifiers that runs from the certifiably dangerous male pedophile to the presumably safe female teacher. This is the logic of the symptom and the dream, the logic of substitution, collapsing, and synecdoche, where a part can stand for the whole and the similar becomes the identical. Written as a mathematical equation, it would be: pedophile = gay male = all males = all adults who work with children. Putting this ideational chain into everyday language, it would go something like this: pedophiles, by definition, are dangerous to children, so all gay men are potentially dangerous since they share perverted desires with pedophiles. Straight men are also dangerous, since, after all, they are men, and men have such strong sex drives. And if men are dangerous, how can lesbians be safe, since butch women imitate predatory male sexuality? And what about straight women, since they often fall under the sway of the perverted desires of men?

The pervert lurking in the cracks and on the fringes of the world of early childhood education is a spectre that haunts our thinking and practice, distorting the way we see ourselves and each other and the decisions we make about practice. For example, to explain her reaction to a story about children playing naked in a sprinkler, a teacher in Honolulu invoked the figure of the child pornographer: "I guess the worst-case scenario that could develop here and that I have in the back of my mind as I think about how I'd handle this situation—well, actually it's not the worst case, but it's a bad case—would be if some weird man with a camera with a telephoto lens took pictures of our children running around naked in the sprinkler. Does that sound like a ridiculous concern to you? Well, five years ago it would have sounded like a ridiculous concern to me, but that's the kind of thing I have to think about these days."[9]

Child pornographers and others who sexually abuse children must be identified and stopped. But our zeal to protect children from pedophiles has led to a morally panicked suspicion of all men who work with young children. James King, in Chapter 6, makes the point that because the care and education of young children are still considered to be women's work, men in early childhood education are seen as intruding into a world where they do not belong. Why would a normal man want to be around young children anyway? But this distorted logic is contagious. In the wake of the McMartin case, women are no longer beyond suspicion. Considering the low pay, poor working conditions, and threat of liability, why would a normal woman want to work in this field? Suddenly, we all are suspect.

One way to expose the illogic of the current reasoning is to take the implications a bit further: Because gay men are attracted only to people of their own gender, wouldn't it be safe for a gay male teacher to hold a girl on his lap? Wouldn't it make sense to have straight male staff members change the boys' diapers and

---

9. The story to which the teacher was responding:
When it gets really hot here we always used to put out some wading pools and sprinklers, and we'd have the two- and three-year-olds just take off their clothes and play in the water without anything on. We never thought anything of it, but then a parent pointed out to us that people can see the playground from the street through the fence, and she suggested the children should wear swimming suits. This seems unnecessary for such little kids, but I suppose that's what we're going to have to do.

straight female staff members change the girls' diapers? But what if a heterosexual-seeming male teacher is a closeted gay and a normal-seeming female teacher is actually a lesbian? Male and female workers could be made to keep an eye on each other. But what if, as alleged in the McMartin case, male and female staff are in cahoots in a child abuse/pornography ring? Perhaps we could require that staff be rotated from child center to child center at regular intervals to break up sex rings. Or we could hire under-cover agents to pose as child care workers and move from center to center rooting out abuse. The hysteria is advancing so quickly that I fear that the absurd child-protection scenarios I have put forward here may be realities in the very near future.

When it comes to assuming the worst of men, the Irish are very like Americans. As in the United States, some of this concern is associated with a mounting sense of danger caused by social and moral deterioration. But Irish responses to the story of the male aide suggest that the suspicion of men caring for young children is a more basic, deeply rooted concern in Ireland. The responses suggest that Irish believe men are unaccustomed and inherently ill suited to caring for children:

- Very few men in this country work in primary education.
- [Men] were never to be alone with one boy, to protect both.
- Men rarely disagree with this concern. There's a recognition in men, also, that men are dangerous.
- Kids wouldn't have been touched much by their dads in the old days. They still aren't.
- Because men aren't being nurturant to children, they are more likely to abuse children.
- My friend has a play group and she tells her husband, "Don't come in while the play group is on."
- One parent, a mother, said, "Don't let your husband take my girl to the toilet."
- If you had a son you wouldn't encourage him to baby-sit. Younger girls can be very provocative.

In contrast to the American concern that men are dangerous if they are gay and/or perverted, the Irish are ill at ease with the notion of men caring for children just because they are men. Child care is women's work in both countries. But these focus group responses suggest that in Ireland the separation of men from the world of women and children is more complete and profound than in the United States.

Panopticism and Litigation: Problems Posing as Solutions

Story 5: We have three little toilets in a row in the bathroom, with no dividers in between. Sometimes, when they're all in use, some other kids are also in there, standing around waiting for a toilet or watching the kids on the toilet. Sometimes they even try to look from behind. They laugh and say, "I can see the doo-doo coming out." We try to shoo the watchers away, to give the kids who are going to the bathroom more privacy, but the kids on the toilet usually don't seem to mind the attention. The only time they really mind is when they have a b.m. and one of the other kids tries to flush the toilet.

Story 6: We took a field trip to the zoo today and the zoo's educational director asked me if the kids would like to watch a calf being born. I had to make an instantaneous decision, so I said yes. The kids were fascinated, but it was really intense. The kids were yelling things like, "Look, it's coming out of her butt!" and "The baby cow is all bloody!" I tried to explain things right there on the spot, but obviously there is a lot left to talk about when we get back to school tomorrow. I'm not exactly sure how detailed to get in my explanations or even what words to use. I put a note up for the parents yesterday letting them know what the kids saw, but I'm still kind of worried about getting some negative parental reactions, or maybe I'm being paranoid and no one will complain.

Believing early childhood educational settings to be fraught with sexual danger, Americans resort to a variety of desperate solutions. Richard Johnson's essay (Chapter 3) describes one of the most ludicrous of these solutions: the "no touch policy." Jonathan Silin and James King, in Chapters 7 and 8, analyze the dynamics of another desperate, ethically despicable solution—running men in general and gay men in particular out of the field. In their responses to the masturbating, kissing, and playing-doctor scenarios, we have seen Americans dealing with children's sexual play by calling for medical or child abuse consultations. American discussions of the bathroom and zoo stories reveal two other ways of dealing with dangerous sexuality—panopticism and litigation. The introduction into preschools of tools and perspectives borrowed from the medical doctor, the psychiatrist, the social worker, the policeman, the prison guard, the lawyer, and the insurance agent works to further disempower rather than protect teachers and children, exacerbating the suppression of their pleasures and desires.

We can see in the beliefs and practices of the contemporary American preschool a preoccupation with sight lines and other techniques for making young children constantly visible. Many U.S. respondents offered panopticism (literally, "seeing everything") as a solution to the problems presented in the bathroom, sprinkler, and playing-doctor scenarios:

- I'd let the children know that I was watching. Usually, that's all it takes. Once they see that you are watching, they monitor their own behavior, and usually you don't even have to say anything.
- I'm much less worried about a game like this, which is going on in the dramatic play area, than I would be about the same thing happening behind a closed bathroom door.
- To catch problems before they get started the secret is to set up the room so you can see at a glance right into the dress-up corner. We've totally reorganized our setup here to give us

improved sight lines. Now, right here where we are sitting, if you stand up and turn around you can immediately see where everyone is and what they are doing.

Panopticism as a solution to children's sex play is not without its problems. For instance, in their discussions of how they would handle children's bathroom play, many American respondents found themselves caught between the urge to make the bathrooms visible and thus safe and the children's right to privacy and developmentally appropriate play:

TEACHER A: I would set up a system to limit the number of children in the bathroom at one time. Children should learn that going to the bathroom is a private time, and that they shouldn't be following each other in there to watch.

TEACHER B: But should the teachers be socializing the kids to think of the bathroom as private when the attitude toward privacy in this context is not logical? If privacy were really a concern, then the school should have put in dividers between the stalls.

TEACHER C: What's needed here is more supervision, not dividers.

TEACHER D: There's a natural curiosity that I don't want to turn off. To adults the bathroom is private, but to children it's a social time, especially for kids still learning to use the toilet. In the story the teacher didn't ask why the kids were bothered. Maybe the kids are upset that they don't get to flush the toilet themselves. If so, that's the kind of situation I'd let the children try to work out on their own.

A similar ambivalence came out in discussions of the playing-doctor story. Most of the respondents felt that it was their responsibility, if not to break up the game, at least to keep an eye on it. But several respondents, concerned that their surveillance would change or inhibit this developmentally appropriate play, pointed out the irony that, as teachers of other people's children, they feel compelled to interrupt play that they would choose to ignore at home with their own children:

- It would be totally different if you were the parent at home. You wouldn't blink. It would be nothing.
- I would let it go at home, but in school, teachers are accountable.
- For all I know my daughter plays doctor up in her room with her friends. That thought doesn't bother me a bit. But at school I don't have the luxury of thinking that way.

American respondents reacted similarly to the zoo story, second-guessing the decision of the teacher in the story to let the children watch a calf being born:

- I think she, the teacher, made a mistake by not getting parental consent for this before the excursion. This is other people's children.
- It would be an easy call if it were my own kids. I'd want them to know about it. But I would be very nervous about what parents might say about my decision to let their kids see this.
- Someone is sure to complain.
- This teacher made the wrong decision if she's feeling paranoid afterward about what parents will say.

In the discussion of the story of the male aide with the girl on his lap, an American teacher commented: "I think the director is right to consider how this might look to parents. The director of a child center has to think this way." In each of these situations we see teachers caught in the panoptic trap. Like prison guards, they hold the power of the panoptic gaze over their charges, but they know that they, too, are being scrutinized. Part of the genius of Jeremy Bentham's prison surveillance invention is that the Panopticon does not require constant vigilance: it is not necessary for a guard to be always watching, only for the inmates to know that the guard *could* at any moment be watching. Parents are rarely physically present to watch and pass judgment on their children's teachers. But teachers are nevertheless governed by the power of the parents' gaze. It is all the more intimidating to teachers that this gaze is indirect, refracted through the (often unreliable) reports that children give their parents each night about what went on that day in school.

Many of the American respondents said it was important for teachers to be responsive to parents' concerns. "These aren't your children. At night, if children get nightmares from what you took them to see, it's the parents, not you, who will be up with them." But other respondents felt that teachers' sense of being watched and judged by parents represented a breakdown in trust and respect that served no one's interest. One teacher offered an insightful analysis: "Parents are feeling guilty. Some of this guilt comes from getting attacked for not caring for their own kids. Maybe the mother-in-law, who stayed home with her kid when she was a young mother, gets on her son and daughter-in-law, making them defensive about having the grandchild in day care. So then the parents take it out on me—they show they are good, responsible parents by not trusting me, grilling me." The implied irony here is that if the parents don't trust their children's teacher, then they are being irresponsible to leave their children in her care.

How did we all come to be caught up in this system? The paranoia and panopticism that are eroding the rights and pleasures of both children and teachers and making parents increasingly frantic are not being imposed from above by a central authority. For better or worse, governmental agencies in the United States play a very small role in the regulation and control of preschools. The panoptic gaze is not the all-seeing eye of Big Brother looking down on us; it is something we are doing to ourselves and each other. Foucault teaches us to be aware of the diffuseness of power. Like the other repressive disciplinary practices Foucault describes, panopticism in early childhood education settings has come to seem so necessary, prudent, inevitable, and logical that we don't ask where it came from, nor do we question its costs.[10]

On the other hand, maybe there is a bad guy here. The muscle backing up panopticism comes not from the government but from lawyers. The threat that preschool teachers and directors face as they struggle to protect the rights and pleasures of children and teachers is the threat of litigation and rising insurance costs.

- [Responding to the doctor-play story] At first, I'm thinking, "Isn't that wonderful." Then I think of protection, litigation, and I worry, and it loses its innocence.
- All it takes is one phone call. There's always that fear. It only takes one parent who had a bad day, who has something against your program, and who decides to get a lawyer.
- It all changed after the McMartin case.
- If we had a lawyer here, he'd be screaming "child abuse!"
- It's the liability issue.

Litigation is having a similar effect on many other sectors of society, including health care, where rising malpractice insurance rates have driven some doctors out of business and led most others to change the way they practice. If professionals as powerful as doctors have lost the nerve to follow their professional judgment and practice, no wonder a group as powerless as preschool teachers are running scared. In the face of threats of litigation and rising insurance costs, preschools are deciding to take no chances, even if that means reassigning or firing male teachers, stopping teachers from following their intuition and judgment

10. A problem with Foucault's argument is that it does not acknowledge the possibility of resistance. I believe that the good news about the Panopticon and other totalizing systems is that in practice they don't work as well as theory predicts. Preschool teachers and children, like prisoners, find ways to resist and avoid the panoptic gaze. My fear that preschools will prevent children from having sexual experiences is thus overstated. I think we can find solace in the idea that children will find ways to touch themselves and each other even in the most panoptic of our preschools.

about what is best for the children in their care, and subjecting children to such draconian measures as no-touch policies.

The law plays a complex role here. We can see the greed of the legal and insurance industries reaching into the world of early childhood education and distorting practice. But we also can see preschool teachers and administrators, already swept up in a moral panic about the sexuality of children and adults, using the threat of litigation to retroactively justify uncourageous stances and repressive practices. In some of the focus group discussions, teachers and especially administrators invoked lawyers to excuse and justify their own less than heroic positions. For example, in one of the U.S. discussions of the male teacher's aide, a child center director expressed concern about the danger men can pose to children: "I must say, I would be worried here. We have to face the statistical reality that men are much more likely to abuse children than are women." Then suddenly, as if aware that her position was coming across as sexist and unsupportive of staff, she pulled back by adding, "Because of liability, I would have to not allow a male teacher to be alone with children or to hold them on his lap. You can't be too careful." Our suspicions and anxieties are too easily projected onto lawyers, who represent society's panoptic desire to root out evil. An administrator's failure to do the right thing is justified first with statistics and then by litigation threats. There is nothing that can be done. The argument of this chapter is that something can be done. It comes down to a call for courage and a rediscovery of trust. To escape from our current dilemma, we must begin by believing that things can be otherwise.

Other Places, Other Times

History and anthropology hold out to us the possibility that life somewhere, sometime can be different. Alternatives to the contemporary American morally panicked approach to dealing with children's sexuality emerged in this study in two forms: in the U.S. informants' memories of things having been different in the past and in the Irish informants' relatively unpanicked responses, sug-gesting that they live in a land not (yet) plagued by this disease.

In their focus group discussions, the Americans often reflected positively on how children's sexuality was handled in the past, in phrases such as "We didn't used to have to worry about . . . ," "We no longer have the luxury of . . . ," "As recently as five years ago we . . . ," "When we were growing up it was different . . . ," and "When I was a kid":

> When I was a kid, my Mom didn't work so I didn't go to nursery school every day. I must have been four or five, and there were tons of kids on my block, and we'd gather in my garage. I remember being the doctor, and making some little boys from next door—they must have been younger than me, maybe three years old or so—I remember making them line up and I was the doctor and they were the patients and I'd call out, "Next patient." And when they came over to me I'd pretend to take their temperatures and give them a shot, but really the point of the game was to pull down their pants. Didn't everyone play games like that? My mother was probably in the house, cooking or watching TV. I'd like kids to have the chance for that kind of sex play. But as a teacher, there is absolutely no way I can look the other way and let kids play doctor in my classroom. Do I sound hypocritical?

We should try to avoid idealizing or attempting to re-create the past. I do not believe that children were necessarily happier or that family life was better in the 1950s, when child care was less avail-able and middle-class mothers were expected not to work outside the home. But one thing we might attempt to re-create from this era was what one of my respondents described as "the luxury of not having to feel like you have to be watching the children every second." Conservative Americans who would like to see a return to the patriarchal family relations of the 1950s portray postwar mothers as constantly available to their young children, supervis-ing their every move. These critics of institutional child care argue that a preschool teacher with twelve or more youngsters in her charge cannot give the children the quality of attention a stay-at-home mother can give to her own children. But what if the secret of successful motherhood in the 1950s was not middle-class mothers' constant attention but their *inattention*? I have memories of playing with my brothers and my friends, and with their sisters and brothers, playing in each other's basements, bedrooms, garages, and in the ravines behind our houses, playing doctor and having peeing contests and telling doo-doo jokes, all while our mothers were cooking, doing laundry, running off to the store ("You boys be good—I'll be back soon"). Apparently our mothers did not feel they had to know where we were or what we were doing each minute of the day.

It's not that our mothers were intentionally choosing not to supervise us because they believed in our right to privacy, or because they wanted to make sure we would have opportunities to play doctor and kissing games, or because they were philosophically opposed to panopticism as a parenting technique. The sociospatial norms governing mothers and children in the suburbs at the time just didn't call for surveillance.

I suspect that in some contemporary American families, in some communities, children still enjoy such unsupervised play. But many families have concluded that ravines behind their houses and neighbors' basements and garages are not safe places for their children to be without supervision. And the increased use of child care means that in the 1990s many American children spend the majority of their waking hours not under the supervision of their mothers, who have the luxury of not scrutinizing their every move, but in family home care or preschool settings with adults who feel compelled to be vigilant, ready at a moment's notice to intervene in disputes or to break up a kissing game.[11]

11. For a discussion of the costs of teachers intervening too readily in children's disputes, see Tobin, Wu, and Davidson (1987).

What Ireland (still) has that the United States has lost is a sense of trust. In contrast to the American early childhood educators' feeling of being scrutinized and second-guessed, the Irish respondents expressed a sense of being trusted and respected by parents and the larger community:

- I trust myself to be physically close to children and to take them to the loo. These leaders [the American teachers in the stories] have no confidence. Where's the trust?
- I have the notion there's a certain amount of goodwill in parents who send their children to you. I'm aware of risks of litigation because I'd be a fool not to [be]. But if I become so alert to these concerns that I couldn't trust in goodwill and be affectionate with children, I couldn't go on.

Irish early childhood educators believe they are moving down the same road that Americans are traveling, but they aren't as far along: "We haven't yet gone totally mad like you Yanks, but we're well on the way!" Some Irish communities are much further down this road than others. In the Irish responses, we find a split along a complex of regional, ideological, and social class lines. At one end of the continuum there's the "Dublin 4 set." "Dublin 4," a postal district, has come to refer to Irish yuppies, whether or not they live in the district. The Dublin 4 parents and teachers I spoke with reacted most like the U.S. respondents in their combination of liberal views on sex and their sense of creeping social deterioration, orientation toward litigation, and belief that preschool teachers should scrutinize children's sex play. Next on the continuum come the members of the Irish Pre-School Playgroups Association (IPPA), self-employed women who run small child care centers in their homes. They tended to be somewhat more conservative than the Dublin 4 set on lifestyle issues but a little less worried about children's sex play and the possibility that their judgment might be second-guessed by parents. The staff of a day care center serving children from the housing projects on the western edge of Dublin had perspectives and concerns much like those of American early childhood educators who work with the urban poor. These teachers, who work with children of young single mothers, regularly come face to face with evidence that the children have been physically, emotionally, or sexually abused at home. But in contrast to their U.S. counterparts, these Irish teachers feel trusted and supported in their judgments of how to work with these children. At the furthest end of the continuum from the values and concerns of teachers in the United States and Dublin 4 are the teachers of rural Sligo on Ireland's western coast. No country bumpkins, these are educated women, some who were born in the west, some who moved there to escape the urban problems of Dublin and Cork. Living in the Irish countryside also allows them to live in the Irish past—free, for a while, from the perception that sexuality is dangerous to young children and their teachers. The sense that at least in rural, western Ireland things are not (yet) as bad as in the United States emerged most clearly in the Sligo discussion of the story of the male aide with the girl on his lap:

TEACHER A: I'm not quite clear. Why would the director be uncomfortable with this? Would it be the whole sexual abuse issue?

TEACHER B: Of course it would. . . . If you're not sure what the story's about, it's because we've been more protected from it so far than they are in the States.

TEACHER C: I would be concerned in bathing a child, you know, that you shouldn't be alone. But then I worked for a while in London.

TEACHER D: Is it getting to be a concern here, about teachers needing to be careful about being physically affectionate with children?

TEACHER B: There's a greater awareness, but not paranoia here. Not as bad as in America.

TEACHER D: Would you hesitate if you were asked to take on a male student as an aide?

TEACHER E: No, but I know why Americans would. We're not as bad as Americans yet.

Over tea, in our postsession socializing, I told the Sligo teachers more about my study and my central concern that Americans, by overreacting to the threat of the sexual abuse of children in child care centers, are reducing the opportunities children and their caretakers have to experience pleasure. Anne responded, "Oh, when we heard an American was coming to talk with us about children's sex play, we assumed you were taking the opposite position." Mary explained, "The truth of the matter is that we aren't all that nervous here about how we interact with the children or about them kissing and such. But we didn't want to appear naive, so we went on a bit more about being concerned about sexual abuse and all than we really are. We didn't want you leaving here telling people we are behind the times."

PLEASURE AND POWER

To reverse the erosion of sexuality in American preschool settings, we must begin by addressing early childhood educators' powerlessness. This powerlessness is not just the inability of teachers to stand up to accusatory parents, supervisors, advisory boards, lawyers, and the court of public opinion. More insidious, it is the inability of teachers of young children to resist the construction of themselves and the children they care for as sexually dangerous and endangered. Preschool teachers and administrators have collaborated in their own deprofessionalization. They have come to see not only their students but also themselves as potentially dangerous and thus in need of surveillance and external control. We have come to accept panopticism and other mechanisms for controlling the pleasures of young children and their teachers as necessary to protect us from each other, from ourselves, and from the appearance if not the reality of being guilty of something terrible.

This loss of confidence and trust prevents preschool teachers from following their professional intuition and doing what they believe is best and right for children. As teachers have become increasingly governed by their awareness of how their actions will be second-guessed by the most cynical of possible audiences, they have reduced the freedom they give young children to explore their sexuality, and they have denied themselves and the children the pleasures of each other's touch. What crimes have young children and their teachers committed to be sentenced to this panopticon? And how can we set them free?

REFERENCES

Foucault, M. (1979). *Discipline and punish: The birth of the prison.* (Trans. A. Sheridan.) New York: Vintage.

Herr, C. (1990). The erotics of Irishness. *Critical Inquiry* 17: 1–34.

Marcus, G., and Fischer, M. (1986). *Anthropology as cultural critique.* Chicago: University of Chicago Press.

Mulvey, L. (1975). Visual pleasure and narrative cinema. *Screen* 16 (3): 6–18.

Scheper-Hughes, N. (1979). *Saints, sinners, and schizophrenics: Mental illness in rural Ireland.* Berkeley: University of California Press.

Sedgwick, E. (1991). Jane Austen and the masturbating girl. *Critical Inquiry* 17: 818–837.

Silin, J. (1994). *Sex, death, and the education of children: Our passion for ignorance in the age of AIDS.* New York: Teachers College Press.

Tobin, J., Wu, D., and Davidson, D. (1987). Class size and student/ teacher ratios in the Japanese preschool. *Comparative Education Review* 31 (4): 533–549.

——. (1989). *Preschool in three cultures: Japan, China, and the United States.* New Haven: Yale University Press.

Zizek, S. (1992). *Looking awry: An introduction to Jacques Lacan through popular culture.* Cambridge: MIT Press.

FIVE

Carnival in the Classroom
Elementary Students Making Videos

Donna J. Grace and Joseph Tobin

It is a sunny October morning in Pearl City, Hawaii. The third-graders at Waiau Elementary School are seated on the floor, ready to watch the videos they have made. As the room is darkened and the monitor lights up, the students' eyes widen and grins appear. The children giggle, squirm, and nudge one another as they recognize faces on the screen.

The first video, *The Dog Who Knew How to Play Tricks*, is about a dog and a cat who enter a talent show. Enjoying seeing their peers pretend to be animals, the children chuckle at the silly antics performed before the camera. Next, there is *The Planet Knick-Knack*, a musical about a dog named Beethoven, who runs away from home and gets lost. The video closes with the cast singing the familiar childhood song "This Old Man." The audience spontaneously joins in a chorus of slightly off-key voices. The third piece is called *Chase Master Monster*. The video opens with three boys playing the parts of little monsters who live on the very hot sun. They wake up one morning, put on their air-conditioned shoes, and begin playing the game Chase Master Monster. The narrator then informs the viewers that the little monsters "fall on their butts" and burn them on the hot sun. On screen, the actors are running around in imaginary agony, swatting at their buttocks and shouting, "Ooh! Ouch! Ooh! Ouch! My

An earlier version of this chapter was published in *Teaching Popular Culture: Beyond Radical Pedagogy* and is reprinted here with permission of the editor, David Buckingham, and the publisher, Taylor and Francis.

buns are burning! My buns are burning!" They keep running until they find some ice, which they rub on their burning rear ends. In the next shot, their eyes roll upward and they sigh with deep relief. Their expressions are those of pure bliss.

The class finds this scene hilarious. Performers and audience are fused in a surge of camaraderie, a spirit of oneness joined by laughter. The adults in the room exchange uneasy smiles. This festive moment is formed in relation to us, the authority figures, and fueled by the knowledge that classroom norms have been transgressed. The moment passes, and the next video begins. The children are quiet, focused on the new images appearing before them. The adults, however, are left with lingering doubts and questions. The equilibrium of the classroom has been unsettled. Taken-for-granted boundaries have blurred before our eyes.

Video production in the Waiau classrooms provided an opportunity for students to incorporate their own interests, experiences, and desires into schoolwork. A space was allocated in which they could explore the limits of speech, behavior, and humor allowed in the classroom. In our three years of doing video work with children at Waiau, we saw many examples of students pushing the boundaries and transgressing the norms of everyday life in school. Alongside the many entirely acceptable and non-problematic scripts the children wrote were a number of more questionable scenes and story lines containing words, actions, and situations that challenged classroom decorum. For the children, these moments of curricular slippage and excess provided the opportunity to produce their own pleasures, on their own terms, in the classroom. These same moments posed questions and gave rise to tensions for the teachers.

That children are frequently fascinated by things that adults consider to be rude, uncouth, or gross comes as no surprise. Alison Lurie (1990) traces the subversive nature of many popular children's stories, rhymes, and verses, from the Brothers Grimm to the present day, and Tom Newkirk (1992) writes of children's predisposition for poop jokes, farts, and insect mutilation. Peter McLaren (1986) and Paul Willis (1981), among others, have documented some ways that students have found to subvert school control and authority. However, these behaviors usually occur outside the school agenda. Significantly, the transgressions that emerged in the Waiau video project were organized and authorized *within* the curriculum.

This chapter explores the issues and tensions that emerged during the three-year project in which the informal, unofficial, and everyday interests of children were brought into the curriculum through the medium of video production. Drawing on Mikhail Bakhtin's writings on the carnivalesque (1968), and Roland Barthes's (1975) concepts of *plaisir* and *jouissance,* we argue that video production opens up a space where students can play with the boundaries of language and ideology and enjoy transgressive collective pleasures. This boundary-crossing and pleasure-getting activity by the children in the midst of the curriculum pushes teachers to think about their authority in new ways.

THE STUDY

A great deal is known about children as readers and writers in classrooms. Little, in contrast, is known about children as producers of video texts. Video production is a new form of literacy that integrates art, language skills, problem solving, technical proficiency, and performance. Although there are manuals available on the technical skills involved, there has yet to be a critical, theoretically informed study of video production with young students. The small body of work that examines the process of production comes largely out of the United Kingdom and has involved older students (Buckingham, 1990; Buckingham and Setton-Green, 1994; Buckingham, Graheme, and Sefton-Green, 1995). With the use of video technology rapidly increasing in school systems worldwide, research is needed that can help us understand what happens to students and teachers when cameras are put in students' hands.

In light of these facts, we developed a video curriculum project with a group of teachers at an elementary school in Hawaii. In meetings with the teachers, it was decided to begin integrating video production into the curriculum, building upon the children's interests in and prior knowledge of television and movies. This was viewed as a unique opportunity to enhance the elementary language and literacy curriculum while increasing our understanding of children as communicators and meaning makers.

The video curriculum was tested in two third-grade classes during the spring of 1992. It was then introduced to grades one through six in the fall and continued for the next two school years. In all, eight classes of approximately twenty-five children each actively participated in the video curriculum. This chapter focuses on work that emerged in grades one through three.

Our role throughout the project was that of participant-observers. During the pilot study and the first phase of video production, we were actively involved in developing and teaching the curriculum to both the teachers and the students. As the teachers and children grew more comfortable and confident with the process, we increasingly became observers.

Our research method is an ethnographically informed case study of children as videographers. We view children not as a distinct cultural group separate from adults but as an interpretive community, a subgroup within the larger culture, with shared interests, experiences, and understandings that reflect their age, generation, and situation as students. As Anne Dyson (1993) writes, school children operate in a peer social world framed by a sense of "being in this together" (p. 3). Their responses to school authority often include attempts to claim a space for themselves in the classroom and to assert their collective identity as children. Bringing the unofficial into the official is one way of establishing territory of their own and forming networks of peer relationships in the process.

Child-Centered Pedagogy

During the pilot phase of the project, we spent two to three days a week working with the children on scripting, storyboarding, using video equipment, and the production process. The children in each classroom were then placed in groups and asked to retell, script, storyboard, and tape a familiar story. The resulting productions included such favorites as *Chicken Licken, Snow White, Jack and the Beanstalk, Henny Penny,* and *The Princess and the Pea.* From an adult standpoint, these productions tended to lack creativity. However, they functioned as good entry points into video production. The retellings seemed to offer the children some safety, security, and predictability while they were working in this new medium with unfamiliar technology. In the second phase of the project, we decided to give the children free choice in content and genre, putting many of our teacherly beliefs about classroom control and the curriculum to the test.

Progressive educators speak of "giving children choice," "building on their interests, background knowledge, and experiences," and "making learning fun." These pedagogical assumptions underlie student-centered, inquiry-based, whole-language, and constructivist approaches to curriculum and instruction. Most often, when teachers tell students, "You can write about anything you want to," the students interpret this invitation to mean "anything you want to that I, a teacher and an adult, will consider appropriate for a school assignment." Yet occasionally, moments arise in the classroom when students do work that ignores, transgresses, or exceeds teacherly, adult notions of appropriateness. Such moments may occur in a writing assignment, a literature circle, an art project, or a science experiment. At Waiau we learned that there is something about video production that elicits an outpouring of transgressive, excessive moments that push us to question how comfortable we are when the curriculum becomes child-centered.

Giving Children Choice

Our intent was to give the students considerable latitude in the content of their videos. The teachers, however, had a hard time relinquishing their right and inclination to guide, shape, and influence these choices. In order to see what would happen if students' unrestrained choices were authorized in the classroom, we asked the teachers to give the children as much leeway as they felt they could. As video production got under way, it became apparent that the scripts created by the children were strongly influenced by popular culture. They included X-Men, ninjas, and characters from the television shows *Saved by the Bell, The Simpsons, Full House,* and *Ghostwriter* and from such movies as *Cop and a Half, Airborne,* and *Jurassic Park.* Themes and characters were also occasionally drawn from more controversial television programs and movies, including *Beavis and Butthead, Studs, Child's Play,* and *Friday the 13th.* Tensions arose. As popular culture entered the classrooms, the unofficial interests of the children shifted from the periphery of classroom life to center stage.

Fear of the Interests and Knowledge of Children

Although child-centered curricula emphasize connecting the world of school to the lives of the children, many of their everyday pleasures and interests lie untouched and untapped in the classroom. Movies, television, videos, popular magazines, fiction, and video games contribute to the shaping of student experiences and subjectivities. However, they must typically leave these interests on the doorstep when arriving at school each day.

As Buckingham (1990, 1994) points out, there are many reasons for the failure to incorporate the popular culture of children into the curriculum. Perhaps foremost is the danger of contagion.

Television, movies, comics, videos, and electronic games have commonly been associated with such negative outcomes as passivity, immorality, poor health, delinquency, a decline in literacy skills, acts of aggression, loss of innocence, and desensitization to crime and violence. Adults consider themselves immune to such effects, but children are believed to be hopelessly and helplessly vulnerable to them. Such concerns and fears have resulted in a growing body of articles and studies on the relation between children and the media. Although Hodge and Tripp (1986), Buckingham (1990, 1993), and other media education scholars have shown that children are sophisticated media viewers, a narrow, often distorted, and limiting view of children's interest in and knowledge about the media persists. The political left and right meet in curious agreement on the disparaging effects of media on children. Where the right faults the media for undermining the morals and values of the dominant society, the left blames the media for perpetuating them. Children are seen as passive and powerless miniconsumers duped by the "culture industry." Gemma Moss (1989, p. 2) writes that teachers tend to accept this view and "assume a wholesale swallowing of popular culture by their pupils." The children's video work in our project provided evidence to the contrary. We found that they used this medium to play with the meanings and messages of the culture rather than absorbing them uncritically.

A second reason for the traditional exclusion of popular culture from the curriculum is the threat it poses to teacher supremacy. Teachers like to feel that they are standing on secure ground when it comes to curriculum. Students often know more than their teachers do about popular television shows, movies, and video games. In this domain, the children are the experts.

A third reason relates to the fear of dissolution of boundaries. When popular culture is brought into the curriculum, lines are crossed between high and low, the official and the unofficial, the authoritative discourses of the school and the internally persuasive discourses of the children. The canon is compromised.

In the face of these concerns, we nevertheless insist that popular culture should be brought into the primary school curriculum. Because school privileges the written word, the knowledge children bring to school about the plots, characters, and genre of what they see on television, for example, is often underestimated and ignored in the classroom. Including popular culture in the curriculum provides another avenue for children to become literate. We also support teaching about movies and television in the primary grades because the role of pleasure has long been overlooked and neglected in schooling. Most children find great pleasure in popular culture. Making a place for such pleasure in the classroom can enrich the school lives of children.

We are aware, however, that bringing popular culture into the official curriculum carries with it the danger that adults will colonize one of the last outposts of children's culture. Once transported into the domain of the classroom, these outside interests are in jeopardy of being rationalized and regulated, purified, homogenized, and reconstituted as curriculum or motivational strategies. When popular culture is co-opted by the teacher, aspects of pleasure associated with it may be destroyed. Our goal, therefore, should be to validate the popular cultural interests of children without appropriating them. Student video production provides an arena for this to occur.

Popular Culture and Video Production

The children's videos produced in our study were greatly influenced by the media and popular culture. But the videos do far more than mimic or replicate remembered plots and themes; rather, children play with aspects of the familiar and conjoin them in imaginative and pleasing ways. In the children's videos, the world of popular culture is interwoven with the world of school. In *Zip and the Ninja Turtles,* for instance, a group of first-graders turned a favorite classroom book about a lost dog into a tale involving a runaway worm who is eventually rescued by three

Ninja Turtles. Another group of children from the same class created a story entitled *The Nine Astronauts and the Revenge of the Slimy Earthlings.* This tale involves a shoot-out with drool-covered, earthling-eating aliens and ends with the cast singing a song they had learned in school about the planets. A third-grade group did a takeoff on the *Wizard of Oz* called *Dorothy Goes to Candyland,* in which Dorothy visits a land where candy grows abundantly on trees. There she is threatened by a slime-breathing, rock-spewing blob that she eventually destroys with a magic candy gun. These are but a few examples of how children imaginatively combined their interests in movies and television with classroom literacy and knowledge.

These videos were not unlike the stories children might write if given free choice of content in a language arts assignment. However, the medium of video, along with the dynamics of the collaborative group process, worked to enhance children's sense of freedom to explore and transgress. The extralinguistic elements of gesture, facial expression, sound effects, and performativity carried the written words into a new and sometimes forbidden realm. As the students incorporated their own interests and pleasures into the videos, they pushed at the borders of propriety, reminding us of the fragility of classroom equilibrium.

Clearly, the children's sense of audience influenced the type of videos they produced. When the intended viewers included parents, relatives, or other community members, their videos took on quite different forms. This was demonstrated in videos the students created for the school's open house, the sixth-grade graduation, and for competition in a video festival, all of which were very well received. However, when the videos were produced with their peers as the anticipated audience, the content noticeably strayed from adult-pleasing fare. Fueled by the desire to surprise, amuse, and entertain, the content of some of these videos was of questionable taste, including depictions of drool, burps, blood, dripping mucus, butt jokes, aggression, violence, and severed body parts. These scenes were enormously appealing to the children and the source of a good deal of transgressive excitement. What was most popular with the children tended to be unpopular with the teachers.

Video Production and the Carnivalesque

In analyzing the children's videos, it became apparent that they did not fit neatly into traditional categories. They hovered in sort of a literary homelessness in the classroom. Genres were collapsed and borders erased. The videos, to use Bakhtin's term, were "carnivalesque." In *Rabelais and His World* (1968), Bakhtin described the world of the carnival as one of laughter, bodily pleasures, hierarchical inversions, and bad taste. He categorized the manifestations of carnival humor as ritual spectacles (feasts, pageants, and marketplace festivals), comic verbal compositions (oral and written parodies), and billingsgate (curses, oaths, slang, profanity). The laughter provoked by such humor was bawdy, crude, and irreverent. Rank and privilege were temporarily overturned. The people portrayed kings as fools and peasants as royalty. It was the official world as seen from below.

Over time, the carnival of the Middle Ages was gradually suppressed. It became licensed, regulated, and tamed. Its remnants survive today in Mardi Gras, the Carnival of Brazil, and Germany's *Fasching*. Elements of the ancient carnivals, Bakhtin reminds us, live on in our everyday life as well. These carnivalesque moments emphasize freedom, pleasure, and desire. They unsettle the existing order of things. They use satire and laughter to imagine how things might be otherwise. Mary Russo (1986) writes that "the masks and voices of carnival resist, exaggerate, and destabilize the distinctions and boundaries that mark and maintain high culture and organized society. . . . They suggest a counterproduction of culture, knowledge, and pleasure" (p. 218).

Like the carnivals, fairs, and marketplaces Bakhtin wrote about, the classroom may be viewed as a site of conflicting agendas and desires where the high (teachers and the curriculum) and the low (children and their interests and desires) meet. Carnival offered peasants opportunities to symbolically invert the usual hierarchies and imagine different roles and relationships. Video production at Waiau offered many such opportunities. With the click of a button, students could become rock stars, royalty, or superheroes. Tiny children might portray giants or all-powerful rulers. The academically marginalized had the opportunity to choose roles as scholars, teachers, or wizards. Serious children could play parts in comedies and parodies, and the quiet and shy could blossom under the guise of fantasy. Through the medium of video, the students were able momentarily to acquire the power of the represented.

The children's video productions often featured the parodic, the fantastic and horrific, the grotesque, and the forbidden. These scenarios enabled the children to locate a space where collective pleasures were produced. As with carnival, however, there were also darker sides to the merriment. Without this darker side, carnival would lose much of its potency and seductive power. In our project, the darker side emerged when students discussed making videos involving cruelty and hurtful stereotypes—portrayals of animal cruelty, racial caricatures, a stuttering singer, and a blind man who stumbles into various objects around him. In some cases, the groups themselves dismissed these ideas, and in others the teachers exercised their veto.

Laughter and Parody

For Bakhtin (1981), parody, the "laughing word," is a corrective of reality. Embodying dual intentions, it contains both the meanings of the author and the refracted meanings of the parodied text or situation (p. 324). Parody can bolster cultural barriers as well as break them down. In some situations, parody functions to release tension, thereby preserving the status quo. In others, it offers opportunities for opposition tempered by humor. Regardless of the outcome, parody provides a space for critique and change. It may pose questions, challenge assumptions, and offer new possibilities.

Our students fully appreciated the pleasures derived from humor and parody. In the wink of an eye, the serious became comical in their videos. The driving force in the children's script-writing was the desire to make the audience laugh. Several of the student groups incorporated parody in their videos. They produced ridiculing and humorous versions of television shows, movies, books, classrooms, and field trips. Two videos parodied marriage (*The Three Stooges Get Married* and *The Rock and Roll Marriage*). A second-grade group, which began to script a serious research report on the Gila monster, wound up with the lizard eating the reporter. A third-grade production of *The Magic School Bus Visits Plant Quarantine* parodies a class field trip. The video begins with students sitting in a row, frowning and slumped over with their heads in their hands. In a dreary, singsong monotone, they say in unison that school is boring and they want to go on a field trip. Miss Frizzle, played by a boy wearing an outlandish wig, agrees. They go to Plant Quarantine, where animals are held on their arrival in Hawaii. There, such scenes as a student getting his hand sliced off by a piranha alternate with very scholarly reports on toucans, flowers, and fire ants. In other videos, laughter is produced through humorous depictions of tyrannical teachers, ridiculous rules, and rebellious students.

The very ambiguity of parody is the source of its power and pleasure. Initially, the teachers wondered how they should take such parodies. However, rather than view these scenes as threatening or subversive, the teachers eventually came to perceive them in a generally prosocial light. They were able to overcome their initial fears and join in the pleasures of the carnivalesque. The teachers eventually realized that the children were not attacking them or their school routines and practices—these teachers did not have deadly boring classes, nor had they sent children to sit in the corner. It was the stereotype, the comic-book representation of school, that was the object of ridicule.

The Fantastic and Horrific

The students' videos demonstrated their fascination with these genres. They overwhelmingly wanted to make videos that were scary, funny, or both. Their video plots were full of monsters, ghosts, aliens, beasts, werewolves, and giant scorpions who frightened, threatened, and eventually were conquered by the protagonists. Inevitably, these conquests provided an opportunity for the usually forbidden play-fighting and produced a great deal of transgressive excitement for the children. In portraying such awesome, fear-inspiring creatures and characters, the students experienced power, agency, and control. Neither size nor gender determined who would play these roles. One of the smallest children in a first-grade class portrayed Magneto, a powerful villain and enemy of the X-Men, and girls frequently chose to play fierce ninjas, creatures from outer space, or mummies and vampires awakened from the dead. Although the hero and monster roles are traditionally figured as masculine (strong, brave, tough, fearless) in the movies and television programs the children see, this was not necessarily the case in their own productions. Traditional masculinity and femininity were frequently muted and blurred in their video stories.

The horrific beings in these scripts usually wound up being more humorous than terrifying, more like the "gay monsters" of the Rabelaisian world and less like the terrifying creatures typical in films of this genre. They tended to be inserted into very child-like plots and in a context of play, providing the children with an opportunity to explore their fears and fantasies in the safety of the group, surrounded by laughter.

The Grotesque Body

A central concern of carnival is the body. According to Bakhtin (1968), the grotesque carnival body represents a lowering of all that is high, privileged, sacred, or ideal. In this oppositional form, the body serves as a site of resistance to regulation, social control, and definitions of normalcy. The grotesque body is ugly and monstrous in comparison to the classical body represented in Renaissance statuary. Where the classical body is pure, clean, finished, beautifully formed, and with no evident openings or orifices, the sensual, earthy, grotesque body is protuberant, excessive, impure, unfinished. It emphasizes the parts of the body that open up to the world: flared nostrils, gaping mouth, the anus, and what Bakhtin termed "the bodily lower strata" (belly, legs, feet, buttocks, genitals). The grotesque body is overflowing and transgresses its own limits. In the Renaissance, these images represented becoming and growth, a phenomenon in transformation, an unfinished metamorphosis. In this sense, the grotesque body has much in common with childhood. Not yet fully formed nor matured, children typically do not share the revulsion adults feel toward sweat, runny noses, dirty bodies, or germ-spewing sneezes and coughs. Rather, they are full of interest and curiosity about their bodily orifices and functions, as their videos make clear.

Images of the grotesque body were prominent in the students' videos. Their works provided many examples of the gaping, oversized, overflowing body. Some scripts also contained suggestions of cannibalism, or the swallowing up of bodies by other bodies. Stam (1989) refers to this as the ultimate act in dissolving the boundaries between self and other (p. 126). In a first-grade production of *Chicken Licken Goes to Jupiter,* for example, the story ends with Chicken Licken getting eaten up by a mean space creature before she is able to complete her journey to reach the king. In *The Nine Astronauts and the Revenge of the Slimy Earthlings,* another group of first-graders created a script involving a confrontation between several astronauts and the aliens they encounter on the planet Saturn. Upon seeing the astronauts, the aliens begin rubbing their tummies, licking their lips, and trying to capture the astronauts to feed to their babies. In enacting this script, the aliens worked up a healthy supply of saliva, which oozed profusely from their chomping, hungry mouths. Like all other examples of the grotesque body, such scenes produced the intended surprise, delight, and laughter in their viewing peers.

The Forbidden

Scatological, parodic, and grotesque elements in children's videos have the power to offend adult sensibilities, but they can be dismissed as typical amusements of childhood. We shake our heads and convey our disapproval but assume that with increased maturity such interests will fade. Fighting, aggression, and suggestions of violence in children are more disturbing to adults. In many homes and schools, play-fighting is forbidden, on grounds of safety. Yet more children are injured by falling off playground equipment or participating in sports than in play-fighting. The fact that ballgames are rarely banned suggests that something other than safety underlies adults' concerns about play-fighting. Aggressive behavior in children taps into deeper fears about crime, violence, and the moral decline in society as a whole. Something about children's delight in mock violence threatens adult authority and disrupts culturally constructed notions about childhood innocence. Thus, we impose rules and prohibitions and attempt to socialize children away from such behaviors. Nancy King (1992) writes that in education the goal has been to create environments and situations in which children will produce only "good" play, consisting of socially approved behaviors such as rule following, cooperation, turn taking, inclusion, socially approved uses of imagination and conversation, and good sportsmanship. Clearly, "good" play has little in common with the everyday nonrestricted play of children. As any parent or teacher of young children knows, toy guns may be banned, but fingers can be used as pretend gun barrels; play-fighting may be prohibited, but rough-and-tumble activities rarely disappear.

A predisposition to play-fighting was clearly evident in the children's video stories. Group after group incorporated such scenes, usually involving some form of martial arts. These usually forbidden behaviors produced high levels of transgressive excitement in both the performers and their child audience. In a third-grade production of *The Four Ninjas* these scenes turned out to be the story's driving force. This tale began with fighting practice for the ninjas (three boys and a girl). Soon they discover that their father has mysteriously died and their mother has been kidnapped. Preparing to avenge their father's death and rescue their mother, they go back to fighting practice. The next day, the enemy ninjas, played by two girls, invade the classroom, and the big battle begins. It goes on until the evil ninjas are eventually conquered. The four victorious ninjas end the night with a celebration at Pizza Hut.

In this video, as well as in others with similar themes, the fighting scenes were greatly elaborated. In each scene, good triumphed over evil, and there was no intent to harm. Enacted in a spirit of play, these scenes have a comic character and begin and end with laughter. Bakhtin (1968) writes that in the carnivalesque, "ruthless slaughter" and death are "transformed into a merry banquet," and "bloodshed, dismemberment, burning, death, beatings, blows, curses, and abuses—all these elements are steeped in 'merry time'" (p. 211). In neither classroom nor carnival are such scenes meant to represent or transfer to the real. That children find pleasure in these mock battles does not mean that they enjoy violence in real life. As with the grotesque body, they find power, pleasure, and opportunities for resistance in portraying these strong, bold, and courageous characters.

In acting out hand-to-hand combat, the children were also able to enjoy a physical closeness with one another that they are otherwise denied. The body-to-body contact characteristic of the carnivalesque crowd appeared to be a source of pleasure for the children in their video fighting scenes. Once past the preschool hand-holding stage, students have few opportunities for touch. Yet such sensations are still needed, desired, and enjoyed. Play-fighting provides a space for this while producing a very intense form of transgressive pleasure.

Another area of the forbidden that surfaced in the video projects was the notion of animal cruelty. This occurred as a third-grade group of two boys and two girls were trying to decide on a topic for their script. Portraying a mad scientist and doing crazy experiments had been suggested, so the group members were flipping through science books looking for ideas. One of the boys asked if they "could do some animal cruelty," adding, "or is cruelty not allowed?" The rest of the group did not appear to be surprised, concerned, or even interested in this query. They just shrugged and indicated that they preferred to go ahead with the mad scientist idea. As observers of this scene, we experienced competing impulses. On one hand, we wanted to question the boy about his intentions. On the other hand, we were disturbed by what we had witnessed. The taken-for-granted had been unsettled, and the familiar had suddenly become strange. This overheard bit of conversation had denatured the ordinary and brought us face to face with the tenuousness, contingency, and uncertainty that lie just below the surface of classroom pedagogy and practice. Why had this boy suggested animal cruelty? Why weren't the others surprised by this suggestion?[1]

In contemplating the parodic, horrific, fantastic, and forbidden elements in students' videos, it is important to remember that they occurred in a playful context. The video stories were not empty reproductions or mirror reflections of their perceptions of reality. They were more like funhouse mirrors, where all is exaggerated and distorted for comic effect. The very *unreality* of the children's stories contributed to the enthusiasm and enjoyment associated with them. The videos gave students the chance to represent their

1. Although the notion of animal cruelty affronts most adult, middle-class sensibilities (ours included), it is not an uncommon feature of games and sport. For more than two centuries, the middle class has accused the lower classes as well as children of cruelty to animals. Harriet Ritvo (1987) points out that during the nineteenth century the treatment of animals was considered to be an index of the extent to which a person had managed to control his or her lower urges (p. 132).

desires, work through their fears and concerns, and play with their identity as children. In the process, collective pleasures were produced. The teachers, however, were less sure about what to do when school became not just fun but pleasurable.

Fun Versus Pleasure in the Classroom

Schooling has traditionally been defined largely in instrumental terms. Along with the explicit goals of imparting knowledge, skills, and information, the school has also been implicitly mandated to transmit the norms, language, styles, and values of the dominant culture. School has typically been a place to learn, work hard, and develop such traits as punctuality, perseverance, conscientiousness, self-discipline, and initiative. In earlier times, fun in school was incidental. Play was considered frivolous, nonproductive, and indulgent. However, discourses surrounding children in school have changed.

Today there is an emphasis on "making learning fun" through child-centered, playlike activities. Play is now considered to be an activity contributing to the cognitive, psychological, and social development of children. Play is used to motivate and reward children. Typically play in school is defined, planned, and monitored by teachers. Studies by Nancy King (1979) and Maria Romero (1989) have demonstrated that young children and teachers tend to have very different perspectives on play in school. Teachers define play as being "creative, fun, pleasing, and rather easy" (Romero, p. 406). Children consider activities play when they are voluntary and self-directed; all activities assigned or directed by the teacher are work. Teacher talk of "making learning fun" masks play's motivational and disciplinary purpose and its intent of preparing the child for the later world of work. Play is rarely valued by teachers as an end in itself.

For the students, video tended to blur the lines between work and play. In their journals, they wrote repeatedly about the fun of video production, yet they often mentioned how much work was involved. Video production seemed to represent a type of work that was fun and in which the children located spaces to play. In their collaborative groups, they read, wrote, problem-solved, and gained technical skills, yet they also found ways to produce pleasure in exploring the boundaries between rules and freedom. Such pleasure frequently moved beyond what we typically think of as fun in school. Spontaneous and sometimes transgressive, the students' videos privileged community, festivity, and solidarity. The pleasures experienced in the video project existed in and of the moment and had a life of their own.

In *The Pleasure of the Text* (1975), Roland Barthes presents his twofold notion of pleasure as *plaisir* and *jouissance*. Plaisir represents conscious enjoyment and is capable of being expressed in language. It is more conservative, accommodating, and conformist than jouissance. Where plaisir is a particular pleasure, jouissance is more diffuse; it is pleasure without separation—bliss, ecstasy, pure affect. Jouissance is an intense, heightened form of pleasure, involving a momentary loss of subjectivity. It knows no bounds. Fiske (1989) sees the roots of plaisir in the dominant ideology. Plaisir produces the pleasures of relating to the social order; jouissance produces the pleasures of evading it (p. 54).

In school, fun is much like what Barthes describes as plaisir: conservative, connected to curricular purposes, and usually organized and regulated by adults. The intent is either to provide a momentary release of tension or to induce the students to engage in the activities on the academic agenda. Pleasure, like jouissance, is produced by and for the children, in their own way and on their own terms. It exhausts itself in the present: the human interplay is all that matters. Where plaisir is an everyday pleasure, jouissance is that of special moments. At times, in the video work, jouissancelike pleasures were created. At these moments, the teacher temporarily disappeared, and the children were united in a spirit of camaraderie, a celebration of "otherness" organized around laughter.

Is the Carnivalesque Transformative?

Several colleagues who read earlier versions of this chapter questioned our celebration of the carnivalesque classroom. One commented, "So some kids made butt jokes in a school project. That doesn't mean they've overturned the power structure of the school." Another warned, "I think you need to be careful not to idealize the transformative potential of the carnivalesque." To avoid being misunderstood, we need to clarify our view of the significance of opening spaces for pleasure and the carnivalesque in the curriculum.

Our colleagues' concerns reflect a deep ambivalence and a long debate among progressive educators about the naughty, resistant, and transgressive behaviors of students. Viewing schools as sites where capitalist, patriarchal societies crush and indoctrinate students, some theorists argue that playing with and even flaunting school expectations, norms, and rules represents a meaningful and even desirable form of resistance (McLaren, 1986; D'Amato, 1988; Britzman, 1991). Some neo-Marxist and feminist theorists, however, are suspicious of claims that naughtiness accomplishes anything.

In *Learning to Labor* (1981), for example, Paul Willis argues that the antiauthoritarian antics of the "lads" in a British secondary school work to support rather than overturn the antiegalitarian structure of the school and more generally of the larger society. The scatological humor, sexual banter, and, most disturbing, the mock and real acts of violence that characterize the everyday lives of the boys in and out of school function in the end to further legitimate the school's authority and to sentence the students to reproducing their families' position in the economic system as an inexpensive source of labor. By antagonizing their teachers and ignoring their schoolwork, the lads take themselves out of competition, giving their better-behaved middle-class peers a less contested path to educational opportunities and better jobs. The lads' transgressive talk and behavior supports not just capitalism's need for a labor pool but also patriarchy and misogyny, as their sexual banter supports the objectification of the girls in their school.

In a study set in a nursery school, Valerie Walkerdine (1990, p. 4) finds the roots of patriarchal violence against women in the sexual banter of two four-year-old boys who verbally assault first a female classmate and then their thirty-year-old female teacher:

TERRY: You're a stupid cunt, Annie.

SEAN: Get out of it Miss Baxter paxter.

TERRY: Get out of it knickers Miss Baxter.

SEAN: Get out of it Miss Baxter paxter.

TERRY: Get out of it Miss Baxter the knickers paxter knickers bum.

SEAN: Knickers, shit, bum.

Walkerdine argues that such talk, though resistant and transgressive, is far from progressive or emancipatory. The boys succeed in resisting the authority of the teacher and the school, but only by reproducing the patriarchal power available to them as a male birthright.

The arguments of Willis and Walkerdine are disturbing and persuasive: there is nothing inherently emancipatory or progressive in students' acts of resistance and transgression. Nevertheless, it is our position that educators in general and media educators in particular have erred in discounting the significance and value of opening up space for transgressive and carnivalesque moments in the curriculum. Our argument is that children's sexual, grotesque, and violent play and expression can be ways of working through rather than just reproducing dominant discourses and undesirable social dynamics, and ways of building a sense of community in the classroom.

Video projects that include representations of violence, racism, and other objectionable subject matter may merely reproduce the sources they imitate, or, through parody, undermine them. As Bakhtin argues, "Of all words uttered in everyday life, no less than half belong to someone else" (1981, p. 339). Applied to children's video production, this suggests that children's videos will necessarily imitate and cite images, plots, and characterizations borrowed from sources in popular culture. But in the process of remaking a movie or television show and imitating previous forms, there is also, always, an element of newness and thus the potential for transformation.

In her reflections on the pornographic memoir of the gay African-American writer Gary Fisher, Eve Sedgwick (1996) raises the possibility that even sadomasochistic relationships have the potential to be transformative. In a disturbing memoir, Fisher speculates that sexual encounters in which he was hit and called nigger by a white man did not just repeat the dynamics of slavery and racism but also allowed him a chance to (re)experience these dynamics and potentially to rework them. Performance (sexual as well as video) has the potential to be transformative—a way of coming to understand through doing/acting/reflecting. As Freud argued, the dream dreamt, remembered, and retold simultaneously reproduces and transforms the emotional impact of disturbing life events.

We can use this logic to analyze a takeoff on the television show *America's Funniest Home Videos* produced by a group of third-graders. In *Waiau's Funniest Kids,* a sneezing, nose-blowing, mucus-dripping master of ceremonies presents segments featuring a blind girl who repeatedly walks into a wall, a stuttering boy who cannot get through his rendition of a popular song, and hula dancers who clumsily bump into one another, knocking off their grass skirts. These segments can be seen as performative attempts to acknowledge, comment on, and work through issues and tensions of everyday life at Waiau. A "full inclusion school," Waiau is home to a great variety of children, including some with physical, cognitive, and emotional disabilities. Some visit the speech therapist for help with stuttering. There are blind and deaf children, and children in wheelchairs. During the years of our project,

Waiau was also home to the Hawaiian Language Immersion "school-within-a-school." The children who made *Waiau's Funniest Kids* were in a classroom next door to a classroom of immersion children who spent the day speaking Hawaiian and who often performed the hula (although their skirts, to our knowledge, never fell off). The content of *Waiau's Funniest Kids* thus reflects what Bakhtin would call the stratified, heteroglot character of the school. The children's parodic, silly representations of disabled children and of Hawaiian culture are contrary in content and in tone to the authoritative discourse the school imposes on discussions of difference. When given the opportunity to make their own video, these children chose to deal with the variety of Waiau's student body in a satirical, irreverent way. Their representations made the adults who viewed the video uncomfortable. But whether they produced discomfort in their student audience, whether the disabled and Hawaiian children represented in the video felt gratified or abused by being included as characters, and whether the parodies reflect the presence of prejudicial feelings in the children we do not and perhaps cannot know. The videos produced by the children at Waiau are complex social texts that cannot be tied to the beliefs of their producers or audience in any simple way.[2]

Our sense is that in most cases, the videomaking and video watching brought the children and the school together. *Waiau's*

2. Not all parodies and satires are inclusive and harmless. Teachers have to use their intuition and judgment. We intervened, for example, to block the development of a proposal to make a video about "Arnold Schwartzennigger." Perhaps this video would have ended up lampooning racists rather than African-Americans. But we decided to veto it because our intuition suggested that the topic was more likely to turn out badly than well. Teachers must make case-by-case decisions. In this case, our prior experience at Waiau, a school with only a handful of African-American students, suggested to us that this project was more likely to widen racial divisions than to narrow them. The other project we discouraged, based on our concerns about the need for separation of church and state, was a proposal to make a video about Jesus. In retrospect, we wish we had allowed this project to go forward.

Funniest Kids and similar videos lampooning boring teachers, befuddled kindergartners, and school bullies, though not artistic hits, proved to be great audience favorites. By subjecting the foibles of everyone from teachers to kindergartners to the same parodic treatment, these videos worked to reduce, though not erase, distance and hierarchy. In the carnivalesque spirit of the videomaking, everyone could be laughed at and everyone could laugh. No disability was too terrible to be lampooned, no difference too great to be represented.

These videos addressed the diversity and inequity of life at Waiau not in the modern liberal mode, which dictates that no one should be laughed at or treated as different, but in the Bakhtinian, carnivalesque mode, in which everyone is laughed at and differences are to be freely acknowledged. There is a fear in schools, and in society in general, that if differences and inequities are frankly acknowledged, the already frayed social fabric will be torn further apart. In the carnivalesque atmosphere that reigned during the period of our video production project, in contrast, there was a sense of confidence that differences and tensions, even if talked about openly, would not harm the children's and teachers' sense of community.

Another example: in our first round of videomaking, as described above, most of the children did remakes of their favorite books and movies. Several of the groups chose to make versions of recent commercial films, with Disney cartoon features the most popular source material. The casting of these Disney remakes often made us uncomfortable, as the children tended to reproduce stereotypical views of race, gender, and physical attractiveness. For instance, during a casting discussion for a second-grade production of *The Little Mermaid,* we overheard the following conversation: "Tina is the prettiest, so she should be Ariel." "Yeah, and you're the fattest, Angela, so you be Ursula." As adults and as teachers, our impulse was to intervene, perhaps by giving a lecture on how everyone is pretty in different ways, or on the importance of not hurting people's feelings by talking about their appearance. But the reality, which the children seemed to accept even if we could not, was that Tina was the prettiest and most petite girl in the group and thus the most like Disney's Ariel, and Angela was the fattest and thus the most like Ursula. The children know, as we do, that such realities govern how real movies are cast, animated characters drawn, and notions of slimness and attractiveness work in our society. Nothing we could say or do could make it otherwise.[3]

In some instances, the children cast their movies against type, with little boys playing giants, girls playing men, Native Hawaiians playing pilgrims, and African-Americans playing Chinese brothers. In these productions, children gave each other latitude to play parts with or against physical, temperamental, and racial type. But whichever way they handled it, the children seemed unafraid to acknowledge their differences, even when those differences are sources of unequal treatment in the larger society.

Marxist, neo-Marxist, feminist, and liberal democratic views of social stratification and inequality share an agenda of reducing difference by making people and the conditions they live and work under more alike. Bakhtin offers a different view of stratification and power, a view which, while not inconsistent with an agenda of progress toward social equality, sees stratification and inequality as inevitable but not totalizing. In Bakhtin's worldview, power and status differentials are characteristic of all complex, stratified, heteroglossic societies; societies are better or worse according not to their degree of stratification but to the quality and quantity of the interactions and the openness to dialogue that

3. We do not mean to suggest that there is nothing teachers can do to intervene in the circulation and reproduction of sexism and racism. We believe that the antibias curricula that have the most chance of succeeding are those that begin by acknowledging the students' prior knowledge and experience with racial and gender distinctions in the larger society. For sophisticated approaches to this problem see Gemma Moss (1989), Bronwyn Davies (1989), and Deborah Britzman (1991).

exists between high and low, and between diverse subcultural groups. Like the marketplace and the carnival, media projects can provide a safe place for satire, parody, and social laughter. Such contexts where high and low meet in a stratified society make life more bearable and meaningful and work as a form of checks and balances on the power of those at the top. Classroom media projects no more erase the power differential separating teachers from students than carnivals erase the power and wealth differential that separates the rulers from the people. But media projects, like carnivals, have the potential to bring the high and the low together. And in modern societies where the poor are kept not just down but also away from the middle class and the rich, increasing interaction between the powerful and the powerless is a significant accomplishment. Schools are highly stratified societies. They can be run like totalitarian states, banning satire, parody, and protest, fearing the open discussion of difference, heterodoxy, and inequality, and erecting emotional barriers between students and their teachers. Or they can be more like Bakhtin's vision of feudal societies, in which the rulers did not fear acknowledging their common humanity with the classes below them or creating spaces for dissent, satire, and laughter.

Over the course of this project, our thinking about children in classrooms was challenged and in many ways changed. As the unseen and unsaid in school life materialized, new questions were posed and alternatives presented. These instances represented a temporary break with the everyday and offered multiple possibilities and outcomes. The laughter of the carnivalesque set both the teachers and the children free and provided an interval in which the terrain of the classroom could be renegotiated. As borders were shifted and redrawn, the unofficial interests, pleasures, and humor of children were acknowledged and given a more equal footing. As Bakhtin (1981) suggests, we are always creating ourselves and our world, moment to moment, in our speech and our actions. It is here that change takes place—not in sweeping waves, movements, or mandates, but in the minute alterations in our day-to-day lives and relations.

Like carnival, video production has no essential nature. Classroom video endeavors play out and are interpreted in different ways at different times and places. As video production becomes institutionalized in school curricula, it is possible that these carnivalesque moments will be tamed, controlled, or stamped out completely. Uncertainty and trepidation accompany the exploration of uncharted territories. However, the possibility for new understandings also exists. As the space is broadened for students to explore, experiment, and construct their own meanings, we stand to learn more about the children, ourselves, and the relationship between us. As we let go of some of our fears about children's behaviors and inclinations, the classroom may become not only a more democratic place but a more pleasurable one as well.

Our point is not to celebrate or romanticize the children's transgressions of classroom norms and values or to suggest that we should write them into our curricula, with, say, butt jokes scheduled right after morning recess. Rather, it is to validate the humor and everyday interests of children and to suggest that they have a place in the classroom, in the delicate, fragile, and shifting balance between excess and constraint. Victor Turner's notion of "spontaneous communitas" helps to illuminate this position. Turner (1977) defines this term as freedom coexisting within structure (p. 129). He writes that communitas "transgresses or dissolves the norms that govern structured and institutionalized relationships and is accompanied by unprecedented potency." Yet, the immediacy of communitas gives way to structure in a dialectical fashion. He suggests that "wisdom is always to find the appropriate relationship between structure and communitas under the given circumstances of time and place, to accept each modality when it is paramount without rejecting the other, and not to cling to one when its present impetus is spent. Spontaneous communitas is a phase, a moment, not a permanent condition. It is nature in dialogue with structure" (1969, p. 140).

Thus, these carnivalesque pleasures are ephemeral. They appear in unexpected places and begin to close at the very instance when they open. As soon as an attempt is made to rationalize and regulate them, they lose their essence and begin to vanish. Yet they will continue to materialize, for these pleasures have value and importance in the school lives of children. They are sites of energy and powerful affect and can be a rejuvenating and creative force for all involved. They can live briefly in the interstice between freedom and structure until their moment is spent, and pleasure can be enjoyed in and of the moment, for itself and nothing more.

REFERENCES

Bakhtin, M. (1968). *Rabelais and his world.* (Trans. H. Iswolsky.) Cambridge: MIT Press.

——. (1981). *The dialogic imagination: Four essays.* (Trans. C. Emerson and M. Holquist.) Austin: University of Texas Press.

Barthes, R. (1975). *The pleasure of the text.* (Trans. R. Miller.) New York: Hill and Wang.

Britzman, D. (1991). Decentering discourses in teacher education: Or, the unleashing of unpopular things. *Journal of Education* 173 (3): 61–80.

Buckingham, D. (1990). *Watching media learning: Making sense of media education.* New York: Falmer.

——. (1993). *Children talking television: The making of television literacy.* London: Falmer.

Buckingham, D., Graheme, J., and Sefton-Green, J. (1995). *Making media: Practical production in media education.* London: English and Media Centre.

Buckingham, D., and Sefton-Green, J. (1994). *Cultural studies goes to school: Reading and teaching popular media.* Bristol, England: Taylor and Francis.

D'Amato, J. (1988). "Acting": Hawaiian children's resistance to teachers. *Elementary School Journal* 88 (5): 529–543.

Davies, B. (1989). *Frogs and snails and feminist tales: Preschool children and gender.* Sydney: Allen and Unwin.

Dyson, A. (1993). *Social worlds of children learning to write in an urban primary school*. New York: Teachers College Press.

Fiske, J. (1989). *Understanding popular culture*. London: Routledge.

Hodge, B., and Tripp, D. (1986). *Children and television*. Cambridge: Polity.

King, N. (1979). Play: The kindergartners' perspective. *Elementary School Journal* 80: 81–87.

——. (1992). The impact of context on the play of young children. In S. Kessler and B. Swadener (eds.), *Reconceptualizing the early childhood curriculum: Beginning the dialogue* (pp. 43–61). New York: Teachers College Press.

Lurie, A. (1990). *Don't tell the grown-ups: Subversive children's literature*. Boston: Little, Brown.

McLaren, P. (1986). *Schooling as a ritual performance: Towards a political economy of educational symbols and gestures*. London: Routledge and Kegan Paul.

Moss, G. (1989). *Un/popular fictions*. London: Virago.

Newkirk, T. (1992). *Listening in: Children talk about books (and other things)*. Portsmouth, N.H.: Heinemann.

Ritvo, H. (1987). *The animal estate: The English and other creatures in the Victorian age*. Cambridge: Harvard University Press.

Romero, M. (1989). Work and play in the nursery school. *Educational Policy* 3 (4): 401–419.

Russo, M. (1986). Female grotesques: Carnival and theory. In T. de Lauretis (ed.), *Feminist studies/critical studies* (pp. 212–229). Bloomington: Indiana University Press.

Sedgwick, E. (ed.) (1996). *Gary in your pocket: Stories and notebooks of Gary Fisher*. Durham, N.C.: Duke University Press.

Stam, R. (1989). *Subversive pleasures: Bakhtin, cultural criticism, and film*. Baltimore: Johns Hopkins University Press.

Turner, V. (1969). *The ritual process: Structure and anti-structure*. Chicago: Aldine.

——. (1977). Frame, flow, and reflection: Ritual and drama as public liminality. In M. Benamou and C. Caramello (eds.), *Performance in postmodern culture* (pp. 125–146). Milwaukee: Center for Twentieth-Century Studies, University of Wisconsin–Milwaukee.

Walkerdine, V. (1990). Sex, power, and pedagogy. In *Schoolgirl fictions*. London: Verso.

Willis, P. (1981). *Learning to labor*. New York: Columbia University Press.

SIX

Sexist and Heterosexist Responses to Gender Bending

Gail Boldt

One fall day, I found one of my eight-year-old students outside our classroom sobbing. It was several minutes before Stephen could stop gasping and tell me what was wrong. Even later he continued to feel so distraught that he called his parents and went home early. Stephen was upset by a conversation he had had with Nicole and Sarah, who had been his best friends since kindergarten. Sarah and Nicole told him that because he was a boy, he could no longer come to their houses for sleepovers and, as the girls put it to him, "It's time for you to start playing with boys and for us to start playing with girls." Stephen's response was, "It's not fair."

By the end of school that day, I had worried the exchange and Stephen's responses into a scenario that went far beyond the afternoon and left me feeling upset and helpless. I imagined Stephen as a high school student, effeminate and confused about his sexuality. I was certain that Stephen would find, at some point, that his sexual desire was for males and that he would have little preparation and support to know how to respond to this. I pictured him having to endure harassment and having to make his way mostly alone. I wondered whether his parents would accept or reject him. I felt cowardly and desperate over the realization that I didn't feel prepared to address homophobia in my classroom, and I hadn't thus far had the courage to deal with it

A version of this chapter was published in *Curriculum Inquiry* in summer 1996 and is reprinted by permission.

without the support of my larger school community and especially the administration.

Quite coincidentally, at the time this happened I was involved in a university reading group that had begun to study works by the queer theorists and feminists Judith Butler and Eve Sedgwick.[1] These writings enabled me to begin composing a story that made sense of what had transpired between Stephen, Nicole, and Sarah as well as many other events I witnessed daily in my classroom. They helped me to understand that this chapter could not be the story of a young, effeminate, possibly gay boy, of how he came to be who he was that day, and of who he would be in the future. Rather, it had to be about my attempt to understand how my own entwining of gender norms and sexuality were actually part of the heteronormative constructions of reality that so worried me. Stephen's choice to play with girls did not predict his future sexuality, and neither his gender performance nor his sexuality predicted his future state of well-being. As I came to understand from Judith Butler's writing, heterosexism and phallologocentrism are articulated, strengthened, and enforced through each other. To be "normal," to have the well-being, privilege, and sanction that goes with normalcy, one must enact one's physical sex, gender, and sexuality in particular ways. One must be a masculine male who desires (or is expected to grow up to desire) females or a feminine female who desires (or is expected to grow up to desire) males. Thus, the regulation of gender and that of sexuality go hand in hand.

This does not mean that I believe the problems of straight women, lesbian women, gay men, tomboy girls, and effeminate boys are all the same, and I don't wish to imply by having begun

1. I wish to extend my deepest gratitude to Joseph Tobin, Donna Grace, Richard Johnson, Anne Phelan, and Elisabeth Fowkes-Tobin for our reading-group discussions on Butler and Sedgwick, and to all of the above as well as Lynda Stone, Aaron Levine, Jonathan Silin, Diane Stephens, Judith Newman, and Cynthia Ward for discussion and feedback on this chapter.

with the story of an effeminate boy that I am more sympathetic to that situation than to others. I am a feminist and am particularly concerned with the way heterosexism and phallologocentrism continue to construct "male" and "power" as synonymous. Nevertheless, it was through taking the time to grapple with my own response and the responses of others to Stephen that I began to develop what feels like a more powerful way to understand sexism and the concerns and causes that should be shared among feminists, both lesbian and straight, "gender bending" men and women, gay men, and, indeed, anyone who is concerned with the narrow demands of gender and sexual "normalcy."

My chagrin at realizing the blindness of my own responses, good intentions notwithstanding, makes me finally claim this as a chapter more about myself than my students. Although I will use the essay to analyze my students' constructions of gender and sexuality, the question that always falls to me as their teacher is, "What will be my pedagogic response to this?" Addressing that question will occupy much of the second half of this chapter.

Finally, although in this essay I read the episodes with the children for ideologies of gender and sexuality, I do not take this to be an exhaustive reading. The students and adults in these scenes have multiple identifications at every moment.[2] We are not only male or female, feminine or masculine, straight or gay, within or without the norms of proper gender and sexuality; we are also positioned by race, class, age, physical size, and countless other identificatory possibilities. I have chosen incidents that show struggles and negotiations carried out in terms that point to constructions of gender and sexuality, but other positions and interests are often enacted and disputed through events that at first glance seem to be primarily or exclusively about something

2. There are several discussions of multiple subjectivities offered in education theory books and articles. See, for example, Moss (1989); Walkerdine (1989); and Davies (1989b).

more obvious.[3] The focus on gender and sexuality is for me a jumping off point, a place to begin grappling with a few issues of subjectivity. Examination of the same episodes through different lenses provides different and even conflicting readings. It is my belief that subjectivity is almost always a massively contradictory affair, and in the final section of this chapter I shall discuss some of the troubling but apparently necessary problematics created by my attempts to take profeminist or antihomophobic stances in my classroom.

IDEALIZED GENDER NORMATIVITIES

One afternoon I was sitting with some kids who were watching and commenting on a game some other kids were playing. Our conversation went like this:

BRIAN: I wonder who will win this time, a boy or a girl.

JOHN: It has to be a boy. There are only boys left.

Several of the children in and outside the circle smiled and nodded, including the one girl who was clearly in the game.

ME: What do you mean there are only boys left? Kelly is still playing.

JOHN: Oh, well, Kelly is a boy.

ME: Really?

KELLY: Yeah, I'm a boy, a tomboy, and Stephen is more like a girl.

Several classmates confirmed this observation with nods and "Yeahs."

3. This is a case made exceptionally well in Savigliano (1995). Savigliano uses neo-Marxist, feminist, poststructuralist, deconstructive, world systemic, and postcolonial theories to analyze the colonizations of Argentina, of the tango, and of herself as a self-described "Third World Intellectual Woman" living in exile. She demonstrates how the same text can be read convincingly in terms of racism, sexism, heterosexism, classism, and colonialism.

After three more rounds, Kelly emerged the winner of the game.

BRIAN: A boy won, a boy won!

ME: What do you mean, Kelly is a boy and Stephen is more like a girl?

BRIAN: Kelly's tough and she likes to play with the boys. She plays like a boy.

ME: How does someone play like a boy?

LANI: She doesn't cry.

JOHN: She plays kinda rough.

FISHER: She pretends she's a horse or dog and pulls the girls around.

KEITH: She likes doing boy things. She just seems more like a boy.

KELLY: I don't like all that stuff like Sarah and Nicole like. I like to play more like the boys, like sports and adventures. And I'm rough.

ME: What about Stephen?

Stephen was across the room from the group I was questioning. The children's responses about him seemed more hesitant and were spoken in quieter voices.

MARK: Well, he only likes to play with girls. He's been that way since kindergarten. Nicole and Sarah have been his best friends since kindergarten, you know.

KELLY: Stephen doesn't like sports and he's terrible in P.E.

LANI: He likes to write and make plays and do art and music.

MARK: He never plays with us at recess. He only plays with Nicole and Sarah, and they only play girls' games, like pretend house. And they pretend they're taking a trip to Japan.

ME: Have you talked about this before?

SEVERAL CHILDREN: Yes.

BRIAN: We talk about this all the time, how Kelly is a boy and Stephen is more like a girl.

ME: Kelly, do you like them saying you're a boy?

KELLY: I don't care. I am more like a boy.

ME: Does Stephen know you say this about him?

SEVERAL CHILDREN: Yes.

ME: Does he like it?

JOHN: No, he just gets mad and tells us it's not very nice to talk about people and that he doesn't talk about us.

LANI: And sometimes he says he is a boy, but boys or girls can do whatever they want.

It appears to me that my eight- and nine-year-old students have the expectation that there are certain ways in which boys *by nature* feel and behave and certain things they like and that these are often different from the behaviors, feelings, and likes that girls *by nature* have. They have told me that boys are rough and girls are nice; boys are tough and girls are emotional and cry easily; boys like sports, disgusting things, fighting, and scary adventures; girls like cute things, stories about animals and friends, and happy endings; boys are messy and girls are neat; boys are loud and girls are quiet; boys are naughty and girls are good.

My students' descriptions of these interests, desires, and feelings are curious because they are rarely accurate when applied to the individuals who make up our class. When I protest these descriptions by saying things like, "But Lani likes sports and she is a girl, and Tony doesn't like sports and he is a boy," the students answer me with exasperation: "But Ms. Boldt, *mostly* boys like sports." I believe that the reason for the exasperation is that I am not getting what they are really saying. My students are not describing anyone individually; they are, rather, describing an *idealized gender identity*. For the students, the expectation exists that there is something real that it means to be a boy and something it means to be a girl. Though the students' ideals differ because of the variety of identities that construct them, there is much consensus within my class on these ideals. All the children, regardless of the specifics of their ideals, are constantly performing (or failing at performing) the roles that are ascribed to them and that they ascribe to themselves by virtue of their physical bodies. As Judith Butler (1990) writes: "Gender is the repeated stylization of the body, a set of repeated acts . . . that congeal over time to produce the appearance of substance, of a natural sort of being" (p. 33).

In the tradition of Foucault, Butler is arguing that it is not possible to talk about a true or a real gender, sex, or sexuality; one can only describe the acts that constitute the illusion of a natural gender, sex, or sexuality. The illusion operates to create a sense that what we are experiencing and doing has a basis in truth. Truth is made up, in part, by ideas and beliefs that are understood to be natural, normal, commonsensical, even intuitive, that are supported by custom and tradition, and that are researched, tested, protected, and enforced by science and epistemology. The critical point here, however, is that such truths can also be understood to be, finally, not "natural," "normal," or "true" but, rather, constructions that create and reiterate the sustaining logic of any exercise of power.

In other words, that my students experience, describe, and attempt to act out unified, consistent genders does not mean that such genders exist; rather, it indicates their participation in and reiteration of systems of power relations that produce us all as gendered subjects. If we believe that there are gender roles that are natural, normal, or true, then we are justified in seeking or creating laws, policies, scientific and medical explanations, and practices that protect those spheres from violation. These exercises of power are not neutral or accidental—they create and protect the power of some and work against others. Butler (1990) describes this point of view on the nature of gender:

Gender ought not be construed as a stable identity . . . from which various acts follow; rather, gender is an identity tenuously constituted in time, instituted in an exterior space through a stylized repetition of acts. The effect of gender is produced through the stylization of the body and, hence, must be understood as the mundane way in which bodily gestures, movements, and styles of various kinds constitute the illusion of an abiding gendered self. . . . The appearance of substance is precisely that, a constructed identity, a performative accomplishment which the mundane social audience, including the actors themselves, come to believe and to perform in the mode of belief. (pp. 140–141)

My students perform gender norms in behaviors, desires, gestures, talents, interests, and stylizations that are so naturalized for them that they feel like and appear to be their own, an internal identity. They wear clothes and hairstyles, play games, speak, move, and express emotions in ways that identify them as masculine or feminine. Their sense of a gender ideal tells them it is normal for boys and for girls to behave in certain ways and alerts them when those norms have been transgressed.

Butler's analysis informs me, however, that what the children are experiencing and doing is *performing gender,* and that gender is a performance that is not chosen but forced and enforced from the time the social interpellation "It's a boy" or "It's a girl" is made (Butler, 1993, 231–232). That gender is performed rather than possessed means that the illusion of its reality must constantly be reiterated through the performance and that violations of the performance norms pose the threat of exposing gender as less than real. The children in my class, like the adults all around them, have learned to ignore most of their own and others' violations in action and contradictory opinions regarding gender norms. They sometimes "catch themselves" or are caught doing or saying the wrong thing, like when a boy in my class suddenly realized that what he had been reading was a "girl's book" and threw it down in disgust. But for the most part, the children's constructions of their own identities make it difficult and upsetting to perceive the slip ups that constantly occur. This makes their awareness of Stephen and Kelly all the more urgent. In fact, Kelly and Stephen are undoubtedly read as presenting a more consistent gender-bending performance than they do; the gendered identities we perceive them as having are also reflections of an idealized gender identity, this one pointing to the "abnormal." As Butler (1990) points out, power comes through the existence of norms, and it requires aberrant identities in order for the norms to function; notions of normal femininity and masculinity have neither intelligibility nor power without the contrasting presence of "abnormal gender" (p. 17).

Although both "normal" and "abnormal" gender identities are constructed and enforced within the same sexist/heterosexist power matrix, they are not equal identities. The descriptions of Stephen and Kelly at times seem neutral and matter of fact, but they carry a cost. Kelly and Stephen were often teased and regarded as "not quite normal" by classmates and adults alike. They were often excluded, whether they wished to be or not, from same-sex play groups and subjected to attempts by adults to make them perform in more "gender-normal" ways: suggestions to Kelly to change her clothing and hair style, her way of playing, and her voice and gait, and suggestions to Stephen to play more with boys, act tougher, and get involved in sports.

In the dialogue between the children and me above, Kelly said that she liked and accepted her role as "boy," but I have seen other evidence that this is a role she sometimes plays with discomfort. I suspect that the role of "tomboy" is different, in many important ways, from the role of "effeminate boy." Tomboys may of course experience difficulties with the regulatory system operating around gendered identity, but the role of tomboy appears to be more accepted than the role of effeminate boy and does not seem to generate nearly as much concern. This is not to downplay the difficulties that tomboys may experience. But for the moment at least, Stephen's discomfort with the role in which he is cast appears to be much greater than Kelly's. While Stephen likes many things that the girls like, these are things that are not valued by the boys and often not by the larger context of school and society. To be a girl called a boy often carries with it the promise of increased opportunities, but to be a boy associated with girls' interests and desires is construed as a move away from power and possibility. Calling someone a girl is an insult that the boys hurl at one another with some frequency. Stephen feels insulted and assaulted when his classmates say he "is more like a girl." The boys explained that to be called a girl is a terrible insult, on a par with calling someone stupid or ugly, a "really a gross thing to be." I don't believe that Stephen's problems around this devaluation of the female and all things feminine are the same as those that face girls in general. After all, girls are perceived as *being* by nature inferior, whereas Stephen's problem is one of *acting* in an inferior manner. Nevertheless, this is a moment when we can see sexism revealing itself in relation to a male.

If it were true that gender has natural and recognizable actions and boundaries, or that gender is a performance that is played out *as if* it has recognizable actions and boundaries, then the children may be describing Stephen accurately when they say that he is "more like a girl." However, there is a critical difference between saying that the boundaries are natural and saying that we only perform as if they were. If gender truly has such boundaries, then Stephen is a freak, some kind of failure who needs help. But if I understand that what appears to be "true" or "natural" is not true but a function of power, I can understand that it is the description of gender that fails Stephen and not Stephen who fails gender.

The Co-Construction of "Intelligible" Gender and Sexuality

Central to Butler's (1990) argument is the realization that the power of gender norms derives strength from the linkage of gender, physical sex, and sexuality: "'Intelligible' genders are those which in some sense institute and maintain relations of coherence among sex, gender, sexual practice, and desire" (p. 17). Butler argues that the appearance of naturalized gender and sexuality and the linking of gender performativity to expectations about sexuality—that the effeminate boy grows up to be the gay man, for example—are in the service of (among other things) both sexism and heterosexism. The normativities of gender and sexuality define those who are "inside," those who reiterate the norms sufficiently and consistently, as well as all those who are "outside," those whose gender or sexuality is not consistent with the norms for their sex. Those inside often have certain officially sanctioned and recognized privileges of power, and those outside are generally marginalized in at least some ways.

With Stephen and his peers, I never had to deal directly with the seemingly inevitable and usually cruelly intended connections that are made between gender performance and sexuality. To my knowledge, Stephen was never called "gay" or "fag" by his peers when he was in my class. But I know that the connection had already been made in the minds of adults because I had made them myself, when I pictured Stephen's future as a gay teenager. On several occasions I heard other adults comment that Stephen had better start playing with boys or he would grow up to be gay. I expected that Stephen's classmates would soon begin to make overt connections and call him names in an accusatory or shaming way. Although I considered my own thoughts on the subject to be nonhomophobic—I supported Stephen's decision to play with girls and I was not troubled by the prospect of his growing up to be gay—I felt that the responses of the other adults as well as those I imagined from the kids in the future were motivated by homophobia.

Butler's writing, however, calls into question any linking of gender performance and sexuality. The same logic that supports a sense of naturalized, normative gender supports a sense of naturalized, normative sexuality; as surely as gender is constructed as following in a certain way from physical sex, so sexual desire is constructed as following from gender and from physical sex. If Stephen's body is male, his so-called normal gender would be masculine and his desire would be for females. That Stephen's gender appears to be at least in part feminine seems to raise the (horrifying) possibility that his desire might someday be for males. This logic must be called into question on several counts.

In "How to Bring Your Kids Up Gay," Eve Sedgwick (1993) explores some of the ties between effeminate boys and gay men. She points out that the 1980 edition of the *Diagnostic and Statistical Manual* (DSM-III), published by the American Psychiatric Association, was the first that did not list homosexuality as a pathology. It *did,* for the first time, include a category called "Gender Identity Disorder of Childhood." Under this category, a girl can be regarded as pathological if she asserts that she is anatomically male, whereas a boy can be treated as pathological if he asserts that "it would be better not to have a penis" or displays a "preoccupation with female stereotypical activities as manifested by a preference for either cross-dress or simulating female attire, or by a compelling desire to participate in the games and pastimes of girls" (p. 71). Sedgwick notes that the depathologization of homosexuality and the simultaneous pathologization of gender identification (particularly of effeminate males) have, ironically, occurred even as the APA and gay activists were making the potentially subversive assertion that sexuality does not follow from gender, that one can be masculine and desire a man, or feminine and desire a woman.

Sedgwick makes the case, however, that the pathologizing of gender roles conceptually positions psychiatry at the very least as a participant in the denigration and isolation of effeminate boys and men and, worse, as a potential ally in the cultural fantasy of the elimination of homosexuality. Under post-DSM-III accounts, effeminacy in boys and men can be seen as a pathology, a failure to consolidate the proper masculine "Core Gender Identity." This serves to continue the tradition of maintaining sexist (genderist?) hegemony through the belief in normal gender. Stephen may or may not grow up to be an effeminate man, and he may or may not grow up to be a man who has sex with other men. To see his adult sexuality, regardless of what it is, as normal while seeing his current and potential genders as a developmental failure is a troubling victory at best.

IMPLICATIONS FOR EDUCATIONAL PRACTICE

It would be gratifying if I could now reveal how a concerned teacher can help the children in her or his care to become more accepting of a broader range of gender and sexual identities, both for themselves and for others. Yet I have always been aware of the ways the children have resisted me when I attempted to do these things myself and of how the solutions I was offering participated in reinscribing the assumptions about identity, gender, and sexuality that led to the troublesome exclusions in the first place. In other words, simply shifting the boundaries of identity did not cleanly resolve the problems created by identity as we currently construct it. Both difficulties, those of the students' resistance and of identity, are worth exploring further.

As in the broader society, there is a commonly held belief in education that one of the causes of stereotype and prejudice is lack of exposure to a broad and positive range of images, or exposure only to negative images of those who are "other." It is popularly held that children will grow up with less prejudice and be more accepting of difference and open to a broader range of possibilities for themselves if they are exposed to difference in a positive way. It has been suggested that this take place in schools through literature, discussion, artwork, and curricula showing people from around the world as "the same" in such important ways as caring for others and having basic needs, and as "different" in a way that promotes acceptance of difference as exciting, creative, and even ingenious. This is the logic of "multi-cultural education." The "antibias curriculum" goes a step further in arguing that it is not enough to talk about difference; children need to consciously inhabit a world of difference in schools where there are teachers and children of many ethnicities and where the differences and similarities are openly explored and discussed; where teachers discuss, deliberately act out, and encourage the children to act out nontraditional gender roles; and even some-times where gay and lesbian teachers are encouraged to be out, with antihomophobia as part of the school agenda.[4]

I hold to the belief that schools committed to an antibias posi-tion are trying to offer a more moral choice for society than schools in which the assumptions continue to reflect more exclu-sive and biased approaches to what counts as worthwhile. These are the kinds of commitments I attempt to uphold in my class-room—for example, by continuing to refute through words and actions the exclusivities of definitions of *girl* and *boy, masculine* and *feminine, homosexual* and *heterosexual.* The evidence is plenti-ful that boys and girls continue to receive differential treatment in classrooms, which daily reiterate for them the realness of gen-dered norms. It is important that I continually work to find not just the simple things, like how boys are called on many times more often than girls, but the more difficult things, like how epistemology and pedagogy may actually be based on gendered, exclusivizing binaries such as active/passive, understanding/ memorization, risk taking/conforming. I not only have to con-cern myself with providing equal opportunities for my students, eliminating sex as a basis for participation or opting out of par-ticipation; I also have to be aware, when variations arising out of gender performativity do occur (as they constantly do because the children are performing differentiated gender roles), of the

4. See, for example, Marsh (1992), Hernandez (1989), and Derman-Sparks (1988).

temptation to attach value judgments to behaviors, interpreting a child as better or worse, more or less successful, more or less normal or likable, on the basis of how much I value the norms the children are replicating or failing to replicate.[5]

My hope is to open up the categories of boy and girl, to give the children reasons to accept the solution Stephen offered them—that "boys and girls can do whatever they want"—so that Stephen's version of boyness and all others would become intelligible and so that the category of girl would be opened up not only to include Kelly but to avoid a devaluing or horrified rejection of anyone and everyone who occupies it. I also hope to help the children realize that it is permissible and even desirable to want possibilities they didn't previously know they wanted or even rejected wanting.

These are my hopes, but thus far I haven't had much reason to celebrate. My students have proven resistant, perhaps sometimes rightly so, to my versions of gender and sexuality. I have had long discussions about gender biases with my students. I have been careful to present them with literature that reflects a variety of gender models, and I have initiated and led conversations when stereotypes have come up in classroom materials. I have been conscientious in trying to reexamine treatment that is differentiated by gender and have sharply revised the terms in which I evaluate students, no longer assuming that silence and passivity are necessarily indicative of lack of knowledge, or that activity denotes understanding or potential. When I find myself attributing some quality such as active participation primarily to boys, I work to understand why I am not seeing the same in girls and to change my attitude and actions; likewise, when I find myself admiring primarily girls for sensitivity and fairness, I force myself

5. For examples of some of the more overt kinds of discrimination that goes on in classrooms, see Sadker and Sadker (1994). For a discussion of the re-inscriptions of sexist binarism in "child-centered" pedagogy, see Walkerdine (1989).

to understand and remedy my failure to credit the boys with the same.

The children's behaviors and beliefs about themselves, their families, and peers appear to be largely unaltered. Students' comments suggest that they understand what I want them to believe. They point out some instances of stereotypes in stories they are reading and agree that women and men, boys and girls, have the right to like and do what they want. However, these sentiments often turn out to be spoken but not enacted. For example, one of the girls talked about a stereotype in a book and shortly thereafter identified math as a "boys' subject" and "too hard for girls"; a boy explained in a discussion why it was OK if boys liked to dance, then was upset when some of the girls asked him to join them in dancing; after the boys reported angrily that "junk girl players" were "ruining" their recess soccer game, they reluctantly admitted that some of the "junk girl players" played as well as or better than they did—but the next day they still did not want to let the girls into the game, claiming that the girls were no good at soccer and would ruin their play.

One obvious explanation for the contradictory words, beliefs, and actions is that the children have learned what they are supposed to say to make their teacher happy. They can play the school game of giving the right answers to leading questions without altering their own systems of power and understanding. Even when children think they believe the words, they often believe them about other people, not about themselves, their peers, and their families. They continue to feel the need to hold themselves and those around them to different standards. The children have much evidence that the traditional approach is the safe one, that I am wrong in my beliefs. If I or one of the students say, "Boys and girls are equal," or "Boys and girls can do whatever they want," the children know that it is not true. The adult world has presented them with few models in equity, and they know that many of the liberties I try to promote in my classroom do not extend beyond our four walls. One day, for example, a student explained his reasoning that it is better to be a boy than a girl by insisting that a female cannot be president of the United States. This child's life experiences told him that boys and girls are different and unequal.

I want to believe that I can influence my students' beliefs and actions around gender and sexuality because I believe that they would be happier and our society would be more just if we could come to value a broader range of performances as worthwhile for others and for ourselves. That my students often resist my efforts in relation to their own identities and the identities of those who matter most to them is not surprising; identity is usually constructed in Western discourse as unitary and noncontradictory. To be something is meaningful only in relation to all that one is not. To identify oneself as a girl one has to be all that is "not boy." To identify oneself as heterosexual one must be all that is "not homosexual." These identities count for something; they exist within a sexist and heterosexist matrix that accords power and privilege only to those who possess the correct identity.

The children have a great deal invested in their gendered identities and often find much pleasure in being who they are. When I asked how many boys would rather be girls, there were no volunteers. When I asked how many girls would rather be boys, only Kelly thought that she might like to try it for a short while. The power differential between the boys and girls seems to be operative once again. Even Stephen, who seems to derive such pleasure from "girl things," refused to consider the possibility of being a girl. Perhaps his stance reflected awareness that the trade would be a step away from power or that a public admission of such an interest would be an impossible position for a boy to take up, whereas Kelly could express the corresponding interest with no obvious negative repercussions. It is also important to note, however, that Stephen, along with all the other boys, and Kelly, along with all the other girls, were able to come up with many examples of ways in which they derived a great deal of pleasure from many stereotypical aspects of their roles as boys or girls. I insist on everyone's having equal access to all the materials and activities in the classroom, yet many of the girls simply do not enjoy the games and attitudes that many of the boys enjoy, and many of the boys do not enjoy the games and attitudes that many of the girls enjoy. I understand how this comes to be in the mandatory formation of identities.

I recognize that to use the identity categories boy and girl as referents continues to imply that these are real or natural categories. Butler (1993) refutes the logic that the solution is to eliminate identity categories. To attempt to do so would suggest that it is possible to come up with a category that is all-inclusive. Such a strategy is ridiculous precisely because it renders identity itself unintelligible (p. 22). Even moving to make categories less exclusive creates new difficulties; in opening up some possibilities for identity, one inevitably closes others. I must ask such questions as: For whom has this become an impossible identification? Who is now excluded from this definition because it conflicts with other identificatory norms, such as race, ethnicity, class, or religion? Further, new identifications threaten to displace some individuals who previously had greater power owing to their closer identification with or performance of the ideal. To include Stephen as a "real boy," for example, throws into question the status of other children and adults who currently experience popularity and success because they closely approximate the dominant idealization.

To attempt to get children to accept a more partial and contradictory sense of identity is problematic in other ways. It moves them into an arena of discourse that they have learned to deny; that is, all the children enact and witness constant contradictions to the ideal identities they perform and uphold, but they have learned not to notice or to be bothered by these contradictions except for cases such as Stephen's, which are understood as unusual and abnormal. Further, we are asking children to take on ideas that do not have strong societal support, sometimes putting them in the position of having to chose between home and school values, or to take positions that are not shared by powerful adults in their lives.[6] A boy who began to exhibit some of the "girlish" behaviors at home that he was encouraged to accept and explore at school could be subject to humiliation and punishment. In Stephen's case, his parents became alarmed by the amount of time he spent with girls at school and decided to "balance things" by enrolling him in a football program. Stephen, who hated sports and rough play, reported much unhappiness over this "corrective action."

It would be possible to argue that my failure to come up with a satisfactory conclusion for this essay, one that would give concerned educators direction for helping children to broaden their understandings of gender and sexuality, simply reflects a lack of imagination or intellect on my part. It is worthwhile to consider, however, that the problem might lie with the expectation for a certain kind of conclusion. Tom Newkirk (1992) argues that in order for a case study to appear successful and satisfying, it must follow a narrative form we are familiar with: beginning, middle, and end; present problem, research it, resolve it. According to Newkirk, the characters that inhabit case studies in the field of education are often familiar to us; a common form casts the heroic teacher as Annie Sullivan, the Miracle Worker, and the struggling

6. Bronwyn Davies (1989a) reports on an incident where a boy in preschool was allowed by his teachers to paint his nails with red nail polish. This provoked an angry note back to the school from the boy's father as well as the four-year-old boy explaining forcefully to his teachers the next day that "he was a good boy" and "boys don't wear nail polish." At one point, the boy exposed his genitals to his teachers to make his point that he was a boy. Davies comments that the teachers were "introducing one form of discourse here in which the possession of male genitals and 'feminine' behavior were incompatible" and that "the child's father found this a serious threat to the boy's achievement of masculinity as he understood that term" (p. 237).

or difficult student as Helen Keller, the child with great potential just waiting for the right teacher to provide the right outlet. Newkirk says that these narratives are inherently conservative; they cater to the demand for emotionally familiar endings that place the sympathetic reader in a gratifying moral position. But such unproblematic solutions do not exist in reality.

Stephen's story begins with a tragedy in the making, his heading unknowingly down the road toward inevitable oppression and suffering. The next step should be for fate to intervene and for Stephen to be assigned a heroic teacher who recognizes what is happening, values Stephen for what he is, and finds a way to help everyone love and value him (and others like him) as much as she or he does. The problem with this conclusion is that I cannot find an unproblematic way to write myself as a miracle worker and Stephen as my Helen Keller.

Such a morally gratifying narrative not only glosses over many problems, including problems the proposed solutions themselves would create. The demand for a coherent narrative reflects a central theme in the sexist and heterosexist power matrixes that this chapter is all about. That is, in telling the story about a child called Stephen, who is troubled, I created for myself and possibly for my audience a sense of tragedy, of the inevitability of present and future suffering for Stephen because of his gender transgressions. I have said that he will almost certainly be persecuted for the assumptions made about his sexuality on the basis of his gender performance. What I have not done to this point is grapple seriously with the implications of Butler's argument that the belief in the inevitable connectedness of sex, gender, and sexuality (and of all three with happiness) is itself part of the power of heterosexism. Perhaps it is the sense of inevitability, which is often constructed through the narrative telling of lives, that must be called into question.

Stephen's perception of his exclusion from play with Nicole and Sarah as "unfair" is certainly accurate, but what are the stakes in implying that this experience is one small step down a lifelong path of injustice and hurt related to his performance of gender and sexuality? The statistics (Gibson, 1989; Proctor and Groze, 1994) on attempted suicides among gay and lesbian teens are alarming, as are accounts I've heard from gay and lesbian adults about their difficult school years. Yet writing about them is a two-edged sword. The pain and suffering created by denigration are important aspects of the power of heterosexism, a warning for any who would stray too near or beyond the outer limits of normative performance. Ironically, my story serves as a frightening reminder of what happens to people like Stephen. Moreover, that it seems impossible for me to make any large-scale, meaningful changes for Stephen may further confirm the overwhelming power of heterosexism. What began as an attempt to tell a story outside the heterosexist power matrix ends up as a fixture within it.[7]

Therefore, it is important that I tell a more complicated story, one that calls into question my tragic narrative of Stephen's life. Most children suffer in school from the demands of identity norms related not only to gender or sexuality but also to race, class, ethnicity, standards of beauty, evaluations of success, and much more. As a teacher I see kids being treated cruelly every day. Why is Stephen's particular kind of suffering so compelling to me? Shouldn't I be suspicious of my inclination to see it as more tragic than other school stories? The suffering of gender-bending kids like Stephen or of gay and lesbian teens is real and needs to be

7. In fact, at least one piece of research (Shaffer, Fisher, and Hicks, 1995) challenges the belief that gay and lesbian teens are more at risk for suicide than heterosexual ones. I have no way of knowing whether Shaffer et al. are correct. Gibson's argument that gay teenagers are subject to frequent physical and verbal abuse and to rejection and that they are therefore more likely than nongay teenagers to attempt suicide is meant to rally support for gay and lesbian youth. One can see, however, how the belief that these teens are more likely to be abused and rejected and more likely to attempt suicide can function to heighten young people's concerns about being gay and make parents and teachers of gay young people worried on their behalf. This concern, in turn, can lead us to wish that a young person's gayness would be otherwise.

addressed, but both telling the stories and responding to them need to occur in ways that do not affirm the sexist and heterosexist conviction that nonconformity to gender or sexuality norms means certain unhappiness, failure, rejection, perversity, pathology, psychosis, or suicide. Yes, it is hard to be a boy who prefers to play with girls, but to focus on Stephen's struggles as a gender bender may wrongly imply that to be such a boy is an inevitable guarantee of unhappiness and that gender-conforming kids find their performance of gender less problematic and more satisfying.

As bell hooks (1990) suggests, I need to listen for stories that proclaim the margins as a place of resistance, power, and joy, a place where one can struggle for freedom of expression (pp. 150–152). Stephen's story is not one of unrelieved misery in school; far from it (and here we could speculate about how *being* a boy, in spite of sometimes *performing* like a girl, may have contributed to Stephen's positive experiences). When he was in my class he claimed to love school and often insisted upon coming to school even when he was sick. Stephen was an excellent student, and his talent in writing and performance gained him much positive attention. He was hard-working, smart, and articulate; progress reports and awards he received in all grades show that teachers evaluated his abilities very positively. In our class, Stephen was recognized as a capable leader by his peers, was consistently chosen for small group work, and was even elected class president. There were, in fact, many kids in the class who liked coming to school much less than he did, including the boy with large front teeth and a learning disability who was taunted as "Beaver" by the other kids and the fat girl who wore unstylish clothing. Even if Stephen had disliked school, to attribute all his problems in school to his gender performance would be a misrepresentation of the situation.

The sense that lives have trajectories that we can discover, predict, recognize, and intervene in, for better or worse, is very much part of the modernist construction of the intelligibility of human lives. I cannot, as a concerned teacher and researcher, know in advance how Stephen will interpret his childhood experiences of gender or sexuality, nor can I devise interventions that I know with certainty will change his life for the better. How Stephen experiences school now and what stories he will tell when he grows may not in the end be the same. The stories he remembers and counts as significant enough to tell may have more to do with who he perceives himself to be at that future time than with what he is experiencing now. He may tell a story of how he got to be who he feels he is that does not reveal all the other stories that contradict that inevitable narrative form of beginning, middle, and end. The stories he tells about his life will change depending upon the context he is in. To think that I could unproblematically intervene now and create a better future or that if I do not intervene now Stephen's future will inevitably be tragic is to participate in the myth of inevitability and to claim the right to determine what constitutes a worthwhile identity.

What does this leave me? The idea that because I cannot assure the future I will do nothing is not tenable. I will continue to try through curriculum and classroom practices to make my students aware of some of the biases and limitations of dominant discourses. But I must also go back to the image that began this story, of Stephen crying in the hall. That moment was the time to act compassionately on Stephen's behalf. Realizing how little I can or want to predict the future has caused me to appreciate anew the things I can do in the present, the ways I can respond to the little and big things that happen daily in the classroom that the kids really care about, like who has to work in what group, who gets most of the time and attention from adults, how to make sure that the good sports equipment and time on the computers are not dominated by a few boys, and how to help the children deal with cruelty. I want my students to feel happy, safe, and respected at school. Therefore, I must work diligently and with passion to figure out how to help particular children in particular situations, in the present, knowing that I sometimes make things better and trying with all my heart to avoid making things worse. I will do well to remember and appreciate that the children often experience pleasure in acting out the roles they have been given, and that those performances predict neither future suffering nor future happiness. I also know that there will always be children who are troubled and hurt by the ever-changing landscapes of exclusions that train children in the power regimes of adults. My efforts to expand the children's acceptance of broader gender and sexual identities will continue because I believe that this offers many positive possibilities for the children in the present. It is necessary, however, for me to remember that no solution is unproblematic, and that I must constantly make reassessments with each new child and each new situation, looking to help create the only happiness I can be reasonably certain of affecting—that of the present.[8]

I will never solve for my students the difficulties that our construction of identity creates, but this does not make me feel hopeless. Indeed, the partiality of any solution I construct is something I must embrace as the best hope. The pleasures and hurts of my students will always be there, to show me the inclusions and exclusions that have been instituted, to remind me that my values and beliefs are always only provisional, always only partly successful, and to challenge me to be fully present and aware of

8. I am particularly impressed by the descriptions offered by Gemma Moss (1989) of the power that her female high school students already have to "hold their own" against the attempts of boys to "do power" over them. Moss describes her own efforts to support the girls in what they are already doing rather than worrying them into being passive, helpless victims who can be saved only by the efforts of a heroic teacher. Moss's writing has helped me to focus more on the real issues that are actually at hand with the children, rather than worrying and daydreaming about the future or about seemingly "bigger" issues. I have also become aware of the way that I often speak for the girls rather than encouraging them to speak for themselves (p. 237).

the endless variety of ways in which my students may need me to advocate for their happiness at that moment.

REFERENCES

Butler, J. (1990). *Gender trouble*. New York: Routledge.

——. (1993). *Bodies that matter*. New York: Routledge.

Davies, B. (1989a). The discursive production of the male/female dualism in school settings. *Oxford Review of Education* 15 (3): 229–241.

——. (1989b). *Frogs and snails and feminist tales: Preschool children and gender*. Sydney: Allen and Unwin.

Derman-Sparks, L. (1988). *Anti-bias curriculum*. (Video.) Pasadena, Calif.: Pacific Oaks College.

Gibson, P. (1989). Gay male and lesbian youth suicide. In *Report of the Secretary's Task Force on Youth Suicide,* vol. 3 (pp. 110–142). Department of Health and Human Services, DHHS Publication no. ADM 89–1623. Washington, D.C.: U.S. Government Printing Office.

Hernandez, H. (1989). *Multicultural education: A teacher's guide to content and process*. Columbus, Ohio: Merrill.

hooks, b. (1990). *Yearning, race, gender, and cultured politics*. Boston: South End.

Marsh, M. (1992). Implementing antibias curriculum in the kindergarten class. In S. Kessler and B. Swadener (eds.), *Reconceptualizing the early childhood curriculum* (pp. 267–288). New York: Teachers College Press.

Moss, G. (1989). *Un/popular fictions*. London: Virago.

Newkirk, T. (1992). The narrative roots of case study. In G. Kirch and P. Sullivan (eds.), *Methods and methodologies in composition research* (pp. 130–152). Carbondale: Southern Illinois University Press.

Proctor, C., and Groze, V. (1994). Risk factors for suicide among gay, lesbian, and bisexual youths. *Social Work* 39: 504–513.

Sadker, M., and Sadker, D. (1994). *Failing at fairness*. New York: Charles Scribner's Sons.

Savigliano, M. (1995). *Tango and the political economy of passion*. Boulder: Westview Press.

Sedgwick, E. (1993). How to bring your kids up gay. In M. Warner (ed.),

Fear of a queer planet (pp. 69–81). Minneapolis: University of Minnesota Press.

Shaffer, D., Fisher, P., and Hicks, R. (1995). Sexual orientation in adolescents who commit suicide. *Suicide and Life-Threatening Behavior* 25: 64–71.

Walkerdine, V. (1989). Femininity as performance. *Oxford Review of Education* 15 (3): 267–279.

——. (1990). *Schoolgirl fictions*. New York: Verso.

SEVEN

The Pervert in the Classroom

Jonathan G. Silin

Americans are alternately expansive and silent about the place of sexuality in the early childhood classroom. We cannot stop talking about the need to screen day care workers for criminal histories, to promulgate regulations about when teachers may (and may not) be alone with students, and to legislate how and where children may be touched. At the same time, few words are spoken about HIV/AIDS, sex education, and desire among children or between children and adults in the classroom. Many of the contributors to this volume document ways in which popular and professional discourses frame sexuality as a dangerous force that must be vigilantly monitored and barred from children's lives.

In this chapter I argue that at the heart of the silence about human sexuality and the talk about child abuse is a heretofore unacknowledged pair, the homosexual and the child. As an educator, I explore how our notions about adult sexuality are linked to beliefs in childhood innocence and ignorance. As a gay man, I ask how these characterizations of children as ignorant of sexuality are reinforced by popular stereotypes of the homosexual as a predatory pedophile. Over time the homosexual-child dyad has become the primary subtext of the absent discourse of desire in early childhood education. If we do not uncouple it we will see increasingly restrictive legislation with respect to adult-child interactions and the proliferation of harmful child abuse–prevention curricula. Most insidiously, continued moral panics

Sections of this chapter were published in chapter 8 of *Sex, Death, and the Education of Children: Our Passion for Ignorance in the Age of AIDS* and are reprinted here with permission of Teachers College Press.

will divert attention from more pervasive forms of physical and social violence perpetrated against children in our country.

THE TRUTH OF SEX

The history of sexual identity may at first appear to have little direct relevance to early education. But on closer inspection these seemingly discrete fields are linked by structure and content and by the meaning and significance of their central texts. For both, the nineteenth century marks a watershed period. The essentialist strategy central to the project of groundbreaking sexologists like Magnus Hirschfeld (1946), Richard von Krafft-Ebing (1931), and Karl Ulrichs (Kennedy, 1988) was similar to that employed by nineteenth-century "child savers" (Takanishi, 1978). The sexologists argued that homosexuality was not a sin of willfulness or an indication of innate depravity but rather a natural aberration, to be accepted as part of the spectrum of human behavior; the child savers rationalized their work by asserting that there were universal aspects of childhood that they undertook to protect. Both sought legal remedies to protect the rights of those for whom they advocated and used scientific arguments to make their claims.

But in spite of the best intentions of progressive sexologists and child savers, the new scientific disciplines of the nineteenth century pathologized the homosexual and the child as special beings, members of discrete populations, who could be observed, classified, explained, and ultimately controlled. Both were regarded as suffering from the need for immediate gratification of undeveloped, egocentric impulses. Both required constant surveillance to check an assumed surfeit of erotically suspect energies. Professionals produced an ever-expanding and infinitely complex taxonomy of human potential, while sustaining their own power to pass authoritative judgments on its meaning. In the twentieth century these expert evaluations have intensified, and the interventions designed to correct various assessed abnormalities have expanded. The extensive consideration given to the deficiencies of children and homosexuals suggests that both pose especially strong challenges to accepted ways of being in the world.

But how did sexuality become central to our sense of identity and definition of personhood? Where exactly is the story of the pairing of child and homosexual written?

To answer these questions we turn to those who tell the story of the body and the regulative apparatuses through which it is controlled. The classical scholar and queer theorist David Halperin (1990), for one, describes the construction of sexuality as an autonomous domain of personal identity. He argues that although it was possible to assess and classify sex acts before the nineteenth century, it was only then, with the assumption of "sexuality" as a singular drive, that sex acts were elevated to a basic organizing principle of character. Although it was understood that individuals experienced sex differently, no one believed that there were different kinds of sexuality—that is, differently structured psychosexual states or modes of affective orientation. Not until the introduction of heterosexual and homosexual types was universal sexuality challenged by the claim that there were two opposing sexual orientations, two different ways of being in the world. Michel Foucault (1978) most aptly describes the appearance of the modern homosexual: "The psychological, psychiatric, medical category of homosexuality was constituted from the moment it was characterized . . . less by a type of sexual relations than by a certain quality of sexual sensibility, a certain way of inverting the masculine and the feminine in oneself. Homosexuality appeared as one of the forms of sexuality when it was transposed from the practice of sodomy onto a kind of interior androgyny, a hermaphrodism of the soul. The sodomite had been a temporary aberration; the homosexual was now a species" (p. 43).

By juxtaposing the sodomite with the new homosexual, defining the former as one who engages in discrete aberrant acts and the latter as a person with a unique psychological structure, Foucault implies that this story can be told solely in terms of gender inversions, reversals, and contradictions. But only in the last quarter of the nineteenth century was the centrality of object choice itself introduced into the discourse. The homo/heterosexual dichotomy gave birth to a new set of sexual taxonomies based on the biological sex of one's partner rather than on such distinctions as age, active/passive role, or conventional/unconventional activities. The emphasis now was on not what one does but with whom.

Foucault documents more than the invention of the modern homosexual. He charts the progress through which sexuality achieved its ascendancy in our lives. Sex is constituted as having a secret, hidden meaning that, once uncovered, reveals the omnipotent cause of who and what we are: "Between each of us and our sex, the West has placed an unending demand for truth: it is up to us to extract the truth of sex, since this truth is beyond its grasp; it is up to sex to tell us our truth, since sex is what holds it in darkness. But is sex hidden from us, concealed by a new sense of decency, kept under a bushel by the grim necessities of bourgeois society? On the contrary, it shines forth; it is incandescent. Several centuries ago, it was placed at the center of a formidable *petition to know*. A double petition, in that we are compelled to know how things are with it, while it is suspected of knowing how things are with us" (p. 77).

This "petition to know" announces Foucault's challenge to the traditional view of the nineteenth century as a period of repression during which our essential sexuality was denied and blocked from expression. In contrast, he asserts that, beginning in the eighteenth century, medical, pedagogical, and psychiatric discourses began producing a proliferation of new forms of knowledge framing sexuality. Sex was transformed from a matter of sensation and pleasure, law and taboo, to a problem of truth that could be interrogated through science.

The Western world does not produce *ars erotica;* it practices *scientia sexualis.* Scientific techniques for seeing inside the soul evolved from the older discourse of confession. A relational strategy once confined to religious penance, the confession now characterizes expectations of personal disclosure between child and parent, student and teacher, patient and psychiatrist, delinquent and social worker.

Linked to science and the confession, sexuality extends its influence as the basis of knowledge/power. That is, the new knowledge of the body permits more subtle and intensive regulative techniques. Power that functioned through law and prohibition, liberty and sovereignty, now becomes an effect of knowledge and the new technologies of the self, promoted by psychologists, psychiatrists, social workers, and educators. The direct exercise of force and the use of punishment are replaced by the normalization of behavior and surveillance of the body. Once public and visible, power now hides and is invisible. With Foucault we move out of the great halls of state and public tribunals and into the university and school, hospital and clinic, where knowledge is produced and reproduced. We also move into the bedrooms and examining rooms of friends and neighbors. The perverse adult, the Malthusian couple, the hysterical woman, and the masturbating child became the privileged subjects of scientific investigation, textual inscription, and the control of sexuality. The effect of this process was not to exclude aberrant individuals from society but to incorporate them through new practices of specification.

The field of sexuality was growing in importance even as the techniques and specialties for surveying its contours were refined. Pedagogical theories and practices developed to explain and control childhood sexuality, modern medicine to map the sexual physiology of woman, psychiatry to normalize the perverse, and demography to control populations. In this process, sex was secularized, removed from the realm of religion and the aura of sin and placed under the protection of the state, in the service of the social body.

The Pairing of Pervert and Child

Foucault's history suggests the importance of looking at seemingly discrete sites of sexual knowing as part of a web of interrelated meanings. Women, children, and homosexuals are linked in a nexus of unfulfilled desires. The emergence of the mental health perspective announced the psychological needs of children and the unique abilities of women to fulfill them; at the same time it defined the homosexual threat to normal development. The homosexual, embodying everything that the child is not, allows us to see the child as innocent and without desire, a blank slate on which we may write at will. Women are charged with protecting the child's (and their own) innocence from those who would seduce them away from their "natural" heterosexuality.

Questions of power in adult-child relations alert us to a less benign dyad than mother-infant: that of pervert-child. Although this is a connection from which we ordinarily prefer to shield ourselves, it too is an inevitable outcome of the petition to know. Our popular as well as scientific notions of perversion link the pervert to children, their innocent victims. The effects of perversion are believed to spread like an unstoppable infection. Willard Waller (1932), a classic educational sociologist, makes clear the diseased nature of the gay teacher: "Nothing seems more certain than that homosexuality is contagious" (p. 147).

Here we must interpret popular ideas that fuel homophobia against the scholarly histories of sexuality. Stereotypes perpetuate stigmatizing and harmful behaviors. Originating in cultural ideology, they reveal the belief systems by which people live (Mohr, 1992). For example, the stereotype of gay men as sex-obsessed child molesters preserves the belief in family innocence. It enables us to locate potentially unregulated and unruly desires outside the home. Sex, according to this discourse, is a simple reproductive activity, not a destabilizing, pleasure-oriented play of complex emotions. The stereotype of homosexuality as a mismatch between a person's biological sex and his or her self-perception—gay men want to be and act like women, lesbians would be men—reinforces the belief in traditional gender roles. The threat posed by the notion of choice in gender identification is disarmed, made ridiculous and unnatural. Homophobic stereotypes are critical preservers of the social fabric, assuring the economic and biologic reproduction of the family through adherence to appropriate gender roles.

The gay teacher comes into the contemporary classroom well aware of these stereotypes and walking in the shadow of the nineteenth-century homosexual. Our historical predecessors, not yet the self-indulgent "clones" who were spurned by gay liberation and who spread physical disease, are the powerfully seductive members of the underworld whose contagion is moral corruption. The classic version of the story suggests that the older, incurable, "true" invert is driven to choose a younger, passive, and (need I add) innocent victim as the object of his attentions. Thus homosexuality is both a repugnant practice and one to which it is all too easy to succumb. Heterosexuality is natural and vulnerable when juxtaposed to the unnatural and powerful claims of homosexuality. In the end no one is safe, least of all the child, the quintessentially defenseless victim.

The most recent version of this story combines the traditional belief in the vulnerable child seduced by the powerful pervert with a new theory of representation (Watney, 1991). In the United Kingdom, the Local Government (Amendment) Act of 1988 bans depictions of gay relationships as equivalent to heterosexual families, tacitly acknowledging that homosexuality is a social identity that does not flow simply from some natural (or unnatural) wellspring of desire. Now media images are assumed to be capable of the seduction once attributed to the individual pervert. The challenge of cultural representation is that it humanizes by individualizing, making the gay experience less abstract and more mundane. Such representations undermine the purpose of the act: to project the premodern image of the homosexual as the sinister Other and to protect childhood innocence from its own desires.

CHILD ABUSE AS MORAL PANIC

It is the yoking of these apparently oppositional images—of childhood innocence and worldly dissipation—that fuels the ultimate moral panic, about sexual abuse of the child. The escalating concern about child abuse is evidenced by multiple day care scandals, stringent new hiring regulations in educational settings, and a rash of legislation requiring recently released sex offenders to register and make public their place of residence. Entire sections in bookstores are now devoted to books on prevention strategies, after-the-fact therapeutic interventions, and popular accounts of abuse suffered in childhood, often repressed or denied, now described in discomfiting detail (Tavris, 1993).

Tracing the history of family violence from its "discovery" in the last half of the nineteenth century to its "rediscovery" during the 1960s, Gordon (1988) places our current preoccupations in context: family violence was originally defined as cruelty to children requiring the charitable efforts of child savers; subsequently it was transformed into a problem of child neglect needing the intervention of professional social workers, or a medical crisis requiring a physician's diagnosis and treatment. Young people suffer more often from ambiguous forms of neglect than from direct assault. The waxing and waning of interest in the topic reflects pervasive anxieties about the health of the family; violence is frequently the result of power arrangements within a given relationship. Best (1990) describes the recent focus on abuse in terms of a broad spectrum of threats to childhood that began to emerge in the late 1960s: child pornography, satanic cults, adolescent prostitution, runaways, missing children. The fears for our own children, natural symbols of the future, were a projection of a more general anxiety about the future of society sparked by the

civil rights movement, the Vietnam war, and Watergate. We identified with the child's vulnerability and marked the abusive parent, the sexual pervert, and the pathological day care worker as
scapegoats, allowing us to avoid considering such intractable issues as poverty, health, and education. This served as a spring-
board for congressional hearings and political rhetoric on the
subject of "our most valuable resource."

In spite of the public debates, little was done to effect the
programmatic changes that would actually make this a safer
world for children. The publicity functioned to distract us from
the difficult reality that the vast majority of abuse—93 percent
of reported incidents—is perpetrated by an adult who is familiar
to the child (Laumann et al., 1994). Jenny, Roesler, and Poyer
(1994) found that 82 percent of accused abusers are in a heterosexual relationship with a female relative of the abused child, and
the chance of a child's identifying a gay man or lesbian as the
abuser is 0 to 3.1 percent, well within the current estimates of
homosexuality in the general community. Most abuse takes place
in the home, with fewer than 1 percent of the reported cases
involving school personnel (Nowesnick, 1993).

But child abuse panics reflect more than a projection of social
anxieties onto the fate of children. They also instruct us about the
line between licit and illicit behavior, which reinforces the family
as the locus of safety, the place where appropriate desires are
shaped by two loving, heterosexual parents. The lesson is clear:
legitimate desires are not sexual desires, sanctioned emotions do
not include jealousy or anger. Erotic attachments to children,
erotic attachments of children, must not be admitted, or must be
admitted only in the presence of a trained professional or for the
purposes of control and abnegation. Abuse is the result of abnormal development, development that can be regulated through the
caring instruction of the family circle. By heightening a focus on
individual pathology and the role of parents in producing acceptable psychological characteristics, the moral panic diverts us from

the intense emotional fabric of the isolated nuclear family in which the overwhelming majority of abusive situations originate.

The child abuse panic uses the outsider, the deviant, to highlight the normative ideal. The ideology of the innocent child, developing free from adult interference but always under close protective surveillance, is punctured most radically by the image of the intrusive adult deviant. The menacing adult underscores the defenselessness of the child. Media stories frequently refer to the potential dangers of the unknown adult, even though most crimes against children are perpetrated by people they know.

Kitzinger (1990), analyzing newspaper accounts of child abuse, documents its depiction as an attack on childhood itself rather than as a crime against individuals. Abuse is seen as the theft of innocence, and who knows more about this form of theft, the initiation of the young into the world of erotic desire, than the homosexual? Homosexuals are seen as placing themselves outside the traditional family and reproductive cycle, without respect for the age-related boundaries defining the law of succession. Kitzinger argues that our assumptions about childhood innocence, passivity, and vulnerability help to perpetuate child abuse and are part of the political process through which children are made an oppressed group. Placing the phenomenon of abuse in this context, she advocates a deconstruction of childhood as we know it so as to clarify the way that power circulates among adults and children and to recognize the forms of active resistance through which children defy their oppression and fend off abusive adults.

Moral panics are not just a conservative resistance to professionalized early care. Rather, they are part of a larger compulsion to control and rewrite sexuality in a way that distances adults from children and alienates us all from questions of sexual desire. Describing the sexual aversion-displacements that have intensified with the HIV epidemic, Bersani (1988) confirms that these have been realized through heightened images of the innocent child and the seductive pedophile: "Adult sexuality is split in two: at once redeemed by its retroactive metamorphosis into the purity of an asexual childhood, and yet preserved in its most sinister forms by being projected onto the image of the criminal seducer of children. 'Purity' is crucial here: behind the brutalities against gays, against women, and, in the denial of their very nature and autonomy, against children lies the pastoralizing, the idealizing, the redemptive project. . . . More exactly, the brutality is identical to the idealization" (p. 221).

KEEPING THE STORY ALIVE

In his explication of Victorian fiction and scientific treatises, Kincaid (1992) helps us to see that the figure of the sinister, corrupting pedophile, created through hysterical talk of child pornography and prostitution, incest and mysterious abductions, is an inevitable byproduct of the pure and fragile child of our imagination:

> If the child is desirable, then to desire it can hardly be freakish. To maintain otherwise is to put into operation pretty hefty engines of denial and self-deception. And that is what we have done. By insisting so loudly on the innocence, purity and asexuality of the child, we have created a subversive echo: experience, corruption, eroticism. More than that, by attributing to the child the central features of desirability in our culture—purity, innocence, emptiness, Otherness—we have made absolutely essential figures who would [make] this desire [possible]. Such figures are certainly not us, we insist, insist so violently because we must, so violently that we come to think that what we are is what these figures are not. (p. 4)

The pedophile, whom we demonize even as we construct, marginalize as we normalize, distance as we bring closer, has become a primary vehicle for expressing/repressing our own erotic interests in children. The innocent child is always ignorant, empty of knowledge, in need of protection: the perfect receptacle for the adult's imaginings. The child-pedophile dyad emerges from the Foucaultian strategy of highlighting the normal through the abnormal, reading the text by deciphering the barely legible notes in the margins. The intensity with which we pursue the pedophile, the campaign to root out evil, tells the story of our own desires, not of a subversive sexuality located in others.

In our overzealous attempts to protect children, we deny their sexuality and their agency. Focusing on the corrupting power of the pedophile allows us to enjoy the role of defending the hapless child. Kitzinger (1990) suggests that we would be more effective advocates for children if we empowered them to come to their own defense, to realize their own strategies and skills of protection—if we saw them as strong rather than as weak, sexual rather than without desire.

The nineteenth-century interest in pedophilia was expressed in literary and scientific texts; today our desires are performed in a variety of venues, including movies, television, schools, athletic fields, playgrounds, day care centers, and courtrooms. It is in this last setting that James Kincaid patiently situated himself, as a recorder and witness to the McMartin preschool case, the longest court trial in U.S. history. The case originated in more than two hundred counts of child molestation involving forty-two children, four members of the family that ran the school, and three additional teachers. After exhaustively reviewing the history of the improbable—at times fantastic and salacious—accusations, Kincaid (1992) concludes that the trial could not be construed as a search for truth or closure; rather, it gave the public what it thirsts for—new narratives of childhood innocence and its violation. It is the strength of our denial, the eight-year duration of the trial itself, that signals our desire: "We keep the story alive and before us, being told over and over. At the same time, we find ways to deny emphatically that we are authoring this story, much less serving as its leading players. By creating Gothic melodramas, monster stories of child-molesting, and playing them out periodically (often), we provide not just titillation but assurances of righteousness. Demonizing the child-molester . . . we can connect to a pedophile drama while pretending to shut down the theater" (p. 341).

The dichotomy of the innocent child and the predatory adult seems to be about age, not gender. But although the gender of the object of desire is a matter of relative indifference (the delicate, vulnerable child is desexed), the desiring subject is inevitably imagined as male, reflecting the ongoing association of sex with social power. But from the perspective of homosexual stereotypes rather than pedophilia per se, the belief in the older man preying on the younger boy continues. In fact, with a wider public acceptance of homosexual relationships among adults, a conservative minority would intensify the association of pedophilia with homosexuality, rekindling homophobic attitudes and reinforcing prohibitions against men caring for young children (King, 1995).

Educational Pederasty

Ironically, in classical cultures the prototypic and only sanctioned sexual relationship between men celebrates differences in age. The pederastic model encourages the older partner, the one who is presumed to know and to be able to act, to fill the younger, passive partner with his own desire. The youth, who is without intentionality, is made a desiring and knowledgeable adult when penetrated by wisdom and age. The teacher is a unique phallic presence; students are many empty receptacles.

But have our biblical morality, laws of consent, and new psychosexual categories proscribed the pederastic relationship, or has it become so fundamental to our way of socializing children that we have lost sight of its pervasive presence? Have we been so blinded by the preponderance of female teachers in the early grades that we cannot see the degree to which our classrooms, with their didactic teaching methods, preplanned curricula, and high teacher/pupil ratios, replicate ancient pedagogical models? Perhaps this is not a matter of blindness. After all, contemporary educational critics have been eager to point out the passive role assigned to students in our schools, the assumption that the adult must motivate the child, and the focus on quantitative rather than qualitative assessments of progress. They have also signaled their preference for less personally threatening metaphors to be extracted from the economic arena. Freire (1970), for example, has condemned traditional educational dynamics as reflecting a banking model of teaching and learning. But such talk sanitizes the pedagogical discourse, transforming the sexual economics of adult/child interactions into the political economics of capital accumulation. Although both models have only one source of knowledge/desire and multiple accounts into which it may be placed, it would be a mistake to assume that they are the same.

What the banking model does not allow us to talk about, and the pederastic model forces us to grapple with, are the assumptions of innocence or guilt, protection and control that form the boundaries of the childhood closet. With our gaze and our theories of childhood we enclose children in a space not so very different from the closet of the homosexual. As we have seen, the naming of the homosexual and the medical discourse it engendered sprang from the same source as the psychologized child and the proliferation of developmental specialists. Both are part of the nineteenth-century attempt to assert order in a world of unmanageable complexity and disorder. Children and homosexuals have come to occupy the same space. For although desire itself might best be described as emergent—neither homosexual nor heterosexual by design, its components discernible only after the fact—only the homosexual is described in the psychiatric literature as caught in a matrix of unresolved fixations, preoedipal fantasies, and undifferentiated desires that have been unsatisfactorily repressed. By failing to accomplish the work of the oedipal stage, the homosexual fails to achieve the socially sanctioned level of genital sexuality that leads to a heterosexual orientation. As one who does not reproduce, who lives outside the generative family, who subverts his/her own family drama, the homosexual does not know the law of succession.

Until the symbolic order asserts itself through the social organization of phallic desire, the child's polymorphous perversity is greeted with varying degrees of anxiety and control on the part of the adult. But once past childhood, any indications of homosexual desire, literally and figuratively represented by an interest in seeking pleasure from the anus, an organ associated with waste and preoedipal erotic satisfactions, are not tolerated. For the anus has been characterized in our phallocentric world as private, interiorized, and therefore antisocial (Hocquenghem, 1978). As it poses the possibility of multiple sites of pleasure and organizing principles, anal eroticism threatens our entire system of binary oppositions: male/female, adult/child, heterosexual/homosexual. The possibility of homosexual desire, of the expression of childhood's polymorphous perversity, undercuts the edifice on which our reproductive arrangements have been built, in turn threatening the gendered nature of our economic system.

Perhaps it is not surprising that a culture that works so hard to believe that children are innocent, devoid of the corrupting desires of sexuality once past the oedipal crisis, would balk at confronting the measured but relentless way in which children are objectified in schools, filled with the desires of others. Even as we try to protect our children from the touch of strangers, judgments of professionals, and social ills that they are presumed to be unable to manage, we readily place them in institutions that cripple their sense of agency. We are quick to substitute the canonical knowledge of teacher and text for their vernacular knowledge of the domestic world. To treat the student as a knowing subject is to subvert the traditional notion of pedagogical authority, throwing into question the phallic economy of the classroom on which it is based. A multiplicity of desiring actors suggests that there are multiple zones from which to receive satisfaction and toward which to direct one's attention. By legitimizing the engagement of

students with one another, we promote a return to a polymorphous perversity in which pleasure/knowledge potentially ema-
nates from and circulates among all the actors in the classroom
drama.

UNCOUPLING THE PERVERT-CHILD PAIR

All of our research projects, publications, and cyberspace com-
munications attest to one reality: we continue to live under the
petition to know. This is a petition that decrees the power of the
visible over the invisible, the spoken over the unspoken, the
image over the unrepresented. With our computers and cam-
corders we survey the educational terrain, seeking to explore
uncharted regions in our maps of knowledge. Inevitably we have
become part of a larger social debate about representation. While
political conservatives seek to ban the images of offending individuals or groups, progressives promote the visibility of the oppressed as a means of bringing about their fuller participation in
society.

But both conservative and progressive strategies may be naive
and simplistic (Phelan, 1993). Like the past, which determines
how we experience the present, and the silences, which mark
what can be said, the terrain of the invisible marks what can be
seen. As a culture we have inflated the power of the visible, as-
sociating it with notions of masculine sexual privilege (Owens,
1992). The visible and invisible are best understood as part of the
same regime of truth rather than as binary opposites, aspects of
the same knowing ignorance that shapes our social world. Visibility can be a trap leading to new forms of surveillance, fetishism, voyeurism, and violence. Images of minority groups are
seldom controlled by those they depict. As commodities to be
sold and purchased in the interest of capital accumulation, images reflect what their creators desire to see and what viewers
need to see in order to assure their own identity. Identity is always
relational.

The novelist Toni Morrison maintains that descriptions of minority experiences by mainstream researchers and artists are too often judged to be failed attempts to capture the Other. She would view them, rather, as successful constructions of a "serviceable other"—serviceable to the dominant group because it highlights the qualities it values/devalues, desires/eschews, admires/fears. Thus whites define their identity through their portrayals of the African-American. "Africanism is the vehicle by which the American self knows itself as not enslaved, but free; not repulsive, but desirable; not helpless, but licensed and powerful; not history-less, but historical; not damned, but innocent; not a blind accident of evolution, but a progressive fulfillment of destiny" (Morrison, 1992, p. 52).

The concept of the serviceable other has been used to deconstruct images of non-Western peoples, women, and wartime enemies (Sampson, 1993). The pervert and the child may be added to this list, the survival of each ensured through the link to the other. These representations are part of the discursive politics that construct reality. Like most stereotypes, they resist correction through the testimony of science or rational argument because they reflect not the absence of accurate information so much as fundamental ways of interpreting experience.

Deconstructing the serviceable other is not about finding a truth or unmasking false consciousness but rather about reversing the inequitable distribution of power that facilitates the publication of distorted images. The corrective is not to make "the truth" visible but to alter the process through which one group comes to dominate the production and distribution of images that ensure its hegemony. While homophobic legislators have recognized the power of images to shift attitudes through their attempts to control them, lesbians and gay men have only begun to use public representations to their own advantage. Central to this project should be images of our lives as parents, caregivers, and educators—gay people caring and providing for the next generation. Early childhood educators must join in this effort by making educational settings comfortable for gay and lesbian staff and families.

The road to combating moral panics, uncoupling the child-pervert pair, begins with knowing about the importance of touch in early care settings and about the new limitations being placed on practitioners by panicked administrators (see Johnson, Chapter 3). It is incumbent on professionals in the field to speak out. We witness the daily impact of "no touch" policies on the quality of care, the defection of skilled practitioners, and the wasteful expenditure of funds on ineffective prevention curricula. Pedagogy is political and our silences are performative speech acts confirming the status quo.

James King's talks with male teachers (Chapter 8) demonstrate how, in the atmosphere of moral panic, the potential for homosexual accusations affects us all. When possible, it is important for gay and lesbian teachers to be open about their sexual orientation. The immediate goal is to improve their professional lives by allowing them to be more fully present to both their students and their colleagues. Accounts of teachers claiming their gay and lesbian identities within the classroom document the power and pedagogical transformation these radical acts make possible (Garber, 1994; Jennings, 1994). Unfortunately, too many reports in the social science literature also describe the costs of identity-management strategies—self-hatred, nonacceptance, frustration, isolation—among gay teachers (Bensimon, 1992; Harbeck and Woods, 1992). Many judge the practical consequences of a public gay identity to be more negative than positive. Often living in a glass closet, they seek a balance between maintaining a sense of personal integrity and concealing just enough so as not to provoke the hostility of the heterosexual world (Khayatt, 1992).

The long-range goal of coming out is to combat the prevalent stereotypes of gay people and the popular confusions about homosexuality, pedophilia, and child abuse. Making the workplace comfortable for gays and lesbians is everyone's responsibility and to everyone's benefit. Openness is part of establishing an environment that is appreciative of differences. As gay people come out, the threat of blackmail will diminish, encouraging more males to seek employment in this predominately female field.

The growing literature on sexual abuse and its prevention marks the absence of positive research on childhood sexuality. Here, too, educators must actively resist negative messages and promote more open discussions about the body and its pleasures. It is not childhood sexuality that is problematic but adult denials. In his introduction to this book Joseph Tobin enjoins us to examine teacher education curricula for the way they facilitate or foreclose frank discussions of childhood sexuality.

Given the current politics of representation and the history of schooling, it is difficult to move quickly to enshrine a pedagogy of pleasure and desire. I am only too well aware of the increased opportunities for subtle forms of social control presented by an ever-expanding curriculum (Bernstein, 1975; Sharp and Green, 1975). Yet we must attend to feminists who highlight the absence of the body in curricular discourse (Grumet, 1988; Pagano, 1990). Valuing distanced, abstract, and fragmented ways of knowing over the immediate, concrete, and literal, the contemporary school is hardly welcoming to the physically active and knowledgeable children it is supposed to accommodate. Equally fractured and fragmented, our relationships with children deny the lived experiences that have brought us together in the classroom.

When the school is imagined as an erotically barren landscape filled with sexually ignorant children, desire is easily located in the pervert lurking at the playground gates, and sex education is reduced to strategies for protecting the privatized body from the prying touch of strangers. Although schools cannot change a sexphobic society, they can place questions of the body in the context of a curriculum that values multiple ways of knowing the world. And moral panics can be seen for what they are, obsessions with our own repressed sexuality.

REFERENCES

Bensimon, E. M. (1992). Lesbian existence and the challenge to normative constructions of the academy. *Journal of Education* 174 (3): 98–114.

Bernstein, B. (1975). *Class, codes, and control.* Vol. 3. London: Routledge and Kegan Paul.

Bersani, L. (1988). Is the rectum a grave? In D. Crimp (ed.), *AIDS: Cultural analysis/cultural activism* (pp. 197–222). Cambridge: MIT Press.

Best, J. (1990). *Threatened children: Rhetoric and concern about child-victims.* Chicago: University of Chicago Press.

Foucault, M. (1978). *The history of sexuality.* Vol. 1, *An introduction.* New York: Pantheon.

Freire, P. (1970). *The pedagogy of the oppressed.* (Trans. M. Ramos.) New York: Continuum.

Garber, L. (ed.) (1994). *Tilting the tower.* New York: Routledge.

Gordon, L. (1988). *Heroes of their own lives: The politics of family violence.* New York: Penguin.

Grumet, M. (1988). *Bitter milk.* Amherst: University of Massachusetts Press.

Halperin, D. (1990). *One hundred years of homosexuality.* New York: Routledge.

Harbeck, K., and Woods, S. (1992). Living in two worlds. In K. Harbeck (ed.), *Coming out of the classroom closet* (pp. 247–261). New York: Haworth.

Hirschfeld, M. (1946). *Sexual anomalies and perversions.* London: Torch.

Hocquenghem, G. (1978). *Homosexual desire.* London: Allison and Busby.

Jennings, K. (ed.) (1994). *One teacher in ten: Gay and lesbian educators tell their stories.* Boston: Alyson.

Jenny, C., Roesler, T. A., and Poyer, K. L. (1994). Are children at risk for sexual abuse by homosexuals? *Pediatrics* 94 (1): 41–44.

Kennedy, H. (1988). *Ulrichs: The life and works of Karl Heinrich Ulrichs.* Boston: Alyson.

Khayatt, M. D. (1992). *Lesbian teachers: An invisible presence.* Albany: SUNY Press.

Kincaid, J. R. (1992). *Child-loving: The erotic child and Victorian culture.* New York: Routledge.

King, J. (1995). Masculinities, children, and care: Feminist and queer readings of gay primary teachers. Paper presented at the Annual Meeting of the American Educational Research Association, San Francisco.

Kitzinger, J. (1990). Who are you kidding? Children, power, and the struggle against sexual abuse. In A. James and A. Prout (eds.), *Constructing and reconstructing childhood: Contemporary issues in the sociological study of childhood* (pp. 157–183). New York: Falmer.

Krafft-Ebing, R. (1931). *Psychopathia sexualis*. New York: Physicians and Surgeons Book.

Laumann, E. O., et al. (1994). *The social organization of sexuality: Sexual practices in the United States*. Chicago: University of Chicago Press.

Mohr, R. D. (1992). *Gay ideas: Outing and other controversies*. Boston: Beacon.

Morrison, T. (1992). *Playing in the dark: Whiteness and the literary imagination*. Cambridge: Harvard University Press.

Nowesnick, M. (1993). Shattered lives. *American School Board Journal* 180: 14–19.

Owens, C. (1992). The discourse of others: Feminists and postmodernism. In C. Jencks (ed.), *The post-modern reader* (pp. 333–348). New York: St. Martin's.

Pagano, J. (1990). *Exiles and communities: Teaching in the patriarchial wilderness*. Albany: SUNY Press.

Phelan, P. (1993). *Unmarked: The politics of performance*. New York: Routledge.

Sampson, E. E. (1993). Identity politics: Challenges to psychology's understanding. *American Psychologist* 48 (12): 1219–1230.

Sharp, R., and Green, A. (1975). *Education and social control: A study in progressive education*. London: Routledge.

Takanishi, R. (1978). Childhood as a social issue: Historical roots of contemporary advocacy movements. *Journal of Social Issues* 34 (2): 8–28.

Tavris, C. (1993). Beware the incest-survivor machine. *New York Times Book Review,* Jan. 3, pp. 1, 16–17.

Waller, W. (1932). *The sociology of teaching*. New York: Russell and Russell.

Watney, S. (1991). School's out. In D. Fuss (ed.), *Inside/out: Lesbian theories, gay theories* (pp. 387–401). New York: Routledge.

EIGHT

Keeping It Quiet
Gay Teachers in the Primary Grades

James R. King

In the sixth grade, I sang a solo with the men's choir at Christmas midnight Mass. The experience brought me as close to perfect happiness as I could imagine at that time. In the mirror above us I could see the men's choir huddled behind me, nodding approval. Mr. Kane, the choir director and my fifth- and sixth-grade teacher, had selected me to sing a falsetto solo. For two years, I had doggedly followed Mr. Kane, eager to provide any help he might need, supply any voice he desired. He was the teacher I chose to become.

Later, I became a teacher of sixth-graders and the roles were reversed. One of my students, Anton, followed me doggedly, eager to fill my needs before I knew I had them. As a gay man, afraid to recognize Anton's desire and afraid of my own sexuality, I was unable to accept his affection as gracefully as Mr. Kane had my puppy love. When other students recognized my discomfort with Anton's advances, they tortured him as a "teacher's pet wannabe," and I did not intervene. Eventually, he found his bearings and joined the torturers. I was relieved and now wonder about how I might have received Anton differently, more productively.

Last semester, I came out to my undergraduate elementary education majors. Janet had just finished a first draft of a paper and volunteered to read it aloud to the class. She wrote of her pain and embarrassment when her former fiancé broke off their engagement at the last minute. Now they are friends. They cry together, study together. She loves him because he is like her, sensitive. She suspects that he is struggling with his sexual orientation and wonders what it will mean to her, about her, if "he turns out to be gay." Janet looked up to my eyes and stopped. Her eyes widened and she quickly looked away. "Not that there's anything wrong with being gay or anything. . . . Oh, you know . . . I didn't mean . . . I mean, it's OK if you're . . . " I monitored the tenseness in my facial tissue, the narrowness of my eye openings, and decided to enter the swirl of confusion. With my peripheral vision I could see heads swiveling from Janet to me, back to Janet. I heard laughter at what seemed a sincere and embarrassing moment. Janet covered her face and said, "Oh, God!"

I did not laugh. I tried to keep my eyes gently with Janet's, out of respect, out of care for her, and out of fear of the crowd. "You really still care about your ex. It sounds like you two are still good friends. Now that you two aren't going to be married, why would it make a difference to you if he is gay?"

Janet wondered what it would mean if she had been sexually attracted to—willing to marry—a man who was a homosexual. At this point, I realized I could no longer be a detached teacher and counselor. "I'm a gay man, and I was married to a woman for seventeen years." The class became very quiet. "You've heard me talk about my ex-wife and I've also mentioned my partner, though without revealing his name or gender. I think we all have the capacity for affection and love. And we all have an overarching orientation toward our sexual desire. But you all know, and I know, that these categories and behaviors that get labeled by others are never absolutes. The behavior is the behavior, nothing more. How can your warm feelings for your ex-fiancé be anything but good? Linda, my ex-wife, and I have learned to be very good, close friends since our divorce. I still see my 'second family,' go to their graduations, weddings, and funerals, and my partner, Richard, understands my need to do so. In fact, he does the same with his ex-wife and her new husband."

At this point, I pulled back. I remembered the risk of seeming to promote "the homosexual lifestyle" with my class. I framed my retreat in terms of "too much to do and too little time." So we went back to work. Later, in the students' written evaluations of this course, I learned that many had perceived my mention of my sexual orientation as inappropriate.

These vignettes from my experiences in education have several themes. First, they are about homosocial relations between students and their teachers. Opening up pedagogical relations to sexually informed fields of knowledge is powerful. I maintain that to engage with students, any students, as an openly gay man and to name that stance is to engage in homosocial teaching relationships. My teeth clench, my pulse races, and my throat constricts when I reexamine these memories.

Second, to use a queer perspective to understand a homophobic context is to set up conflict. Once the relations are opened, various overlapping and conflicting frames of meaning rush in to fill up the space. Is it ethical to reinterpret previously lived experience from a homosexual perspective (a queer reread)? What would have been an effective teaching solution? Am I pursuing a lifestyle agenda?

Third, the use of silence as a denial/power perspective is common in classrooms. Yet refusing to reopen interpretation to issues of desire and homosexuality is denial. In my acts of denial as part of my teaching, I shunt my person, my desires, and my profession to some other location, some safe place of pristine teachers who never marry and therefore never have sex. Gay teachers are the ones who spend all day teaching from one closet only to be symbolically filed away into another at the end of the day.

Fourth, the notion that primary teaching contexts are havens for sexual silence merits reexamination. Is this assumption true for all teachers of young children? How is it that my sexual orientation as a primary teacher is so important to others when I've never been sexual at my worksite? Or have I? Is being a homosexual being sexual? Or is it only the case if I "act like a homosexual"?

I gradually have come to understand how the cultural constructions of desire, sexuality, masculinity, and teaching combine to police how I act and how I am perceived in the classroom. As a gay man, a primary teacher, and a professor of education, I find this a sobering realization. I want now to use a critique of these cultural constructions to expose the horrible accusations unjustly unleashed on gay men who work successfully with young children.

Can We Talk (About Sex)?

The answer is no. Not in schools. And especially not in the primary grades. And don't even think about sex if you happen to be gay. It is not surprising that talk about males, sexuality, and children is, if not altogether absent, mostly whispered. It is uttered behind fans of fingers, under windshield-wiper eyes. We know with our bodies that this talk can end careers and send people to jail, not just make for a juicy story. Michelle Fine's essay "Silencing in Public Schools" (1987) suggests that silence "permeate[s] classroom life so primitively as to make irrelevant the lived experiences, passions, concerns, communities, and biographies of low-income, minority students" (p. 158). "Primitively"—a root characteristic, deep seated, and immutable. It is precisely to mute passion and to reduce the relevance of our lives outside of the classroom that silence becomes so necessary to schools. Silence is also effectively deployed to control teachers' lives both inside and outside of school. Teachers and students enter a no-talk zone, where our passions are inappropriate. Yet we are encouraged to be passionate about the education of our students. So passion, like silence, is selective and ambiguous. The ambiguity is contained by our silences. But silence that denotes absence can never fulfill its mission. A vacuum violates nature; when nothing is said, our desires, our passions fester. In effect, our silence acknowledges the expectation that our desires will, can, and do become manifest in schools.

Psychoanalysts call this need to locate our desire outside our selves projective identification. As Denis Carpy (1989) writes, "Projective identification is a primitive phenomenon and can therefore only involve very powerful feelings which are only able to be dealt with in this way because the patient is unable to put them in words" (p. 287). That projective identifications are characteristic of erotic transferences makes them tougher to explore. Harriet Wrye and Judith Welles (1994) contend that the "erotic component can be the last [one] of which the patient, the therapist, or the supervisor becomes aware" (p. 68). The silencing of teachers' sexual desires, therefore, can lead to distortions and compromise formations of those desires. What we silence and transfer comes back to us in an exoticized, commodified form. Locating desire for children within gay men hypersexualizes homosexuality and desexualizes teachers. It is an exchange that ill serves both parties.

While a "culture of desire" (Browning, 1993) has opened some space for gay men, it has its costs. As Eugene Goodheart (1991) suggests, the modern insistence upon essentializing sexuality as the purest form of human energy has turned sex into tyranny. To align a cultural movement along a continuum of desire, as Browning has done with contemporary gay culture, is to imprison it.

Of course, transferring desire onto someone else does not quench it. Desire flourishes in displacement. Projecting teachers' desires onto gay men may hide the strength of teachers' attachments to children, but does not diminish it. The desire that is now located in gay men still operates within the teacher. What began as a teacher's attachment to children, an attachment that is potentially productive and healthy, is transferred to some Other, a site of constructed pathology.

But there are other ways to interpret the intentions and purposes behind silenced discourses of desire. Silence can be the language of denial. Arguing from Lacan, Valerie Walkerdine (1990) suggests that in silence and denial about what is different, we find our own desires. Denial makes the production of desire possible (p. 45). This appears to be a double bind. First, desire (sexuality) is the thing that cannot be discussed. Yet the denial of desire is the very production of it. When we establish difference—what is not part of us—that constructed difference assumes the potential, if not the intent, for exoticism; that is an occasion for our desire. According to Walkerdine, it is the simultaneous denial of desire and denial of self, in contrast with the production of desire in the service of the "developing child," that makes teaching an irrational project. While gay men and sexual orientation in general would seem to be minor ingredients in such a salty soup, a wider look at women's desire may suggest otherwise.

Judith Butler (1990) argues against the Lacanian notion that women's experience and especially their sexualities are framed by their performance (masquerade) of what the man is not. In order to instantiate (for the male) what it means to be a male, women perform "not male" to define men's masculinity. "The 'masquerade' is what women do to participate in man's desire, but at the cost of giving up their own" (p. 47). But such a "masquerade" perspective, Butler argues, also opens the possibility for a preperformative female sexuality, or at the least relegates Lacanian notions of women's gender performance to a "parodic (de)-construction" of men's desire. Both Walkerdine's direct description of women's self-displacement in teaching and Butler's arguments for sexual displacement have implications for men's participation in women's teaching space.

The systematic displacement of desire and of self is basic to both the construction of teaching and the construction and maintenance of beliefs about the culture in which teaching is embedded. Thus, enacting the role of elementary teacher may be a different experience for males than for females, even when the behaviors and intentions behind them appear to be identical.

TEACHING IS WOMEN'S WORK

For many, teaching young children is an act of caring. Asked why they chose to become elementary teachers, my undergraduates (almost all of them female) tell me that they just love kids and want to help them. This is a good place to start. But, of course, it is not enough. Or is it? In her interviews with British elementary teachers, Jennifer Nais (1989) found that a common discursive marker was teachers' talk about care and caring for children. These teachers used care to contextualize discipline, curriculum, and professional relations. Similarly, Nel Noddings (1984, 1992) offers caring as a root metaphor for teaching. Care orientation as a way of constructing moral approaches to education is not only encouraged but required by Noddings. She characterizes the professional moves of caring teachers as those that are centered on students, the ones cared for. "When a teacher asks a question in class and a student responds, the teacher receives not just the 'response' but the student" (1984, p. 176). The intent of the response is less important than the psychological engagement between student and teacher.

This is powerful stuff. The use of questioning is a frame within which to connect with students. Teachers are expected to conceptualize these interactions as a complex mix of teacher and student contributions. According to Noddings, a teacher accomplishes his or her focus on a student by being "totally and *nonselectively* present to the student, each student, as he [she] addresses" the teacher (p. 180, emphasis mine). Presumably, teachers are totally available for these moments of connection with their students. Offering one's self nonselectively to each and every student on an individual basis presupposes that teachers have constructed a close, caring relationship with each of their students. It also suggests that teachers are aware of and comfortable with elements of their self-knowledge. "Being there" includes empathic identification with students who need their teacher. Helpful, caring relationships are what guide a "being there" teacher.

While Noddings (1984) acknowledges that men can and do care for others, she believes that the performance of caring comes more naturally to women. In fact, both Nais and Noddings offer descriptions of teaching that parallel Carol Gilligan's (1982) theorizing about women's morality as "connected caring." Women, according to Gilligan, base their moral decisions on an ethic of care, which is grounded in their relationships, remains connected to others, and is sustained by unique processes of communication. These rich, layered relationships also can lead to "a sense of vulnerability that impedes . . . women from taking a stand . . . [a] 'susceptibility' to adverse judgment by others which stems from their lack of power" (p. 66). Gilligan's analysis exposes the underlying effects of marginalizing women's meanings, lives, and language. She characterizes women as "drifting along and riding it out," caught in an opposition between selflessness and responsibility. "Describing a life lived in response, guided by the perception of others' needs, they can see no way of exercising control without risking an assertion that seems selfish and hence morally dangerous" (p. 143). Being connected to the lives of others through relationships, through caring, concomitantly requires the suppression of teachers' personal needs and desires.

If teaching is defined as caring for children, and caring is a woman's way of knowing and being, what does this say about men teaching young children? There are few males in early education. This has led some educators, like Kevin Seifert (1985, 1986, 1988), to argue that we need to recruit more men into primary teaching. According to this argument, men teachers are desirable for children without fathers, as role models of caring and as nurturing male figures. It is unclear what kind of male is desirable for young children. A nurturing, soft-spoken, and caring male may not be the kind of male role model some parents want. In contrast, Noddings calls for teachers—male or female—to embody traditionally feminine rather than traditionally masculine traits. In either case, teaching in caring ways is something that males *can* do. It is less clear, however, that caring teaching is valued when it is enacted by men.

For some, then, teaching children during their early years is isomorphic with caring. Yet to be the one caring involves some personal cost. For Walkerdine (1990), the teacher-mother functions as the container of irrationality. As a primary grade teacher instantiates social control into the minds of young children, she also shunts her own person out of the picture to make way for the "developing child." Like the worker bee who cleans and feeds the larvae, teachers exist to serve children's needs. But these needs are not desires. For an innocent child to have desire is unthinkable. Similarly, teachers constructed in this Victorian classroom mold can have no desire. In fact, Erica McWilliam (1995) has argued that teachers have been severed from their bodies. Without bodies, without desire, teachers can be frozen in a revered state, put in the cloakroom at the end of the school day, and obliged to stay single, or stay childless, or stay home when they are visibly pregnant.

In her analysis of Samuel Johnson's writings on morality and imagination, Patricia Spacks (1990) suggests that for Johnson "desire's power, derived from the dangerous prevalence of imagination, depends on the human tendency to project into the future. To resist the power of the imagined future almost exceeds human capacity" (p. 19). For Dr. Johnson, desire (regardless of its object) must be governed and resisted. Desire is part of nature, which is base and in need of regulation. The eighteenth- and nineteenth-century models of virginal, asexual teachers have been superseded by modernist versions of woman and teacher. Yet we have not fully rejected the notion of teachers as disembodied, desexualized care providers.

The pressures for teachers to be asexual and to defer to men and children are strong in elementary education. Caring as a way of being for females has been criticized for reproducing Kohlberg's male/female moral reasoning hierarchy and essentializing females' character traits (Code, 1991; Broughton, 1983). Joan Tronto (1993) describes care as a morality born of subordination. Teachers, especially teachers of young children, care, but not about themselves. They are passionate, but only about children's lives. They make themselves into vessels for children's lives by emptying themselves of desire. We may know individual teachers to be self-protective and self-indulgent, but the disembodied, idealized teacher defers her desire to make room for the emerging child.

The elementary teacher—always presumed to be female—is praised for that deferral. But such selfless behavior is systematically devalued in a sexist, patriarchal culture. Because "care" is axiomatic with elementary teaching, and because it is believed to be "natural" for females, the work is seen as unskilled and genetic rather than technical and learned. With "care" located within constructions of femininity, men are simultaneously constructed as "at-risk" for providing care. We are at-risk because we are not female, and therefore cannot be caring, or because we cannot be caring without being sexual, or because if we can be caring without being sexual, we upset the economy that entraps female teachers in an early education sweatshop. If care is naturally female, then work differentiation based on care, which is necessary for lowering the prestige and value of women's work (Reskin, 1991), is a "naturally occurring" phenomenon. If men claim that they also care, they risk identifying themselves as "unnatural." Some men *are* recognized for their abilities to care. With careers in caring, these men constitute a threat to gendered work differentiation. To better understand how and why men are dissuaded from this border crossing, it is productive to view masculinity as an intrusion into a female context.

GAY MALE TEACHERS AND WORK DIFFERENTIATION

Gay men are being used to keep all men out of early childhood education. Even while many gay males are providing rich, moral, appropriate classroom experiences for young children, their identities as constructed by others are being used to keep out other men, gay and straight. That sexual orientation is an issue at all is related to a cultural and economic use of homosexuality. Homosexuality is a relatively new construct, a twentieth-century invention created for political and economic control of people, especially men. Following the arguments of Foucault (1978) and Sedgwick (1985), Craig Owens (1992) reasons that homophobia is a ritualized mechanism of social control. He suggests that there is great utility in viewing homosexual men as outsiders or others. Given the public's perception that all men are, or should be, heterosexual, men can be manipulated by accusations of homosexuality. The success of appropriating sexual orientation as a lever for social control depends on creating and intensifying the criminality as well as the feminization of homosexuality. Such homophobic practices are most certainly oppressive to gay men, but Owens suggests that their more pervasive influences are in regulating the behavior of *all* men. "The imputing of homosexual motive to every male relationship is thus 'an immensely potent tool . . . for manipulation of every form of power that [is] refracted through the gender system—that is, in European society, of virtually every form of power' (Sedgwick [1985], pp. 88–89)," (p. 221). Homophobic social control is itself misogynistic in "feminizing" homosexuality in order to devalue it.

A quick comparison of perceptions of elementary teachers and homosexual men will point up some problematic pairings. First, elementary teachers are constructed as selfless and gay men as self-indulgent. Second, elementary teachers are seen as virginal and gay men as promiscuous and sybaritic. Third, elementary teachers are seen as nurturing and gay men as predatory. Of course, most individuals do not conform to these stereotypes. My life, for example, does not fit these gay stereotypes I have sketched. But the devastating fact is that *because* I am gay, many other people use those stereotypes as a way to see me. Returning to the discussion of difference, desire, and teachers may help to explain why.

The category "teacher," especially elementary teacher, cannot contain desire. Our historical legacy from Victorian morality, as well as the modern production of the child (Kincaid, 1992), ensure that a teacher with desire would disrupt the social mythologies of "child" and "teacher." Yet teachers, all of us, do desire, do have sexual lives, and do become passionate about more than our students' learning. Because of our society's notion of a disembodied teacher and its homophobia, gay men provide a ready vessel for our deferred desire. Gay men carry the desire that we all feel for our children.

I am not suggesting that parents or teachers want to engage sexually with children. Nor am I suggesting that men—gay or straight—desire that relationship. I am pointing out that our culture projects our sensual, erotic attachments to children onto the figure of the homosexual.

Within a homophobic stereotype, which constructs me as a self-centered, sexual predator, how can I participate in the intense social interactions that constitute the intimacy of classroom relationships? Rather than attack the social wisdom that undergirds these falsehoods, we are silent. We don't talk about sexual desire, especially the desire of a gay adult male. Our response to hiring gay and lesbian teachers has been "better safe than sorry." To push an insidious question to its absurd limits, how can we allow anyone with a history of carnal thoughts to be associated with our children, who are constructed as innocent? If our answer remains "better safe than sorry," we will have no teachers, male or female, gay or nongay.

ON THE SUITABILITY OF GAY TEACHERS

I am amazed at how much gay and lesbian teachers have in common. We all teach from a space inhabited by fear of disclosure and fear of job loss. We are all sure that most colleagues, many parents, and some children have "figured us out," but few are in our confidence. We are not "out" at work. It is the "don't ask, don't tell" of education.

When I was teaching elementary grades, I remember monitoring my interactions with other teachers. I would blush terribly at sexual innuendo and become shy when spouses were discussed. I monitored the number of geraniums I grew on the windowsill lest they give away my sexual orientation. I remember wondering if my pants were too tight, my voice too high, my hair too long, my touch too light. My teaching was filled to capacity with self-monitoring. I monitored because I knew I could not be gay. The attention I focused on self-monitoring was unavailable for more productive examination of my teaching, or indeed any focus on my students.

Progressive, child-centered education does not overtly control children. Rather, the control is located inside the learner. In child-centered pedagogy, freedom is taken to mean absence of control by the teacher. But what this celebration of freedom conceals is teachers' personal costs in moving children to self-regulation through reason and rationality. Part of the boundary or border crossing for males who enter this space is awareness of the roles that women play in the production of rationality. The suspension of desire and of self, required in the production of rationality, can be very different acts with different costs for men and women. Holding cultural capital for being male, men who teach in the primary grades may feel less vulnerable than women when making space for children's struggles with autonomy and identity. On the other hand, males, taking personal autonomy for granted, may be less able to empathize with children's autonomy and identity struggles. This argument engages gay teachers at the level of beliefs about children's constructions of power, knowledge, and relationships. Gay men who have experienced masculinity as a performance may make the shifts in perspective more easily. It is my belief that gay men who have lived the construction (and deconstruction) of gender on a daily basis are ideally positioned to understand the identity confusion and struggles of young children.

Some female teachers believe that men have an easier time controlling kids, on the assumption that male teachers are more comfortable wielding authority. Such understanding, constructed along gender lines, reinscribes power and control in male teachers and nurturing exclusively in female teachers. We need to move away from and beyond such gender binaries. Like the bilingual teacher in an ESL classroom, gay and lesbian teachers, with a foot on each side of the gender chasm, can be a productive resource for the gender work of other primary teachers. Granted, these suggestions fall under what Deborah Britzman (1992) has characterized as "unpopular discourses." But feminist educational theorists hammer home the necessity of pursuing such unpopular discourses (Barrs and Pidgeon, 1994; Christian-Smith, 1993; Gilbert, 1989; Walkerdine, 1990).

So, while I am arguing for the inclusion of gay males as elementary teachers, others reason that gay men (and lesbians) are unsuitable *because* of our sexual orientation. Some suggest that those who even *act* like homosexuals not be allowed to teach. I owe what understanding I have of children and teaching to the feminine parts of my personality. I learned these things as women do, by sitting in the kitchen, listening to stories, baby-sitting, and caring about and for others. These are good things to know. I also think my knowledge is related to my sexual orientation. I think of myself as a male who is apprenticing in feminism. I have had access to women's lives and stories in ways that are unique because I am not seen as a sexual predator. Yet this learning, which I see as uniquely queer, is not available in a public way. Maybe the covert deployment of a queer perspective keeps it a limited and valued commodity that is productive. I will know only when *what* I know and *how* I know it are no longer whispered behind a fan of fingers and told with windshield-wiper eyes.

In the final analysis, it's about the kids. Every so often, young voices, fresh perspectives, and unrehearsed knowledge disrupt my steady state. My two young neighbors recently debated the ethics and semantics of the life my partner and I share. After verifying that we shared the same house, and the same bed, four-year-old Patrick asked if we were married. Before we could answer, his brother Andrew, older by two years, stated flatly, with a first-grader's wisdom, that, "both boys," we "can't get married." Patrick considered that argument while Richard and I waited. He looked at us, smiled broadly, and turned to his older brother, who was also observing us. Patrick closed the discussion. "Oh, yes they can!" And we all went back to raking leaves.

REFERENCES

Barrs, M., and Pidgeon, S. (eds.) (1994). *Reading the difference: Gender and reading in elementary classrooms*. York, Maine: Stenhouse.

Britzman, D. (1992). Decentering discourses in teacher education: Or, the unleashing of unpopular things. In K. Weiler and C. Mitchell (eds.), *What schools can do: Critical pedagogy and practice* (pp. 151–175). Albany: SUNY Press.

Broughton, J. (1983). Women's rationality and men's virtues: A critique of gender dualism in Gilligan's theory of moral development. *Social Research* 50: 597–642.

Browning, F. (1993). *The culture of desire: Paradox and perversity in gay lives today*. New York: Crown.

Butler, J. (1990). *Gender trouble: Feminism and the subversion of identity*. New York: Routledge.

Carpy, D. (1989). Tolerating the countertransference: A mutative process. *International Journal of Psychoanalysis* 70: 287–294.

Christian-Smith, L., (ed.) (1993). *Texts of desire: Essays on fiction, femininity, and schooling*. London: Falmer.

Code, L. (1991). *What can she know? Feminist theory and the construction of knowledge*. Ithaca: Cornell University Press.

Fine, M. (1987). Silencing in public schools. *Language Arts* 64: 157–174.

Foucault, M. (1978). *The history of sexuality.* Vol. 1, *An introduction.* New York: Random House.

Gilbert, P. (1989). Personally (and passively) yours: Girls, literacy, and education. *Oxford Review of Education* 15: 257–265.

Gilligan, C. (1982). *In a different voice*. Cambridge: Harvard University Press.

Goodheart, E. (1991). *Desire and its discontents*. New York: Columbia University Press.

Kincaid, J. (1992). *Child-loving: The erotic child and Victorian culture*. New York: Routledge.

Kohlberg, L. (1981). *The philosophy of moral development*. San Francisco: Harper and Row.

McWilliam, E. (1995). Touchy subjects: Pedagogy, performativity, and sexuality in classrooms. Paper presented at the annual meeting of American Educational Research Association, San Francisco.

Nais, J. (1989). *Primary teachers talking*. New York: Routledge.

Noddings, N. (1984). *Caring: A feminine approach to ethics and moral education*. Berkeley: University of California Press.

——. (1992). *The challenge to care in schools: An alternative approach to education*. New York: Teachers College Press.

Owens, C. (1992). Outlaws: Gay men in feminism. In S. Bryson, B. Kruger, and J. Weinstock (eds.), *Beyond recognition: Representation, power, and culture* (pp. 218–255). Berkeley: University of California Press.

Reskin, B. (1991). Bring the men back in: Sex differentiation and the devaluation of women's work. In J. Lorber and S. Farrell (eds.), *The social construction of gender* (pp. 141–161). Beverly Hills, Calif.: Sage.

Sedgwick, E. (1985). *Between men: English literature and male homosocial desire*. New York: Columbia University Press.

Seifert, K. L. (1985). Career experiences of men who teach young children. *Canadian Journal of Research in Early Childhood Education* 1: 56–66.

——. (1986). The culture of early education and the preparation of male teachers. *Early Child Development and Care* 38: 69–80.

——. (1988). Men in early childhood education. In B. Spodek, O. Sarancho, and D. Peters (eds.), *Professionalism and the early childhood practitioner* (pp. 105–116). New York: Teachers College Press.

Spacks, P. (1990). *Desire and truth: Functions of plot in eighteenth-century English novels*. Chicago: University of Chicago Press.

Tronto, J. (1993). *Moral boundaries*. New York: Routledge.

Walkerdine, V. (1990). *Schoolgirl fictions*. London: Verso.

Wrye, H., and Welles, J. (1994). *The narration of desire: Erotic transference and countertransference*. Hillsdale, N.J.: Analytic Press.

Contributors

Gail Boldt is an elementary school teacher and a doctoral candidate at the University of Hawaii, Manoa. She has lectured in curriculum and instruction at the University of Hawaii, Manoa, and the Territorial Teachers' Training Assistance Program in Pago Pago, American Samoa. Her research focuses on identity, gender, and sexuality issues in early childhood education.

Donna J. Grace teaches elementary education courses and supervises field experiences at the University of Hawaii, Manoa. Her research focuses on children's understanding and uses of popular media.

Richard Johnson teaches courses in early childhood education, serves as coordinator of a field-based elementary teacher education program, and is graduate chair at the University of Hawaii, Manoa. In his current research, he is bringing a postcolonial perspective to early childhood education.

James R. King teaches graduate and undergraduate students in literacy and qualitative research at the University of South Florida in Tampa. His current research interests include emergent and "at risk" literacies, as well as critical, queer, and feminist theorizing in education.

Robin L. Leavitt is the chairperson of the Department of Education at Illinois Wesleyan University in Bloomington. She is the author of *Power and Emotion in Infant-Toddler Day Care* (1994).

Anne M. Phelan is an assistant professor in the Faculty of Education at the University of Calgary. She is coordinator of the early childhood and elementary education programs. Her research focuses on women and teaching, teacher socialization, and epistemology.

Martha Bauman Power is an associate professor in the Department of Family and Consumer Sciences at Illinois State University in Normal. Her research interests include early childhood socialization and special-needs adoption. She has published in several journals, including *Sociological Quarterly, Social Psychology Outreach,* and *Journal of Contemporary Ethnography.*

Jonathan G. Silin is a member of the Graduate Faculty, Bank Street College of Education in New York, and the author of *Sex, Death, and the Education of Children: Our Passion for Ignorance in the Age of AIDS* (1995). His research interests include early childhood education, lesbian/gay studies, and curriculum theory.

Joseph Tobin works in a field-based teacher preparation program and teaches qualitative research and educational theory courses at the University of Hawaii, Manoa. His publications include *Preschool in Three Cultures: Japan, China, and the United States* and *Remade in Japan: Everyday Life and Consumer Tastes in a Changing Society.*

Index